Deep Exegesis

Deep Exegesis
The Mystery of Reading Scripture

Peter J. Leithart

BAYLOR UNIVERSITY PRESS

Cover Design by Cynthia Dunne, Blue Farm Graphic Design

Cover image © 2009 iStockphoto.com

Oedipus the King by Sophocles, from *Three Theban Plays* by
Sophocles, translated by Robert Fagles, © 1982 by Robert Fagles.
Used by permission of Viking Penguin, a division of Penguin Group
(USA) Inc.

Library of Congress Cataloging-in-Publication Data

Leithart, Peter J.
  Deep exegesis : the mystery of reading Scripture / Peter J. Leithart.
    p. cm.
  Includes bibliographical references and index.
ISBN 978-1-60258-069-5 (pbk. : alk. paper)
Printed Case ISBN: 978-1-4813-1480-0

  1. Bible--Criticism, interpretation, etc. 2. Bible--Hermeneutics. I.
Title.
  BS511.3.L45 2009
  220.6--dc22

                          2009010380

Contents

He is giving a case for Sensus plenior

Preface

Learning to Read from Jesus and Paul

I have two main aims in this book. First, this book advocates a hermeneutics of the letter. That is to say, reading Scripture has to do with attending to the specific contours of the text—the author's word choices, structural organization, tropes and allusions, and intertextual quotations.

That might seem a prescription for minimalism, if not boredom or even murder. The letter kills, after all, while the Spirit gives life. Don't we want our hermeneutics to raise us rather than kill us?

I disagree with the premise of this critique. We get at the meaning of baptism not by ignoring the properties of water but by musing on those properties. Eucharistic theology properly emerges from considering the meanings of meals, of bread and of wine, of broken loaves and full cups. So, too, we get to the rich and richly varied *sensus plenior* of the sacramental word not by moving past the letter to a spiritual sense, not by treating the letter as a husk for removal. We get at the riches of Scripture precisely by luxuriating in the letter, by squeezing everything we can from the text as written.

My first aim is to show that a hermeneutics of the letter ought not to be a rigidly literalist hermeneutics.

My second aim is to learn to read from Jesus and Paul. Almost without exception, most of the questions I attempt to answer in this book arose from my efforts to make sense of how the Bible works, and particularly how Jesus, Paul, and the other New

Testament writers read the Old Testament.[1] In some chapters, my argument does not overtly take this shape. Even when I am beginning from a theory of textual temporality (chapter 2) or considering analogies between textual and musical structure (chapter 5), however, my goal is to describe and defend the ways biblical writers themselves read the Bible. I want to read the Old Testament and the New as a disciple of Jesus, and that means following in the footsteps of the disciples' methods of reading.

I am not satisfied with learning to read only the Bible from Jesus and Paul. As a disciple of Jesus, I want to follow his lead whenever I pick up a text, whether it be the Song of Songs or *Song of Myself*. I begin from the assumption that the apostles are not employing some bizarre form of sacred hermeneutics when they find Christology and ecclesiology around every corner of the Old Testament. They are giving us pointers to the nature of reading itself: clues to the meaning of meaning, the functions of language, and the proper modes of interpretation. To make this point concrete, every chapter includes readings of both biblical and extra-biblical texts.

Throughout the book I return to John 9, the story of Jesus' healing of the man born blind. This chapter is one of the literary masterpieces of the Bible, and therefore superbly embodies many of the points I want to make about texts and reading. Though the chapter functions as an illustration, it is more than that. My aim has not been to develop a theory or method and then apply it to John 9. On the contrary, the theory has more or less emerged from reflecting on the way the texts are put together, and on what I actually do when I set about to read them.

John 9 is also more than an illustration because I want the text to work on the reader as much as the reader works on the text. I aim for the text to do what Jesus did for the blind man—to make new by opening eyes.

One

The Text Is a Husk

Modern Hermeneutics

Picking through the rubble of postwar Poland to find something worth keeping, Nobel laureate poet Czeslaw Milosz came upon the Bible. Though he could not believe the Bible was literally true, he concluded that it was the "common good" of both believers and unbelievers. For intellectuals in the West, the Bible has "provided a standard of authenticity against the pervasive falsehoods of advertising, social engineering, moral uplift, demagogic politics—all the verbal corruptions of democracy, the language of illusion." For Milosz, "the scriptures provided a standard of authenticity against a much more dangerous language, the language of legalized murder."[1]

In his brilliant collection of essays, *Cultural Amnesia*, Clive James reflects on Milosz' remark and wonders if the Bible's importance can only become clear when civilization is collapsing. In our more comfortable surroundings, we fool ourselves into thinking that "the eternal can become outdated, and safely forgotten." Forgetfulness, James argues, is not confined to unbelievers. He chides Christians for the ease with which we have "let the Bible go." Though himself a lapsed believer, James laments the "successful reduction of once-vital language" to the "compendium of banalities" of modern English translations.[2]

Throughout the history of the West, the Bible has been much more than a "standard of authenticity." It has been a civilization-building book as well as a critical tool. During the medieval period, copyists, monks, and later university professors devoted

1

their intellectual energies to preserving and penetrating the biblical text. Pope Gelasius I set one of the cornerstones of Western political life—his "two swords" theory of church and state—in a typological meditation on Melchizedek, the priest-king of Salem, and Alfred the Great was not the only medieval ruler to knit the Ten Commandments into the laws of nations. Music was composed to carry the lyrics of the Psalms, and poets and prose writers drew on the riches of biblical poetry.

Despite their abandonment of medieval modes of reading, the Reformers continued to revel in the beauties and unlock the power of the text. Scripture inspired a rich literary culture within early Protestantism, perhaps nowhere more evident than in Elizabethan and early Jacobean England. Anglican theologians and pastors developed a biblically based genre criticism that was employed by religious poets who were among the major poets of the time (e.g., George Herbert and John Donne). Because Protestants gave attention to the letter of the Bible, they regarded "the particular verbal formulations and figures" as "the precisely appropriate vehicles for conveying truth, whether of natural things or of God." While insisting that the Scriptures have a "single sense," Protestant interpreters, poets, and writers recognized that a variety of applications could arise from a single sense, and the Bible's multifaceted symbols enriched the imaginative stock of religious and even secular poetry.[3]

Protestant biblical interpretation was also broad enough to encompass political and social concerns. Though Calvin seems to have denied that the Hebrew political system should serve as a model for contemporary politics, many of his followers turned to the Old Testament for political guidance. Even Hugo Grotius, normally known as one of the founders of secular political science, examined the similarities between the Hebrew and Dutch Republics in an early work.[4]

Today, the Bible has lost much of this culture-forming power. Lacking a common imagination inspired by Scripture, modernist poets and writers have thought it necessary to invent their own composite mythologies. In the United States, the Bible continues to have some of the political weight it had in the early modern period, but survey after survey demonstrates that even Christians

[Handwritten marginal annotation, left margin:] Social life was stockpiled on the Scriptures, until what was built is torn down, that in the collapse we might renew our knowledge

[Handwritten annotation, bottom:] of what the Scriptures truly mean for all of life, once more and always.

are ignorant of the Bible. Scholars have not helped. Over the last several centuries, the few academics who pay attention to Scripture have kept themselves busy ripping the Bible to pieces, skeptically analyzing its factual claims, mocking the idiocy of the final redactors, criticizing its ethical teachings, and generally treating the Bible with contempt even while protesting their piety. A book whose very letters Jews and Christians once treated with reverence has been reduced to a heap of broken fragments.

It is easy for Christians to blame secularists for "letting the Bible go," but the church is at least as culpable. As James points out, translation is a key symptom of our willingness to emasculate our own Scriptures.

Consider these translations of Psalm 23, the first from the King James Version (KJV):[5]

> The LORD is my shepherd; I shall not want.
> He maketh me to lie down in green pastures: he leadeth me
>   beside the still waters.
> He restoreth my soul: he leadeth me in the paths of righteous-
>   ness for his name's sake.
> Yea, though I walk through the valley of the shadow of death, I
>   will fear no evil: for thou art with me; thy rod and thy staff
>   they comfort me.
> Thou preparest a table before me in the presence of mine
>   enemies: thou anointest my head with oil; my cup runneth
>   over.
> Surely goodness and mercy shall follow me all the days of my
>   life: and I will dwell in the house of the LORD for ever.

Then this, from *The Message*:

> God, my shepherd! I don't need a thing.
> You have bedded me down in lush meadows, you find me quiet
>   pools to drink from.
> True to your word, you let me catch my breath and send me in
>   the right direction.
> Even when the way goes through Death Valley, I'm not afraid
>   when you walk at my side. Your trusty shepherd's crook
>   makes me feel secure.
> You serve me a six-course dinner right in front of my enemies.
>   You revive my drooping head; my cup brims with blessing.

>Your beauty and love chase after me every day of my life. I'm
>back home in the house of God for the rest of my life.

The most obvious difference between these two translations is
diction. While King James English is more archaic now than it was
when it was written, even in its own time the KJV was English
of a high register, not street English.[6] By contrast, *The Message*
is insistently colloquial, with its contractions, its clichés ("catch
my breath"; "back home"), and its contemporary references ("six-
course dinner"; "Death Valley").

The KJV can be faulted for being more formal than the original Hebrew and earlier English translations (Tyndale or the
Geneva Bible), but the slanginess of *The Message* is no solution.
Some of the latter's decisions are quite unfortunate. "Bedded
down" has a distracting sexual connotation. "Death Valley"
might bring to mind the hottest place on earth, but I have a
hard time reading the phrase without thinking of Ronald Reagan and mid-twentieth-century American television. When you
get "back home," you are ready to kick up your feet, but for
David, the "house of the Lord" is the temple-palace of the High
King of Israel. It is not a place of relaxed familiarity but one of
intense worship.

For readers with a smattering of Hebrew, the other contrast is
in the literalness of the two translations. In verse 3, *The Message*
renders "on account of Your Name" (*lema'an shemo*) as "True to
your word," and in verse 4 translates "I walk" (*'elek*) as "the way
goes" and adds to the Hebrew the notion that the Lord "walks"
with David through the valley. *The Message* completely deletes
"table" and "anointing" from verse 5 and gives us a droopy head
that is not present in the Hebrew. From *The Message*, one would
not guess that the God in Psalm 23 has a personal name, Yahweh,
which begins and ends the psalm; the translator uses the generic
"God." "Catch my breath" is not bad,[7] but to get the full sense of
the original, one has to realize that *breath* has far richer connotations in ancient Hebrew than it does in modern English, where it
has to do with oxygen intake.

The most crucial difference, though, is a difference in authority: which language, which idiom, determines the rendering of

the Hebrew into English? For the KJV, the Hebrew text forces itself on the English. "Valley of the shadow of death," now an English cliché, was introduced by Bible translators, as was "my cup runneth over." Older translations refreshed the target language (English) by bringing in the Hebrew as much as possible. The KJV enlarged not only the language but also the conceptual apparatus of English speakers, as more or less common words and concepts like *table* and *cup* and *staff* took on the religious aura of the psalm. For *The Message*, by contrast, contemporary English dictates what the Bible may and may not say. "For your Name's sake" does not communicate in a modern culture where names are much less mysterious than in the ancient world, so it gets dropped. "Rod and staff" is redundant, and is reduced to a "trusty shepherd's crook," thus losing an opportunity to enrich English style with Hebraic repetitions. Few of us have seen an anointing, and the Hebrew idiom, literally rendered "You fatten my head with oil,"[8] was too strange even for the KJV translators. So *The Message* has a drooping head revived, but neither fattened nor anointed.

The problem can be put this way: imagine an artistic rendition of *The Message*'s translation of 23:5a ("you serve me a six-course dinner"); then imagine that scene in stained glass in a church; and then imagine what that artistic rendition would look like in a century or two. To our great-grandchildren, one hopes, it would look like tawdry, dated kitsch, a step or two above dogs playing poker. If they had any taste, they would follow the Reformers' example and bust out the glass. Then think of the thousands of paintings, drawings, illustrations, and stained glass windows inspired by the KJV.

This example from *The Message* is far from the most egregious example that could be found. But it does go some way toward justifying Dwight Macdonald's complaint that modern Bible translators turn down Scripture's "voltage, so it won't blow any fuses."

My point is not merely aesthetic, and it is not at all nostalgic. I am not pining to hear the echoing, arching rhythms of the KJV ring from pulpits everywhere. My point is theological, and one of the main themes of this book. For *The Message*, the crucial thing about the Bible is the substance of what it teaches us, and many readers and interpreters come to the Bible with the same interests. For translators, commentators, preachers, and theologians, the idioms and cadences, the rhetoric and the tropes, the syntax and the vocabulary of the original have been reduced to mere vehicles for communicating that message. If the vehicle fails to reach its destination, we change vehicles. We substitute, add, or subtract words to make the Bible sound normal. We change idioms to be more familiar. We turn God's names into generic terms of divinity. We fiddle with the Bible's rhetoric so that it fits our rhetoric, rather than letting the Bible's rhetoric shape ours. Once we think we have found the spirit of the text, we feel free to mold the letter as we will.

As the comparison of the two translations indicates, students of the Bible have not always treated the Bible this way. Older translators recognized that no translation can completely capture all the features of the original text. But the goal of Reformation and post-Reformation Bible translators was always to carry over as much of the original text as possible into the target text. When Tyndale found no word for a Hebrew concept, he invented one—atonement—which is having a remarkably fruitful career in the English language, not to mention English theology, psychology, anthropology, and political theory. When the KJV translators found the Hebrew redundant, they made the English redundant: "dying, you shall die." When they found a vulgarity, they (sometimes) kept it in the English: a vulgar man is one who "pisseth against the wall." For most earlier translators, and for commentators, preachers, and Bible scholars, the original Bible set the agenda, while the target language and the target culture were expected to make room for it. They did not believe that the Bible needed to adjust to our prior concepts and institutions.

Scripture once transformed the world precisely because Bible students clung to the letter. Once the letter is reduced to a malleable vehicle, Scripture loses its potency. It no longer shapes our imaginations, our poetry, or our politics, because it is not allowed to say anything we do not already know. We have lost the Bible because we are no longer theologians of the letter.

How did Christians come to think of the specific shape of the text as a husk to be stripped away and discarded? Telling that story, or some of that story, is the burden of this chapter.

BATTLE FOR THE BIBLE

The story begins in the seventeenth century, and it begins in the Netherlands.[9] Among other things, the Reformation was a complicated battle over the Bible—over the canon, over translations, over hermeneutical principles and the interpretation of individual texts. But the battle for the Bible that shaped modern biblical criticism took place in the following century.

In 1666, a now-obscure Dutch Lutheran humanist, physician, and amateur theologian named Lodewijk Meyer anonymously published his *Philosophia S. Scripturae Interpres* (*Philosophy as the Interpreter of Holy Scripture*). His book describes a battle over the Bible. The antagonists are "dogmatists" and "skeptics," the former basing their theology directly on the biblical text, the latter subjecting the biblical text to the rational analysis of philosophy.

It is not hard to see who the dogmatists were. They were the Orthodox Protestants, who agreed with the original Reformers about the final authority and absolute truth of Scripture. Luther had been fond of quoting the conciliarist Nicolo de Tudeschi, known as Panormitanus, who said that "in matters touching the faith, the word of a single private person is to be preferred to that of a pope if that person is moved by sounder arguments from the Old and New Testament."[10] Luther went further even than the conciliarists, arguing that infallible interpretations did not reside in councils any more than in popes. He exhorted his followers to leave "all human books" in order to "steep ourselves in Scripture." Scripture would not mislead, since it was "most certain, simple and open." Luther protested that he was not more learned than others and that "Scripture alone should reign," and he wished to be judged by Scripture and "by its spirit."[11]

By the seventeenth century, the Reformation doctrine of Scripture had been refined into a strong doctrine of inerrancy. According to Lutheran theologian Johann Andreas Quenstedt (1617–1688), the Bible contains

no lie, no falsehood, not even the smallest error in words
or in matter, but everything, together and singly, that is
handed on in them is most true, whether it be a matter
of dogma or of morals or of history or of chronology or of
topography or of nomenclature; no want of knowledge, no
thoughtlessness or forgetfulness, no lapse of memory.[12]

For his part, Meyer shared the Orthodox assumption that
Scripture is true. Any correct interpretation of the Bible is necessarily true. This identity of meaning and truth is found only
in Scripture, not in any other text. Meyer's intention was not to
undermine the truth of Scripture but to address the lamentable
diversity of Protestant interpretation. In contrast to the Reformers, Meyer did not believe that Scripture is perspicuous. Clarity
is not a quality of texts, but has to do with the reception of texts.
If the receivers of a text differ on its meaning, the text cannot be
perspicuous. The mere fact that interpretations vary falsifies the
Orthodox claim about the clarity of the Bible.

To solve the problem of diverse interpretation, Meyer challenged another of Protestant orthodoxy's central beliefs, the claim
that Scripture should be its own interpreter. As Meyer saw it, not
even the Orthodox really let Scripture interpret itself. They did
not simply allow the clear passages of Scripture to interpret the
unclear passages. Rather, they used reason to determine which
passages were to be "understood and interpreted properly, and
which improperly and figuratively."[13]

Paying attention to Orthodox practice, rather than Orthodox theory, pointed toward reason as a solution to the problem
of diversity. Cartesian philosophy could save the Orthodox from
hermeneutical confusion. According to Cartesian doctrine, one
should accept as true only what is clear and distinct to natural
reason, and this criterion of truth should be applied to the Bible.[14]
Though often described as a Cartesian, Meyer did not consistently
hold to Cartesian views.[15] What he shared with Descartes and the
Dutch Cartesians was an assurance that philosophy and science
could yield virtually infallible truth.

In part, Meyer's argument is about language. The Orthodox, he
asserts, view language as "mathematical formulae" with invari-

ant meaning (Preus' formulation). Language does not work this way. Each text, Meyer argues, must be interpreted in the light of its own context, and specific words and phrases might vary in meaning from one passage to another. The Orthodox will make progress only when they recognize that biblical language is ordinary language and, as such, inherently ambiguous.[16] Because of its ambiguity, Scripture's own language is inadequate to harmonize the diversity of the Bible. To discover what the Bible means and to agree about that meaning, readers must move beyond the language of Scripture to the metalanguage of rational philosophy. That is to say, interpretations must pass through rational review.[17] Meyer holds to the axiom that "Nulla verae philosophiae dogmata theoligicis esse contraria" (no true philosophy can contradict dogmatic theology). It is an axiom that might be taken in the Orthodox sense that philosophy has to be judged by the deliverances of revelation. Meyer means it in the opposite, Cartesian sense. Because true philosophy cannot contradict theology, theology must be assessed by the light of true philosophy. Meyer reverses the Orthodox view of the relation of philosophy and theology, giving primacy to philosophy.[18]

In the end, Meyer does not resolve the problem of diverse interpretation. His single criterion of exegesis is that "exegesis must contain truth," but he recognizes that this truth is "inexhaustibly varied."[19] Any number of interpretations of a passage might thus be true, and the test of their truth is their consistency with philosophy, that is, with the clear and distinct deliverances that arise from Cartesian method. Some interpretations are ruled out because they are unreasonable or self-contradictory, but reason gives its imprimatur to many readings. Meyer's solution to diversity is less a philosophical solution than a political one. Interpreters will still come up with different readings, but Meyer argues that all interpretations that pass rational scrutiny should be tolerated. Like Spinoza after him, Meyer aligns a hermeneutical theory with a democratic political theory.

The dogmatic implications of Meyer's biblical criticism were vast. He mocked theologians who debated the Trinity, arguing that philosophy demonstrated "the dispute to be both meaningless and superfluous."[20] Trinitarian interpretations of Scripture must be wrong interpretations because the conclusions violate reason.

Meyer's book touched off a debate throughout Europe, spreading from the Netherlands to Germany, Scandinavia, and England.[21] Widely and roundly condemned by the Orthodox, it remained a touchstone of Enlightenment thinking about the Bible for a century. Jonathan Israel writes,

> Anxious to spread the debate to the vernacular and "enlighten" the people, Meyer followed up the Latin version the following year with a slightly expanded 137-page Dutch translation he prepared himself, and which was again published clandestinely by Rieuwertsz. Vigorously suppressed by the city governments, this vernacular edition seems never to have been subsequently reissued. The Latin version, by contrast, reappeared in 1674, frequently distributed bound together with Spinoza's *Tractatus*. Later, during the High Enlightenment in 1776, a remarkable third, Latin edition appeared at Halle, with extensive critical notes and a new preface (but again without any attribution to an author) by Johannes Salomo Semler, one of the founders of modern Protestant Bible criticism.[22]

For my purposes, Meyer's book is important because in it, he initiates a hermeneutical method that detaches the truth and meaning of Scripture from its verbal expression. For Meyer, the evident claims of the text are to be taken as true only if they are judged reasonable. Subjecting the Bible to a rational test, Meyer treats the surface of the Bible—its ordinary language, poetry, metaphor, and narrative—as dispensable. The Bible's truth is found in the rationally justifiable message and not in the rustic letter; it is the rational core that remains after the husk is removed.

SPINOZA THE PROTESTANT

Like his friend and promoter Meyer, the Jewish philosopher Benedict Spinoza also used the labels "dogmatists" and "skeptics" to describe the seventeenth-century battle over the Bible. For Spinoza, though, the dogmatists were dogmatists of reason, who believed that the Bible should be interpreted according to the canons of (usually Cartesian) rationality. Skeptics, on the other hand, were

Who are the Skeptics? [handwritten]

The Text Is a Husk Of *Reason and* [handwritten] 11

skeptics concerning the powers of reason, who subjected their reason to the sheer authority of Scripture. For skeptics, if Scripture contradicted rationality, so much the worse for rationality.

[handwritten margin note: *authority to interpret Scripture*]

It is fairly clear whom Spinoza had in mind when he spoke of skeptics. In a clever rebranding, he attacked the dominant Reformed orthodoxy of the Dutch Republic as a scrum of skeptics. Spinoza was charier about revealing the identity of the dogmatists. When he attacked them, he used the names Maimonides and Rabbi Alpakhar.[23] It is most likely, though, that he was aiming at Meyer, whose treatise was published four years before Spinoza's own *Theologico-Political Treatise* (1670, hereafter cited in text as *TPT*).

Spinoza's contribution is at once more Protestant and more radically anti-Protestant than Meyer's. Spinoza came by his Protestant views honestly, befriending Dutch Collegiants who formed independent quasi-Pietist "colleges" for Bible study in the wake of the acrimonious Arminian controversy of the early seventeenth century. The Collegiants turned against Orthodox dogmatism in favor of the "inner light" of the Spirit, an emphasis that transmuted in the early Enlightenment into the inner light of natural reason.[24] Like the Collegiants and other Pietist groups throughout Europe, Spinoza condemns the idolatry of the letter, appealing to 2 Corinthians 3 to emphasize the primacy of heart piety (*TPT*, 172).

Spinoza's rhetoric is that of a Pietist. He inverts the meanings of pious and impious, claiming that the "impious are not those who point out the contradictions in the Biblical text but those who bludgeon others with their Bibles" (*TPT*, 168, 189). From the preface of his treatise to the end, Spinoza insists that the keynote of faith is not orthodox adherence to dogma but practical fruit and obedience to the divine law of justice and love. He finds it shameful and incomprehensible that Jews, Christians, and Muslims differ not at all in their lives, but only in their doctrines. In all this, he assumes the mantle of "reformer" (*TPT*, 189).

[handwritten margin note: *woe to those who put light for darkness and darkness for light*]

Beyond the rhetoric, Spinoza adapts a number of characteristic Protestant themes in his treatment of the Bible. Against Meyer, he argues that Scripture should not be subjected to the judgment of reason, but should be interpreted in the light of Scripture (*TPT*, ch. 15), apparently affirming the Orthodox notions of *sola scriptura* and Scripture's self-authentication. He takes up the Reformation argument that Scripture does not belong to a clerical or academic elite, but should be, and is, accessible to the common man. Neither philosophers nor theologians should claim monopoly on the interpretation of Scripture. Again against Meyer, he argues that the central teachings of Scripture are perspicuous.

More subtly, he uses the Calvinist notion of accommodation to explain the idioms and wording of Scripture. Calvin said that the Scripture's rough and simple form was a result of the gracious condescension of a God who "lisps" to human beings as a parent babbles to a baby. In his famous letter to the Grand Duchess Christina of Tuscany, Galileo had also used accommodation as a device to harmonize Scripture with the discoveries of science. Taking Scripture literally at every point could only lead to "serious heresies and blasphemies," Galileo argued, since it would imply that God has "feet. Hands, eyes, and bodily sensations, as well as human feelings like anger, contrition and hatred, and such conditions as the forgetfulness of things past and the ignorance of future ones." These expressions in Scripture can only be understood correctly if they are understood as "dictated by the Holy Spirit . . . in such a way as to accommodate the capacities of the very unrefined and undisciplined masses." Scripture comes at "the dictation of the Holy Spirit," but "in disputes about natural phenomena one must begin not with the authority of scriptural passages but with sensory experience and necessary demonstrations."[25]

Spinoza appeals to this Calvinist theme in a way of which Calvin and his followers would have disapproved. He explains discrepancies between the prophets on matters of philosophy and natural science by suggesting that "God adapted revelations to the understanding and opinions of the prophets, and that in matters of theory without bearing on charity or morality the prophets could be, and, in fact, were, ignorant, and held conflicting opinions" (*TPT*, 40). Prophet differed from prophet on "philosophical" questions, but spoke with a unified voice on the main point of religion, which is ethics.

The "Word of God" that is contained in Scripture is the divine law of charity and justice, and the Bible deals with "speculative" metaphysical realities only insofar as they support these ethical demands. Spinoza reduces Scripture's doctrinal content to a few basic teachings: the existence of "God or a Supreme Being," the unity of God, his omnipresence, and his "supreme right and dominion over all things." Based on these minimal theological truths, the Bible demands the true worship that "consists only in justice and charity" and promises that those who live according to divine law will be forgiven and saved (*TPT*, 186–87). On these points, the Bible's teaching is perfectly clear.

Triumph of Tropology

Like many of his other themes, Spinoza borrowed his emphasis on the moral teaching of Scripture in part from the Reformation. We can see Reformation interpretation as the triumph of tropology.

Over the course of several centuries, medieval theologians and biblical students had developed what is known as the *fourfold method* or *quadriga*. According to this mode of reading, Scripture as a whole and its particular passages are not single in sense, but have multiples senses, specifically the literal, allegorical, tropological, and anagogical. Interpreted literally, a passage tells us what happened; the allegorical sense teaches us what we are to believe, particularly about Christ and his church; the tropological tells us what we are to do; and the anagogical tells us what we are to hope for.[26] From the time of John Cassian, *Jerusalem* served as a key example of the method. Literally, Jerusalem is the city of David; allegorically, it is the church; tropologically, each of us is a city in which God dwells, so what applies to the whole city applies to each of us; anagogically, it is the future Jerusalem.

Among the Reformers, Luther was the most deeply informed by medieval methods of interpretation. In his early commentary on the Psalms (1513–1515), Luther combines the quadriga with the double literal sense of the French humanist Jacques Lefevre d'Etaples to produce a hermeneutic of eight senses:

> Luther develops this point—playfully it would seem—by
> considering the eight senses which the phrase "Mount

[handwritten marginal note: what Spinoza attempts to do is establish his authority on the bears of God's word, but that detached from dogma doctrine, description and the day of our Lord.]

Zion" might bear, on the basis of this scheme. Taking the
term in its literal-historical sense—"the killing letter (literal occidens)," as Luther terms it, following Lefevre—the
following four senses may be deduced. In its literal sense, it
refers to the land of Canaan; in its allegorical sense, to the
synagogue; in its tropological sense, to the righteousness
of the law; in its anagogical sense, to the future glory of
the flesh. Taking the term in its literal-prophetic sense—
"the life-giving spirit" (*spiritus vivificans*), as Luther terms
it—four very different senses may be deduced. In its literal sense, it refers to the people of Zion; in its allegorical
sense, to the church; in its tropological sense, to the righteousness of faith; in its anagogical sense, to the eternal
glory of the heavens.[27]

Even Calvin, though very hostile to medieval flights of
fancy, came close to a Protestant version of the quadriga with
his hermeneutics of promise and fulfillment. What is most distinctive about Calvin is his attention to the historical context
of the text. When he read Joel or Daniel, he made every effort
to discern what the text meant for the original hearers and how
the prophecy was fulfilled close to the time it was delivered.
Yet Calvin also made room for multiple fulfillments, so that a
prophesied deliverance of Israel came to fuller realization in the
deliverance achieved in the cross and resurrection. Beyond that,
Calvin believed that prophecies could also be applied to his own
time, since the church of the sixteenth century existed within the
unfolding history initiated by Jesus. These multiple fulfillments
were all, for Calvin, contained in the literal sense, since the literal
sense spoke not of isolated moments of time but of the "historical succession" of the kingdom's expansion.[28] This scheme yields
three wheels of the four-wheeled quadriga: the immediate fulfillment of the prophecy is the historical sense (say, the restoration
from Babylon); the New Testament fulfillment corresponds to the
allegorical or christological sense; and the contemporary application amounts to a tropology. And it would not be hard to add the
fourth wheel: prophecies are also anagogies, foretelling the final
rescue from death and the devil.

Overall, however, the Reformation emphasized tropology. The Reformers differed on what tropology was. For Erasmus and Bucer, and to some extent Calvin, tropology was about moral demands placed on Christians, while for Luther, "the tropological sense refers to the gracious work of Jesus Christ in the individual believer, so that the *bonum tropologicum* is to be defined as faith." Luther's tropology concerns "what God does for man, rather than . . . what God expects of man."[29] The primacy of tropology was a "strongly subjective element of Luther's exegesis."[30] In short, the Reformers, in their zeal to open the Bible to their congregations, emphasized the immediate personal application of the text. Hermeneutically, the Reformation represented a turn to tropology. With their personalized reading of Scripture, Pietist groups like the Dutch Collegiants advanced an important Reformation theme, one that Spinoza radicalized.

Spinoza against the Protestants

In the end, Spinoza's treatment of the Bible is deeply hostile to the Reformation and Protestant orthodoxy. The fundamental issue is the truthfulness of Scripture. Spinoza abandons the belief, shared by Meyer and the Orthodox, that truth and meaning are identical in Scripture (*TPT*, ch. 7). He admits that the basic narrative of Israel's history is accurate, as are the Gospels' accounts of the life of Jesus. But the Bible's detailed factual claims are not coherent. Scripture is full of factual errors, contradictions, even blasphemy. The Bible cannot be relied on for truth, and the goal of biblical study is not to arrive at truth, but rather to arrive at the meaning of the original text.

For Spinoza, the factual inaccuracy and philosophical incoherence of the Bible did not rob it of its majesty and authority. Prophets held a variety of opinions about natural science and philosophy, and some had a fairly accurate grasp of historical fact. But that did not matter, since they were united in their demand for justice and love. They are distinguished not by their knowledge of nature or metaphysics but by their piety and faithfulness. A believer is required to honor only the ethical teachings of

Scripture and the basic speculative teaching that supports these ethical demands. According to Spinoza, the husk of history and speculation can be stripped away to get at the mere kernel. The letter is nothing; the ethical spirit of Scripture is all.

Spinoza claimed he was not a dogmatist who wanted theology to bow to reason. He challenged "Alpakhar's" (Meyer's) notion that nothing in Scripture contradicts reason, insisting that Scripture "expressly affirms and teaches that God is jealous . . . and I assert that such a doctrine is repugnant to reason" (*TPT*, 193). On Alpakhar's theory, the Bible's teaching that God is jealous "in spite of all, [must] be accepted as true" (*TPT*, 193). Spinoza disagreed: "theology is not bound to serve reason" (*TPT*, 194).

At the same time, Spinoza believed that reason is the test of truth. Theology need not bow to reason, but that is not because theology is reason's master. Theology need not bow to reason because theology is not concerned with questions of truth in the first place, but with questions of good behavior.

In short, behind the distinction of meaning and truth is a sharp dualism of philosophy and theology, the latter understood as revelation. Theologians should concern themselves with studying the original meaning of Scripture, but these studies take them outside the sphere of reason. Philosophy is a quite separate discipline. Philosophy and theology operate in different spheres, and each should be allowed to pursue its interests without interference: "be it far from me to say that religion should seek to enslave reason, or reason religion, or that both should not be able to keep their sovereignty in perfect harmony" (*TPT*, 192). Spinoza summarizes the distinction:

> The sphere of reason is, as we have said, truth and wisdom; the sphere of theology is piety and obedience. The power of reason does not extend so far as to determine for us that men may be blessed through simple obedience, without understanding. Theology tells us nothing else, enjoins on us no command save obedience, and has neither the will nor the power to oppose reason: she defines the dogmas of faith . . . only in so far as they may be necessary for obedience, and leaves reason to determine their precise truth: for reason is the light of the mind, and without her all things are dreams and phantoms. (*TPT*, 194–95)

Thus, "we may draw the absolute conclusion that the Bible must not be accommodated to reason, nor reason to the Bible" (*TPT*, 195).

Spinoza's theory appears to affirm the autonomy of theology, but in fact he arrives at a conclusion very similar to that of the "dogmatist" Lodewijk Meyer. Reason tells the interpreter what is and what is not properly "religious" (ethical) in the Bible.

Reading with Spinoza

Spinoza's new theory of the Bible implied new ways of reading, and new goals for that reading. Though giving primacy to tropology, Protestants read Scripture not only to learn God's demands but to learn about the nature of things. Orthodox theologians believed that Scripture revealed metaphysical truth. Given his dichotomy between faith and philosophy, Spinoza considered theology a nonrational if not irrational discipline, radically simplified the theological substance of Scripture, denied legitimacy to highly developed theological systems, and argued that the main point of studying and teaching theology was to inculcate piety in the hearers.

Spinoza argued that theology—the study of revelation and Scripture—should have its own subject matter and its own standards. In part, he was advocating a version of the Protestant principle that Scripture interprets itself, a claim he explicitly supports at a number of points in his *Tractatus*. Interpreters of Scripture, he insists, should follow the same methods that a scientist follows in his interpretation of nature: "the interpretation of nature consists in the examination of the history of nature, and therefrom deducing definitions of natural phenomena on certain fixed axioms, so Scriptural interpretation proceeds by the examination of Scripture, and inferring the intention of its authors as a legitimate conclusion from its fundamental principles" (*TPT*, 99).

Examining the history of Scripture means learning Hebrew and Greek, analyzing each book's contents with a view to establishing its meaning, and then researching the setting of the author and book—"the life, the conduct and the studies of the author of each book, who he was, what was the occasion, and the epoch of his writing, whom did he write for, and in what language." The history of Scripture includes reception history, "how it was first received, into whose hands it fell, how many different versions there were of it, by whose advice was it received into the Bible, and, lastly, how all the books now universally accepted as sacred, were united into a single whole" (*TPT*, 103). The mysteries of Scripture are not speculative mysteries, but simply the result of the difficulties of language and history, and the lack of knowledge of these things.

Based on these principles, Spinoza conducted a historical examination of the question of the authorship of the Pentateuch. The internal evidence of the Bible itself demonstrates that Moses could not have been the author. Deuteronomy records Moses' death, and the Pentateuch refers to Moses in the third person, includes place names that were not introduced until much later, and uses phrases like "until this day" that indicate the author of the work is living at a time much later than the events themselves. History, as evidenced by the text itself, was turned against traditional claims about the text.

Ultimately, Spinoza's interest in Scripture was not theoretical, but political and cultural. As he argues in the preface to the *Tractatus*, social agitations generate superstitions, as people flounder for something to hold on to in an uncertain world. Superstitions in turn lead to schisms and conflicts among sects that have different interpretations of the superstitions they characterize as mysteries. Irrational attachment to ecclesiastics and idolatry of the letter reinforce these superstitions, and Spinoza wanted his method to break the power of superstition by smashing the idols of the letter and relativizing the conclusions of the theologians (*TPT*, 6–7, 166).

Spinoza's "chief conclusion," though, was to defend a political system in which "everyone's judgment is free and unshackled, where each may worship God as his conscience dictates, and where freedom is esteemed before all things dear and precious." He hoped his treatise would show not only that "such freedom can be granted without prejudice to the public peace" but also "that without such freedom, piety cannot flourish nor the public peace be secure" (*TPT*, 6). He developed a social contract theory of the foundation of the state, suggesting that while natural powers and rights to act on one's desires are ceded to the state, the rights and powers of thought and speech are inalienable and cannot be given up. He envisioned a liberal state in which diverse theological opinions and a babel of theological talk would be tolerated, but where the state would have the right to ensure that worship and preaching would not disturb public peace (*TPT*, chs. 16–17). Freedom in Spinoza's liberal state would be the freedom to interpret the Bible as one chooses, and freedom from state enforcement of any one interpretation of the Bible. Picking up yet another Protestant habit, he defended this system by appeal to the Hebrew state, in which, he claimed, the king oversaw and regulated worship in the temple and the priests did no more than administer the king's commands.

Spinoza among the Orthodox

Despite Spinoza's hostility to traditional uses of the Bible, a number of his most radical ideas penetrated the Dutch Reformed churches and were accepted, not without controversy, within the scope of orthodoxy.[31] Ludwig von Wolzogen, a rationalist Orthodox theologian, wrote a response to Meyer in 1668, challenging the "paradoxical fencing-master" Meyer, who had claimed that philosophy interprets Scripture. Wolzogen did not accept the notion that there could be contradictions in Scripture, or contradictions between reason and revelation, but he adopted Spinoza's most characteristic and central theme, that there is a sharp distinction between reason's pursuit of philosophical understanding and the spiritual illumination needed for understanding Scripture.[32] Orthodoxy was catching up with Spinozist dualism.

Christoph Wittich was a Spinozist *avant la lettre*, sharply separating philosophical (or scientific) knowledge from revelation and deploying Galileo's notion of accommodation to show that there was no contradiction between Copernicus and Scripture. Wittich also introduced the notion of intent into hermeneutical discussion. Scripture communicates truth, he argued, but the truth it communicates is the substance that the Holy Spirit intends in any particular text. This substance is communicated

Meyer... philosophy elites interpret scripture

Spinoza.... anyone's interpretation of scripture
∟This is a is valid if it produces charity/justice
smarter me, but not wiser.

in language that embodies a particular worldview, and the worldview is *not* part of what the Spirit intends. In interpreting a passage to discover its universal truth, Wittich said, interpreters "are to see whether a prejudice is perhaps implicit in these expressions, which does not have its origin in the Holy Spirit, but rather in common usage, and whether, therefore, the language is 'vulgar,' or is precise and brings pure truth to expression."[33] The Bible's authors knew nothing of this distinction, of course, but in retrospect, modern interpreters can "distinguish between the intended truth and the form in which this truth is expressed, and thus can transform scriptural assertions concerning 'philosophical' things into philosophical assertions without doing harm to their content."[34] For Wittich, the division of philosophy and theology centered on cosmology and physics. There could be no biblical physics, and the notion that philosophy and natural science should subordinate themselves to theology was nonsense.[35] In 1660–1661, the Synod of Gelder determined that he was orthodox.[36]

ALLEGORY OF PRACTICAL REASON

[handwritten margin note: the ethical to concerns are a moral kernel waiting to be liberated from the husk of the text]

A number of Spinozist themes were further developed and systematized in German philosophy and biblical criticism. Despite its prominence in the biblical scholarship of the last two centuries, Germany was a latecomer to critical scholarship, and was heir to more than a century of English debate.[37] Kant is rightly described as the grandfather of liberal theology, but many of his characteristic ideas were borrowed from elsewhere. *Christianity as Old as Creation*, by the English freethinker Matthew Tindal, was in Kant's library,[38] and many of the fundamental assumptions of his arguments in *Religion within the Bounds of Reason Alone* came from Spinoza and English writers inspired by Spinoza.

English deism—more accurately and broadly, "freethinking"—developed from the latitudinarianism that developed after the Stuart Restoration (1666). Distraught over continuing battles over fine points of doctrine, which fueled the hostilities of the English Civil War, the Latitude-men advocated toleration for non-Anglicans. To overcome these unhappy divisions, they reduced true religion

[handwritten margin note: is this not gnosticism in new shoes]

to a few fundamental truths that could be affirmed by all Christians and tried to demonstrate the rational basis for religion. They believed that human beings have an innate religious instinct, a natural "light" or "inscription" of divine revelation, and this natural religion is simple and monotheistic. This innate instinct is evidenced in the fact that certain religious truths are universally believed. Christianity in its essence is this natural religion, which focuses not on doctrines of ceremonies but on duty and action. According to John Wilkins, natural religion is religion "which men might know, and should be obliged unto, by the mere principles of Reason, improved by Consideration and Experience, without the help of Revelation." Wilkins thought that natural religion could be reduced to belief in God, acknowledgment of his perfection, and performance of the duties of religion.[39] Running through the century's debates was the question of the relationship between natural and revealed religion, a problem often formulated with terminology drawn from the study of law as a contrast of "natural" and "positive" (revealed) religion.

The Latitudinarians were not skeptics about religious truth, but they provided some of the tools that were later turned against Christianity. For John Tillotson, one of the best-known Latitudemen, the fundamental truths of natural religion provided a standard for testing the truth of revelation. Echoing Meyer, he argued that no revelation can be accepted as supernatural "which plainly contradicts the principles of natural religion, or overthrows the certainty of them."[40] Armed with this standard, Tillotson argued that Calvinist predestinarianism and Catholic sacramentalism were irrational, but it was not long before others would use Tillotson's standard against his own brand of gentle and genteel Christianity.

Lord Herbert of Cherbury formulated the most influential freethinking creed. He claimed that natural religion could be reduced to five points: there is a supreme God, he should be worshipped, virtue and piety are the central forms of worship, we must turn from evil, and there are rewards and punishments after this life.[41] For most freethinkers, this was the original monotheistic faith. Over time, self-interested priests corrupted this simple religion of moral goodness by introducing ceremonies, superstitions, sacrifices, and dogmas, and then inserting themselves between God and men as mediators. Priestcraft was the great corrupter of religion. Though Jesus came to restore natural religion, Christianity too has been corrupted by priests. Meanwhile, the natural religion of reason has been preserved by philosophers, but in secret for fear of the priests.[42]

Freethinking was an anti-creed, and there was a good deal of variation among freethinkers. Lord Herbert would not have approved of John Toland's "pantheistic" theology, picked up from Spinoza, and Toland would have disagreed with most of Herbert's articles of natural religion. Yet there are important continuities that persist straight through to Kant. All freethinkers shared an antipathy to priestcraft, a suspicion of the dogmas, rites, and texts of positive religion, and a conviction that the central thrust of religion is morality. But for the diction and some terminology, one might mistake Toland's summary of the gospel for Kant's: "one main design of Christianity was to improve and perfect the knowledge of the Law of nature, as well as to facilitate and inforce the observations of the same."[43]

All freethinkers believed that Christianity's pure kernel had been encrusted and needed to be liberated. So did Kant, and so does the liberal theology inspired by Kant.

Rational Religion

Kant wrote a book entitled *Religion within the Boundaries of Mere Reason* (hereafter cited as *RBMR*). The title tells us a lot. The fact that Kant constructed a theory of "religion" shows that he was already assuming a sharp dichotomy between the form and content of religion. Only on this assumption could he write about religion in the singular, since actual religions come in the form of liturgy, dogma, doctrine, practices, and symbols. Further, Kant already knew what that content was before he ever began looking at the specifics of Christian religion or revelation. For Kant, religion is rational; therefore, like Spinoza, he knew that religion is "moral." For Kant, true rational religion must be natural rather than particular and positive.[44] Though

[handwritten marginalia: "wrong...the glory of God is the main design!"]

[handwritten marginalia at bottom: "→ Maybe the irrationality of the apostles was the wisdom of God? → A critique of Kant's"]

he withholds the crucial definition of religion to the end of his treatise, he assumes the definition from the beginning: religion is accepting the demands of practical reason as if they were the demands of God." *according to Kant* → *end statement*

According to Kant, only a "plain rational faith" with universal extent can be taken as "pure religious faith."[45] Pure religion is to obey commands and do one's duty as the will of God (*RBMR*, 113). It is to do duty for no other reason than duty, to do God's will purely for God's sake, without hope or expectation of reward. But human beings are weak, and we often treat moral action as service to God that makes us pleasing to God. We treat our duties as transactions with God. This is morally impure, but it is necessary. We are too weak to be pure in faith, and as a result, "ecclesiastical faiths" (positive religions) are unavoidable moral crutches.

Ecclesiastical faiths add revelatory demands and duties to the natural moral legislation written on the heart. While these requirements cannot be treated as divine commands, since they are accommodations to human weakness, they do have a temporary value. The rituals and sacraments of "cultic religion" are morally indifferent, but "precisely for this reason, they are deemed to be all the more pleasing to God, since they are supposed to be carried out just for his sake" (*RBMR*, 115). By this process, a community practicing a "positive" religion is formed through cultic participation into a pure ethical community that does what is right for duty's sake only. Ecclesiastical faith provides the elementary principles that the enlightened outgrow; it is a schoolmaster leading to natural religion.

All the evils of religion result from treating ecclesiastical faiths as true religion. It is a mistake, for instance, to characterize post-Reformation struggles as religious wars; they were faith wars, bloody struggles between different ecclesiastical forms that were claiming more than they should—claiming to represent in their statutory and cultic form the very will of God. Faith wars arise from "catholic" faith or "orthodoxy," which "claims that its ecclesiastical faith is universally binding" (*RBMR*, 117).[46] Kant considered himself a faithful Protestant adhering to the Protestant principle that protests Catholic claims to universal validity.

"Religion within the Boundaries of mere Reason"

Redeeming Positivity

Though he borrowed much of the scaffolding of English freethinkers, Kant was also heir to Pietism, and thus wanted to rescue at least one positive religion, Christianity, since it is the religion that most closely resembles true, natural religion. Kant's tack in *Religion within the Bounds of Mere Reason* is to prove that Christianity, stripped of its positive features, is identical to rational, natural religion.[47]

Underlying his entire argument is a strict distinction between form and content.[48] The form of Christian religion, or of the biblical text literally considered, holds no more authority for Kant than it did for Spinoza. What matters for Kant is the rational substance that is communicated through these accommodated forms. The forms of ecclesiastical faiths are only valuable insofar as they lead to the core content of rational religion. Armed with this assumption, he offers a church history and a hermeneutical method for stripping the chaff from the kernel of Christianity.

First, his history of the progress of true religion borrows its terms from the freethinking histories of priestcraft. Christianity succeeded Judaism, but there is no real continuity between them. Ancient Judaism was political, external, and exclusivist. Christianity is completely different, a universal faith that emphasizes truly religious ethical principles. The first Christians stressed their continuity with Judaism only to avoid offense. The history of Christianity, however, is an unhappy one, since the pure faith was quickly undermined by enthusiasm, superstition, and priestcraft. Despite all the efforts of popes and others, the first aim of Christianity has not been entirely abandoned, and the original vision of Christianity is finally being realized in Enlightenment Europe. Kant considered his own era to be the high point of Christian maturity, since it was moderate in its views of revelation and taught the Bible in the interests of morals.

Second, Kant offers a hermeneutical method for moving from the positive, historically bound, and circumscribed to the universal and rational.[49] His hermeneutics is a form of moral allegory, as Kant moves from the narrative and poetry of the Bible to rational, philosophical accounts of the realities in question. The husk of the text (or of the rite, or of the dogma) can be transcended, since it is reinterpreted as a symbol of a truth that can be arrived at without the aid of revelation.

Kant's theory of radical evil serves as an example of the procedure. He opens with a philosophical consideration of evil in human life. Man is free, radically autonomous, and his moral choices and actions are not determined by anything outside himself or even anything within himself other than his own choice. For Kant, freedom is part of the very definition of morality, because if we do not act from free choice, then we cannot be held accountable for our actions. The free will simply is the moral faculty. Sensuously, we are not self-made; morally, we are authors of ourselves. Though our will is free, it takes a specific shape in actual choices and actions as we incorporate good or evil incentives into the maxims that guide our choices. This incorporation of incentives is also a free act (which opens up an unfathomable regression, as Kant admits).

To the Pelagian assumption of free will, Kant adds another Pelagian assumption: if we are commanded to act morally, we must be capable of acting morally. Kant resorts to this claim when, for instance, he denies that evil habit makes us incapable of acting well. No matter how often we have willed and acted wickedly, still we are confronted with the moral law in our every action. If we are confronted with the moral law, we must be capable of obeying it; thus, our evil habits are irrelevant to our capacity to obey.[50] At times, Kant resorts to the semi-Pelagianism of the medieval theologians, whose maxim was that God would not deny assistance to those who do the best with what they have. God comes alongside and helps us to improve morally, but we first have to prove ourselves worthy of that assistance.

If we are free in this way, what accounts for the universal human propensity to evil? Kant does not blame our sensuous nature, since our sensuous nature is a given, not a free choice, and therefore not morally crucial. Nor is corruption of reason the ground of evil, since, following the English freethinkers, Kant believes reason to be incorruptible. The problem is not quite the mixture of sensuous and moral incentives in the maxims of our conduct. Given the kinds of beings we are, this mixture is unavoidable. We are always going to have incentives to do right (moral), as well as incentives to seek our own happiness and self-interest (sensuous).

The crucial moral question is, which incentive conditions the other? Do I choose to do good insofar as it brings happiness or promotes self-interest (which would make adherence to the moral law conditional on fulfilling the sensuous demands of self-love)? Or do I choose the good for its own sake, respecting the majesty of moral law itself, regardless of whether I achieve happiness or not (which makes the moral law unconditioned, and fulfillment of sensuous incentives dependent—if it happens at all—on fulfillment of the moral law)? Someone may by all external measures act morally, but if he acts to achieve some other end (e.g., telling the truth because it is hard to keep track of lies), he is evil. This propensity to invert moral and sensuous incentives is precisely the propensity to evil.

At this point, Kant turns to the Bible. He has already concluded that the origin of human evil must be located in reason, not in time. A free act cannot be constrained by a prior event, because that would deprive the act of its freedom. Above all, Kant insists, the human propensity to evil cannot be inherited (as, say, from Adam), because we cannot be held accountable for the deeds of our fathers. Evil's origin must be considered rationally. Once we make this adjustment from time to reason, we find a remarkable convergence between philosophy and faith. Kant believes he has proven rationally that every evil act is a free, unconstrained choice that involves the inversion of incentives, and this is just what we find in Genesis 3. Of course, Genesis presents this in temporal categories, but Kant sees the temporal/narrative framework of the fall as a husk that can be removed to get at the rational core.

Once we remove the husk, Genesis 3 gives in symbolic and mythical terms the very truths of natural, rational religion: Adam is evil because he does not count the moral law as a sufficient incentive to action; instead, he mixes in other incentives and inverts the order of incentives within his moral maxim.

When he considers sensory inducements—the apparent tastiness of the fruit, the promise of wisdom—he sins. We are all Adam, and every moral choice is a potential fall from innocence. The narrative of the fall even symbolizes the fact that there is no discoverable ground for evil. Evil comes from a choice, yet our predisposition is to good. How, then, does evil arise? Kant concludes that the answer "remains inexplicable to us, for, since it must itself be imputed to us, this supreme ground of all maxims must in turn require the adoption of an evil maxim." Genesis makes the same point, implying the incomprehensibility of the origin of evil.

Kant performs similar allegories on other biblical narratives and Christian dogmas. Reason gives us an ideal prototype of perfected humanity in all its splendid purity, and this is the Son of God. We cannot explain the presence of this prototype. It is as if he dropped from heaven and abased himself for us, as if the ideal became flesh and dwelt among us. The incarnation is a mythical rendering of philosophical truth. Even the career of Jesus as depicted in the Gospels is consistent with reason. A humanity pleasing to God must be a suffering humanity: "a human being willing not only to execute in person all human duties, and at the same time to spread goodness about him as far wide as possible through teaching and example, but also, though tempted by the greatest temptation, to take upon himself all sufferings, up to the most ignominious death, for the good of the world and even for his enemies" (*RBMR*, 80). Practical faith in this Son of God means being conscious of a moral disposition that enables us to believe that, under the same pressures and circumstances, we would do what Jesus did. Only a person with such a disposition should consider himself worthy of God's pleasure.

Ecclesiology gets allegorized as well. Philosophically, the need for a moral community arises from the fact that our actions are shaped by others. As free beings, we are bound to the evil principle through our own fault, but Kant also says of mankind that the "causes and circumstances that draw him into this danger and keep him there . . . do not come his way from his own raw nature, so far as he exists in isolation, but rather from the human beings to whom he stands in relation or association" (*RBMR*, 105). A person living by himself has limited needs, and so can pursue moderation and tranquility. As soon as he is surrounded by others, "envy, addiction to power, avarice, and the malignant inclinations associated with these, assail his nature" (*RBMR*, 105). Thus, we "mutually corrupt each other's moral disposition and make one another evil" (*RBMR*, 105).[51]

If evil has a communal dimension, the moral life must also. We need a society that operates by the principles of virtue and reason. Reason is not only the legislator for human beings but "a banner of virtue" that provides a "rallying point for all those who love the good" (*RBMR*, 106). As Kant's description of this community develops, it becomes evident that he conceives it as a kind of church. What he has in mind is an "ethical community," distinct in various ways from the juridico-civil society. In the political state, the people are legislators. This must be so, since legislation limits freedom and only the people themselves can alienate their own freedom. In the ethical society, however, the people are not the legislators, since "in such a community all the laws are exclusively designed to promote the morality of actions" (*RBMR*, 109). Further, the ethical community is concerned with "something internal," while the political community is concerned with external legality. Only God, therefore, can be the legislator of the ethical community, which takes the form of a church, a people of God.

Kant's view of the ethical community links up with his treatment of ecclesiastic faiths. The people of God should not be conceived as a juridical community ruled by statutory laws interpreted by priests. That would be a theocracy (like Israel) and would qualify as a politico-civil rather than an ethical community. Even if God legislates, so long as the legislation is external, we are still dealing with a civil and juridical reality. The true church is thus an invisible church, which, Kant says, is the "mere idea of the union of all upright human beings under direct yet moral divine world-governance" and which "serves for the archetype of any such governance," the former being "the actual union of human beings into a whole that accords with this ideal" (*RBMR*, 111). He lays out four marks of this ethical church—universality, purity, freedom, and unchangeability—and notes that "In its life it more resembles a family than a state" (*RBMR*, 112). In actual sensuous experience, no combination of human beings ever achieves the "sublime, never fully attainable idea of an ethical community." It is "at best capable of representing with purity only the form of such a community" (*RBMR*, 111). The formation of this community depends on God, but each member of the community must strive as if everything depends on his own efforts, and as that happens, the kingdom of God comes to earth.

Kant's moral allegory turns the text into a husk in several ways. First, he detaches Christian faith, Jesus, and the gospel from the Old Testament. Israel was a political state, not an ethical community, and Israel's history is only loosely related to the New Testament. Israel's history is not a foreshadowing of the coming gospel, not a type whose antitype is found in Christ. Second, and more fundamentally, he strips the temporal husk from the philosophical kernel. According to Kant, the Bible does not give an account of history. It is not telling us what happened, or giving us insight into the patterns of human history. We can get the point of the Bible only by siphoning off the temporal, narrative form and getting to the ethical substance. Kant believes that the Bible gives us reason's conclusions in an accommodated temporal form; he does not consider the possibility that the Bible is pointing us to the historicity of reason itself. He does not consider the possibility that the Bible might be indicating that we reason temporally.[52] Like his Pietist forebears, Kant is interested in the moral message of the Bible and not in its linguistic letter.

Both of these decisions are fatal to traditional reading of Scripture, and both are fateful.

KANTIAN EVANGELICALS

Give the liberals their due. As James Barr points out, liberal critics come to their conclusions and theories about the history of the biblical text by examining the texts in excruciating detail, scrounging for any evidence of a fissure. Barr claims that fundamentalists, not liberals, fall into the husk/kernel, letter/spirit

- Point : Evangelicals are more influenced by liberal thinking then we are apostolic thinking

dichotomies. Barr also insists, against fundamentalists, that the "verbal form of the Bible does not stand in contrast with its meaning, but is the indicator of that meaning."[53] Liberals attend to the specific formulations of the text not because they think they will find an account of actual events but because the specific formulations of the text reveal the theologies of the authors.

All this is true enough, and qualifies the characterization of liberal biblical study under the "text as husk" metaphor. Yet Barr is also quite clearly in the stream of Spinozist/Kantian biblical studies. He openly disagrees with the claims of the Bible and considers the biblical text to be correctable by overriding theological concerns, not to mention historical research. For him, the Bible reveals the theologies of the authors, but the Bible's specific textual shape has little or no authority.

Barr has a point too in charging conservative Christians with being more Kantian than he is. Evangelicals whose overall theology is closer to the Dutch orthodox than to Spinoza and Kant frequently make Spinozist/Kantian maneuvers. In some evangelical systems, the Old and New Testaments are distinguished to the point of separation. Israel is given an identity and history separate from that of the church, an earthly destiny that runs parallel to, but on very different tracks from, the spiritual destiny of the church. Many sources and influences stand behind this form of theology, and Kant is not usually a direct influence. Yet the effect is very similar to that of Kant.

Much evangelical preaching, further, is known for its tropological bent.[54] Evangelicals want to make the Bible practical, and that often means drawing moralistic conclusions from the text. Evangelicals who make morality the primary content of religion may not be affected by Kant directly, but the hermeneutical results are the same: the events are moral allegories. Alternatively, Protestants as far back as the Reformed Scholastics have often come to the Bible looking for doctrinal content or polemical ammunition. Details of the biblical text that do not yield immediate dogmatic results are ignored.[55]

The husk/kernel model appears in more sophisticated and subtle forms in some evangelical Protestant biblical work. In his controversial 2005 book, *Inspiration and Incarnation*,[56] Peter Enns, formerly associate professor of Old Testament at Westminster Seminary, offers an "incarnational" model of Scripture, one that affirms both the divinity and the humanity of the Bible. Because it is a human as well as a divine book, the Bible "was *connected to* and therefore *spoke to* those ancient cultures." The Bible is "encultured."[57] It uses existing languages with their own histories and meanings. It was written within "a world of temples, priests and sacrifice," and it reflects that world. Israel had kings, like other nations surrounding it, and its legal system bore a striking resemblance to ancient Near Eastern codes like the Code of Hammurabi.[58]

Though Enns clearly affirms that the Bible is the word of God, several of his arguments are reminiscent of Spinoza and early biblical criticism. Enns points to commonalities between biblical views of the world and the worldviews of other ancient Near Eastern peoples. When God condescended to choose Abraham, he "also adopted the mythic categories within which Abraham— and everyone else—thought." Israel's account of creation and early history bears similarities to *Enuma Elish* and the *Epic of Gilgamesh* because Abraham and his descendants, being ancient peoples, "shared the worldview of those whose world he shared and not a modern, scientific one." Genesis and other Mesopotamian literature share "worldview categories" that were "ubiquitous and normative at the time."[59]

Much of this is obvious, and obviously true. But the way Enns uses this evidence indicates his proximity to the husk/kernel model we have traced from Meyer and Spinoza through Kant. Enns implies a distinction between worldview and message. What makes Genesis different from ancient myths is not the worldview but the fact that Abraham's God "is different from the gods" of the nations around Israel.[60] The theological message of the Old Testament comes cloaked in an ancient mythic view of the world, a worldview that long preexisted the writing of the Old Testament and even the events that it records. We can affirm the divinity of the message without necessarily submitting ourselves to the humanity of the worldview.[61] The worldview that the text communicates is a husk, part of the letter and not inherently part of the message.

Second, Enns is employing the characteristic device of early modern biblical criticism (and of Calvin), accommodation, to explain how the Bible can be a book from an omniscient and truthful God while also containing claims that are, by modern scientific accounts, simply false. Enns makes the theme of accommodation explicit:

> This is what it means for God to speak at a certain time and place—he enters *their* world. He speaks and acts in ways that make sense to *them*. This is surely what it means for God to reveal Himself to people—he accommodates, condescends, meets them where they are.[62]

Accommodation, as noted above, is a Calvinist theme. But Enns' use is closer to Galileo's. Enns believes on other grounds that some claims of the Bible may not be historically defensible, and accommodation helps him reconcile the Bible's literal claims with the findings of contemporary historical scholarship.

Similar assumptions are evident in Enns' discussion of harmonization. He asks, what did Nathan say to David? 2 Samuel 7 is not identical to 1 Chronicles 17. Which is right? Enns concludes, "I am beginning to suspect that this is not the primary question the Bible is set up to answer."[63] Questions about what happened are not part of the scope of Scripture. Enns explains the practical impact of his incarnational model, saying that "the central function of the Old Testament may not be there to 'tell us what to do,'" but instead to reveal Jesus. Though the core of Scripture for Enns is Jesus, rather than morality, the underlying husk/kernel model is the same as Kant's.

Enns is not the only evangelical to introduce Spinozist and Kantian themes into his hermeneutics. In a widely quoted passage, Richard Longenecker says that we ought not attempt to reproduce the style of Paul's arguments, even though we have to accept their substance:

> But apart from a revelatory stance on our part, I suggest that we cannot reproduce their pesher exegesis. While we legitimately seek continuity with our Lord and his apostles in matters of faith and doctrine. . . . we must also recognize the uniqueness of Jesus as the true interpreter of the Old

Testament and the distinctive place he gave to the apostles in the explication of the prophetic word.

> Likewise, I suggest that we should not attempt to reproduce their midrashic handling of the text, their allegorical explications, or much of their Jewish manner of argumentation. All of this is strictly part of the cultural context through which the transcultural and eternal gospel was expressed. This is fairly obvious where such methods are used more circumstantially and in *ad hominem* fashion. But it is true even when they are not.

And again,

> What then can be said to our question, "Can we reproduce the exegesis of the New Testament?" I suggest that we must answer both "No" and "Yes." Where that exegesis is based on a revelatory stance, or where it evidences itself to be merely cultural, or where it shows itself to be circumstantial or *ad hominem* in nature, "No." Where, however, it treats the Old Testament in more literal fashion, following the course of what we speak of today as historico-grammatical exegesis, "Yes." Our commitment as Christians is to the reproduction of the apostolic faith and doctrine, and not necessarily to the specific apostolic exegetical practices.[64]

That is to say, when the apostles do what we do, we can follow their example. When they do not, we cannot. Longenecker, though, faces the obvious question: exactly what kind of hermeneutical authority does the New Testament have? How is the apostles' reading supposed to form our reading if we are constantly pulling up short and refusing to follow their interpretive hints?

Longenecker places us squarely in the husk/kernel hermeneutics of modern liberal theology, at a somewhat different level. He certainly wants us to acknowledge Paul's theology, and to do theology in the way Paul did. He certainly thinks that Paul had every right to argue the way he did. He wants us to draw the same conclusions Paul drew from the gospel, and to affirm that we are reconciled to God by the grace of Christ through faith. But Longenecker does not always want us to follow the reasoning

Paul used to draw those conclusions. We are supposed to follow Pauline doctrine, but not Pauline exegesis. The kernel of doctrine is detached from the husk of Paul's puzzling and odd, if entertaining, rhetoric and dialectic. We are to follow Paul's doctrine, and in the few instances where he shows us the pathway to the doctrine, we can follow his path. We are not, however, supposed to use the same path elsewhere. Paul may teach us how to read certain texts, but Paul is not supposed to teach us how to *read.*

He disagrees with this stance

Conclusion

The Bible's message is the power of God to salvation, but that message comes to us in a particular form, using particular categories, introducing a particular language. It is the power of salvation for whole humans—for their languages and institutions, their imaginations and poetry, their art and architecture—as much as for their souls. Its transforming power becomes incarnate in human life through various media (sacraments, other believers), but the incarnation of the message occurs largely through words, preeminently the words of Scripture. When we detach the message from the medium, we muzzle the message itself. The message can still get through; the Spirit blows where he listeth. But the message does not get through in its full transfiguring power.

My aim in the remainder of this book is to enrich the reading of individual believers, pastors, and theologians by encouraging devoted attention to the husk. But not only that; my aim is also to contribute to the recovery of Scripture as the world-forming book it was intended to be. To that end, this book will insistently, manically present a hermeneutics of the letter.

That is, looking to the hermeneutics hints of apostolic interpretation of the Jesus gospel event *husk*

My aim is also to contribute to the recovery of Scripture as the world-forming book it was intended to be.

Scribes, Scripture, and Supplication

[handwritten: Typology, what is the event?]

Texts Are Events

Typology

[handwritten: Hirschian Interpretation and How It All Turned Out]

The authors of the New Testament do unconscionable things with the Old Testament. Whatever he might have been thinking at the time, Hosea was, by Matthew's account, referring to Jesus' flight from Bethlehem when he wrote, "Out of Egypt I called My Son" (Hos 11:1; Matt 2:15). Whatever Zechariah had in mind, he was actually prophesying Jesus' triumphal entry to Jerusalem when he wrote, "Behold your king is coming to you" (Zech 9:9; Matt 21:5). Even sober-minded Paul could not help messing with the intended, literal meanings of texts. There is no hint that the "Rock" in the wilderness "followed" Israel; nor is there any evidence that the rock was "Christ" (1 Cor 10:1-4). On the triangle of Abraham, Hagar, and Sarah—and the related sibling rivalry of Ishmael and Isaac—Paul freely allegorizes. At least he admits that he is allegorizing (Gal 4).

What gave him the right? Some think he had no right. He ought not to have done this. Paul was an irresponsible reader, a strong misreader, and so are all who follow him.

E. D. Hirsch has, in the last few decades, been the primary (almost the only) exponent of the view that textual meaning is the meaning intended by the author, and that this meaning is stable through time. Hirsch admits that the significance of a particular text changes for readers in different circumstances, but this shifting significance is rooted in a stable verbal meaning. Any other approach to textual meaning, Hirsch fears, can only lead to relativism. If meanings change, then texts can be made to mean whatever readers want them to mean.[1]

This seems perfectly sensible, even obvious. It would be uncharitable, if nothing else, to attribute to an author things he or she did not mean to say. And if the meaning of the text changes with the seasons, then textual meaning appears pretty much indistinguishable from meaninglessness.

It all seems perfectly obvious, until we read Matthew. A reader of the Old Testament and a writer inspired by the Spirit finds something in Hosea 11:1 that Hosea could not have intended in any sense of the word *intend*. How do we account for that?

As we saw in chapter 1, Richard Longenecker does not want to accuse Matthew or Paul of misreading, and he tries to split the difference. As we also saw, Longenecker's position accepts the husk/kernel model that is the heart of modernist, post-Kantian hermeneutics. That is not going to produce a robust, culture-transforming reading of Scripture. It makes us liberals in method and presumption, even if our convictions about the text and our conclusions are conservative.

If we want to avoid liberalism, we must make sense of apostolic exegesis. How?

THE LOGIC OF APOSTOLIC READING

One option, noted by Longenecker, is to show that the apostles employ some of the hermeneutical techniques of their Jewish contemporaries. They are doing midrash or pesher. Peter Enns also points out, for instance, that Paul did not invent the walking rock, but drew on existing Jewish tradition. Enns, unlike Longenecker, thinks that we can follow apostolic example in our own reading.[2] True as this is, it does not really answer the key questions: Where did those pre-Pauline Jewish readers get that reading of the exodus story? By what logic could they draw that kind of conclusion? And if they could find a walking rock in Exodus and Numbers, could they not find just about anything they fancied? If Paul borrows their conclusions, is he endorsing their logic?

Another legitimate but limited response is to point out that the Scripture is uniquely a double-authored text.[3] In determining the author's meaning of an Old Testament passage, we also have to reckon with the intention of the divine author. Hosea was recalling to the exodus when he wrote of Israel being called from Egypt, but the divine author knew that the exodus was merely a foreshadowing of a new and greater exodus that would be accomplished in the incarnate life and death of the Son of God.

A related response is to say that the apostles were divinely inspired, and so their readings of the Old Testament are correct even when we cannot see the logic of their reading or imitate it. This leads us back to the problem in Longenecker's position: If one can read the Old Testament this way only under the direct and special inspiration of the Spirit, what happens to those of us (i.e., all of us) who lack that apostolic unction? How should we read? And how is the Bible forming our reading at all?

A more complete defense is to say that the apostles were not indulging their penchant for Barthesian jouissance in their interpretations, but were following hints from the Old Testament itself. About that rock: though Exodus never says the actual stone that produced water in the wilderness followed Israel, Exodus does say that something—someone—was following Israel: the cloudy pillar of fire, or fiery pillar of cloud, went "behind" Israel as they passed through the sea (Exod 14:19). When the people complain about the lack of water, Yahweh instructs Moses, "I will stand before you there on the rock at Horeb, and you shall strike the rock, and water shall come out of it, that the people may drink" (Exod 17:6). Moses strikes not just the rock but Yahweh himself with the rod that brought judgments to Egypt, and from Yahweh stricken, smitten, afflicted, flow rivers of living water.[4] But Paul says that the rock followed them. Just so: every Israelite regularly sang the song of Moses, which declared Yahweh to be the Rock of Israel (Deut 32:4, 15, 18, 30, 31; and, tucked in between, v. 13). I cannot prove it, of course, but I strongly suspect that both Jewish midrashists and Paul used something like this line of meditation to arrive at the conclusion that the rock that followed and watered Israel was Yahweh the Rock. "That Rock was Christ" suddenly seems a far more plausible interpretation of Exodus.

Or take the allegorization of the story of Isaac and Ishmael. Is there any hint in Genesis that Ishmael is a type of fleshly Israel or that Isaac is the child of the Spirit? Yes, in fact.[5] For starters,

Genesis is fragrant with foreshadowing of Israel's later history. Abram enters Egypt, the Egyptians suffer plagues, and Abram returns to the land, where he engages in a battle for control of Canaan (Gen 12–13). Isaac and Jacob also go through exodus experiences, and the last thirteen chapters of the book begin the exodus story that continues into the following books.[6] Further, Ishmael and Isaac are born on opposite sides of Abram's circumcision. Ishmael is born while Abram still has his "flesh," his foreskin, but Isaac is born after Abram's flesh has been cut off, after Abram has become Abraham and ritually renounced confidence in flesh (Exod 17). It is one of the high ironies of the Galatian heresy that they have fleshly confidence in circumcision, a ritual that renounces flesh by removing it.

Beyond that, there are evident structural parallels between the story of Ishmael's departure from Abram's camp and Isaac's sacrifice on Mount Moriah:

Ishmael, Genesis 21:8-21	Isaac, Genesis 22:1-19
Cast out, v. 10	Take son, v. 2
Rose early, v. 14	Rose early, v. 3
Journey, v. 14	Journey, vv. 3-4
Shouldering burden, v. 14	Shouldering burden, v. 6
Child in distress, vv. 16-17	Child near death, v. 7
Angel, v. 17	Angel, v. 11
Life boy, v. 18	Do not lay hand on boy, v. 12
God opened eyes, v. 19	Abraham looked and saw, v. 13
Well, v. 19	Ram in thicket, v. 13
Lived in Paran, v. 21	Lived in Beersheba, v. 19[7]

Ishmael's experience thus foreshadows, in great detail, the later story of Isaac.

We can go further, in fact: Ishmael's history is not only a prototype of Isaac's but of Israel's. He goes from Abraham's camp into the wilderness, where God miraculously provides water. Later, he settles in Paran, where he marries an Egyptian and has twelve sons, all of them princes. At a time when Isaac still has to be content with only two squabbling sons, his half-brother is already living the history of the twelve tribes. That Ishmael decreases so that Isaac might increase does not mean that Ishmael was nothing.

Rabbi Paul, bending for decade after decade over the Torah, might well have recognized the melody of Ishmael being transposed into the history of Isaac, and concluded that the whole story foretold a future transposition on a greater scale.

All this is true and helpful, but several of these arguments fail in one crucial respect: if the apostolic reading of Scripture is defended by appeal to the uniqueness of Scripture, how is this method of reading supposed to inform our reading of other texts? Apostolic reading would give us a sacred hermeneutics, applicable to the single double-authored, inspired text of the Bible but inapplicable to every other text. We might read Jeremiah as Matthew does, but we ought not read Marvell that way. Do the apostles teach us how to read double-authored texts? Or do they teach us how to read?

Is it possible to justify apostolic reading—which I will call *typological*—with an argument that applies to texts as such, or at least to all texts of major importance? Can we defend typology as a mode of reading in general, not merely as a mode of reading Scripture?

I believe so, and I believe it can be done by highlighting the crucial factor of time in interpretation. To put it simply, we find typology odd only because we make a prior assumption that texts and their meanings are timeless. That assumption is false. Authors exist in time and take time to write, and any self-aware author will tell you that what he or she means changes and develops as the time of writing passes. Readers are also in time, always a different time from authors and sometimes a vastly different time, and they take time to read. Once texts are written and distributed, many persist through time and are read by readers at different times, many of whom have read not only the text but also the musings of earlier readers of the text. I will take some time to get to this point, but the goal of this chapter is to show that once we discard the false assumption that texts are timeless, typological reading is the most natural thing in the world.

But at our backs we always hear E. D. Hirsch winging near. Hirsch asks, do we not need fixed texts with fixed meanings if we are going to avoid subjectivism, arbitrariness, and eisegesis?

If texts and their meanings are in time, can we not make them mean anything we want them to mean?

The answer is no, but we must answer carefully, and let us answer by clearing the site before we begin building. Let us begin not with texts but with events.

A Changing Past?

Some forty years ago, Arthur C. Danto imagined a historian whom he called the "Ideal Chronicler" or "I.C." The I.C. is blessed with a kind of omniscience as well as infallibility. Though he does not know the future, he knows every event that happens at the very moment it happens and never gets anything wrong. He also possesses the unique gift of "instantaneous transcription." As soon as an event happens, it is recorded in the Ideal Chronicler's Ideal Chronicle.

The I.C. sounds like a perfect historian, but Danto did not think so. Many historical truths would be unavailable to the I.C. He could not, for instance, know that "The Thirty Years War began in 1618." He would know the 1618 Prague Defenestration in excruciating detail, he would know all about the dung hill that broke the fall of the defenestrated, and he would know all the circumstances that made this event the spark for a war. But he could not know that the war would last thirty years. Danto says that the I.C.'s chronicle would be complete "in the way in which a witness might describe it, even an Ideal Witness, capable of seeing all at once everything that happens, as it happens, the way it happens."

But, he adds emphatically, *"this is not enough"*:

> there is a class of descriptions of any event under which the event cannot be witnessed, and these descriptions are necessarily and systematically excluded from the I.C. The whole truth concerning an event can only be known after, and sometimes only *long* after the event itself has taken place, and this part of the story historians alone can tell.[8]

The I.C. could never have said, as Yeats did of Zeus' rape of Leda,

> A shudder in the loins engenders there
> The broken wall, the burning roof and tower
> And Agamemnon dead.[9]

Stories may only be told by those

The I.C., for all his omniscience, could not fully know what happened at the Prague Castle on May 23, 1618, nor what was going on when Zeus raped Leda. <u>He could not tell any stories because stories can be told only by those who know the end.</u>

Danto concluded that our descriptions of past events necessarily change as time moves on. He did not conclude that the past itself is alterable. An event of the past can acquire new properties as related events unfold. After the Peace of Westphalia, we can describe the Prague Defenestration as having the property of being "the beginning of the Thirty Years' War." Over time, it takes on further properties, as it comes into relationship with other events: the political disarray of Germany, the writings of early modern political theorists haunted by the horror of religious war, the rise of the modern nation-state, and so on. But the event does not change because we do not "causally operate on that event." It takes on new properties only because "the event at t-1 [the time it happens] comes to stand in a different relation to events that occur later." Our descriptions of the event necessarily become richer over time, but the event remains stable: "The Past does not change, perhaps, but our manner of organizing it does."[10]

Danto is the E. D. Hirsch of the philosophy of history. For Danto, the past event is fixed and stable, but the significance of that event, and our description of it, grows richer and richer as passing time brings the event into a more and more complex set of relationships. Meaning remains stable; significance changes over time. *Helpful*

This gets us some way, but not far enough. Our descriptions do change over time, but not only our descriptions. Events themselves change over time, taking on new properties because of later events.[11]

Consider an assassination. At 10:00 a.m., the assassin aims, shoots a gun, and hits his target with a bullet to the head. At 1:00 p.m., the victim dies at the hospital.

This event is fixed in certain respects. At 10:00 a.m., the assassin pointed the gun and pulled the trigger, a bullet was propelled through the barrel toward the victim, the bullet flew through the space between the gun and the victim, the bullet entered the victim's head, and so on. That "skeletal event"[12] is done, and in this respect, what's done cannot be undone.

That level of description is not very satisfying, though. If we leave things at that, we are back in the dilemma of the I.C. Besides, in other respects, the event at 10:00 a.m. changes as a result of the event at 1:00 p.m. At 1:00 p.m., we can announce that "an assassination took place, a horrific and brazen murder." We cannot say that at 10:30 a.m. because there has not yet been an assassination or a murder. At most, at 10:30, we can say that there has been an attempted murder. How are we to account for this?

We might be tempted to say with Danto that only the "description" of the event has changed. We have changed our description, from shooting to murder, but that is because the victim died. Shooting and killing qualify as two different descriptions of the same event. That is true in one sense. At 2:00 p.m., we can call what happened at 10:00 a.m. either a shooting or a killing. But those are not alternative descriptions between 10:00 a.m. and 1:00 p.m. They are two different events, and only one of them happens before 1:00 p.m.

We might say that we do not know what happened at 10:00 a.m. until 1:00 p.m. That does not work either. We do know what happened at 10:00 a.m.: there was a shooting and an attempted assassination. Long before 1:00 p.m., the Internet will be buzzing with reports and analysis and probably a cell phone video. Between 10:00 a.m. and 1:00 p.m., we know there has been a shooting, but we do not yet know that there has been an assassination. That is because there has not been one. We can say that we do not know *fully* what happened at 10:00 a.m. This is correct, but it is important to see the reason why it is correct. We cannot know the event fully because we do not yet know how the events of 10:00 a.m. will be modified by later events.

We might say that the shooting happened at 10:00 a.m., while the killing occupied the time between 10:00 a.m. and 1:00 p.m.[13] Or we might say that the shooting took place at 10:00 a.m. but the killing at 1:00 p.m. Neither of these makes sense. The assassin was either arrested or on the run during that period. He was not continuously shooting his victim. While the victim's dying occupied the time between 10:00 and 1:00, it strains language to say that the killing took place over the course of three hours. And the action that caused the victim's death took place at 10:00 a.m., not 1:00 p.m., so it is not accurate to say that the assassin killed his victim at 1:00 p.m.

The cleanest way to answer this conundrum is the most unsettling: the past event changed from a shooting to a murder as a result of a subsequent event, the death of the victim. At 10:00 a.m., there was a shooting; at 1:00 p.m., that original event changed from a shooting to a killing.

Or, to go back to our earlier example: the Defenestration of Prague sparked a war, but it became the spark for the Thirty Years' War only after that war had been fought and brought to an end. This is not simply a change of description but a change of the event. And the event changes for the very reason that Danto said the description changes—because the event is brought into relation with subsequent events and acquires new properties that change the very thing that it is.[14]

In important ways, this takes our actions, and the meaning of our actions, out of our hands. Did the ruffians who threw the two imperial representatives and their scribe, Philip Fabricius (later Philip von Hohenfall), onto the dung heap at the foot of the Prague Castle intend to start a Thirty Years' War? How could they have intended such a thing? Yet, for all subsequent historians, that is what their action was and that is what it meant. This does not mean that intention is irrelevant. We intend our actions. We are not at the mercy of random forces. We might grab hold of someone, lift him off the ground, and toss him through the nearest window. We intend to defenestrate, and we intend to defy the emperor. Once that more or less skeletal event is over, though, what that event becomes, what kinds of properties it takes on, and what it means escape our control.

This does not mean that every event changes every prior event in any meaningful way. Even events caused by prior events do not necessarily change what those prior events were. My musings on the Thirty Years' War were caused by the Thirty Years' War. If the war had never taken place, I would never have commented upon it. But my comments do not have any significant effect on the event.

It is enough, though, to show that some historical events—many, in fact—are changed in fundamental ways by subsequent events. Already we are some way toward typology. What happened when Abraham took Isaac to the altar? We can describe the event in sheer physical terms: Abraham and Isaac walked up the mountain, Isaac carrying the wood; Abraham bound Isaac; Abraham raised his knife; he heard a voice; he stopped. We might even give a thicker description of the event: by delivering Isaac from the knife, Yahweh promised Abraham that his seed would rise from the dead. Once Jesus rises from the dead, though, that earlier event becomes something more specific. It becomes a promise of Jesus, the crucified and risen Messiah, a type and a foreshadowing of the great deliverance of Golgotha, the final sacrifice.[15]

So much for events. What can we say about texts and their meanings? Do meanings change over time?

It appears that the answer is yes. From the earlier argument, we can conclude that texts say new things as they come into relationship with subsequent texts and events. But again, we must answer carefully.

Changing Meaning

In a very obvious and important sense, texts are fixed. Every reproduction of a text should include the same markings on the page in the same order. Any competent reader who reads the text aloud should make the same (or very similar) sounds. If we change the words or the word order, eventually we will have a different text.[16] If the text is a poem, then a single change would, for the poet at least, constitute an assault on his poem. Eliot would not recognize

> April is the cruelest month, breeding
> Roses out of the dead land, mixing
> Memory and desire, stirring
> Dead roots with spring rain.

as his own, because he wrote "lilacs," not "roses," and said the roots are "dull," not "dead."

Nor would he acknowledge paternity of

April is the cruelest month,
Breeding lilacs out of the dead land,
Mixing memory and desire,
Stirring dull roots with spring rain.

"It's all wrong," he would say, even though all the right words are there in the right sequence. The only change is the placement of the participles, but that would be enough to drive Eliot to raving. Moving the participles (breeding, mixing, stirring) from the ends to the beginnings of the lines destroys the meter and rhyme (-ing, -ing, -ing). More subtly, moving the participles rushes past the momentary suspension of the line. "April is the cruelest month" is arresting because we consider spring the season of new birth and hope, of sunshine and Easter lilies. "April is the cruelest month, breeding" is more arresting still, hinting at a paradoxical reason for April's cruelty (how is breeding cruel?), and for a split second leaves us pondering breeding without knowing what is being bred. We first get pure breeding, unqualified breeding, breeding as a Platonic idea, before it closes in on the concrete "dead land" breeding "lilacs." At the same time, Eliot's placement of the participles leaves the reader hanging over a cliff at the end of each line, clinging to a transitive verb with no object. "Breeding what?" and "Mixing what?" we demand of the first and second lines as Eliot wrote them. Changing the order of words changes the reader's experience of the lines.

The text is fixed.[17] Come tide, come storm, if we have *The Waste Land*, we have *these* words in *this* order of *these* lines. Any time *The Waste Land* is read, it is the same text, or it is no longer *The Waste Land* but some cheap knock-off, a bastard and no true son.

And the meaning is fixed too, is it not? This is a much more complicated question, and it depends on what is meant by "meaning."

Questions about meaning are often historical questions: what did this set of words mean to the author who wrote them and to the audience that first read them? To answer that, we make our best effort to study the language of the time in which the text was written, the connotations and associations attached to particular words and phrases and forms and genres, the cultural and political setting in which the text was first issued, and so on. No matter how much research we do, we may miss some important information that would illuminate the text, especially if the text was written in a faraway time, in a language different from ours, in a cultural situation very different from our own. Unless we have textual evidence (and textual evidence is always fragmentary), we will never know that a particular word or turn of phrase in the *Canterbury Tales* was widely understood as fourteenth-century slang for drunkenness. This does not imply that the meaning (in this sense) of an old text is beyond recovery. Recovering the meaning of an ancient text is difficult, but it is possible.

This is the meaning that Hirsch and many biblical scholars are most interested in. In this sense, it is quite true to say that a text means what it says. In this sense, too, it is accurate enough to say that the text has a fixed meaning. Whatever nuances it may have had for Paul, the Greek word *sarx* means "flesh," and that is how we should understand and translate its occurrences in the New Testament. Whatever additional connotations there might be to "April is the cruelest month," it means "April is the cruelest month."

Meaning in this sense is somewhat analogous to the skeletal event we examined above. We can reconstruct a fixed historical event from remaining sources, and we can reconstruct the original meaning of a text from the available evidence.

When we have explored this dimension of the meaning of a text, though, we are only beginning to explore the text's full meaning. It is a necessary beginning, but it is not the end. Interpretation is never simply paraphrase. Expressing the meaning of a text is never simply a matter of discovering synonyms.

Once we go beyond this skeletal notion of meaning, things get interesting because, in most other senses of the word meaning, the meaning of a text is not fixed but mutable. The event of the text is fixed in some respects, but like all events, it is subject to change in the light of later events.

For starters, words can change meaning, and therefore sentences made from the same words can change meaning too.

Uttered in one time period, the sentence "She is nice, glamorous, and gay" would mean "She is an ignorant but cheerful witch." *Nice* meant ignorant, *glamorous* is derived from a word connoting witchcraft, and *gay* meant happy and light and (perhaps) slightly airheaded. Uttered today, the sentence means "She is a pleasant, alluringly beautiful homosexual." Even today, one can utter the very same words in the very same order and mean quite different things. When words take on new meanings, they do not immediately shed old ones. Many of the words we use have many meanings, some dominant and some subordinate, and the relation of dominant and subordinate is changing all the time. Saying "fag" on the streets of San Francisco might be a (somewhat retro) insult to homosexuals; saying "fag" to your buddy with a pack of cigarettes is a (somewhat retro) request for a smoke.

This is simple. The more mysterious and difficult cases are texts in which word meanings remain relatively constant but the meaning of the statement as a whole changes. This is how the meaning of Hosea 11:1 changes from its setting in Hosea to its setting in Matthew 2. Making allowances for translation, the words "out of Egypt I called my Son" mean the same in the original text and in Matthew. *Egypt* means Egypt, the nation to the south of Israel; *call* means call; *my* is a first-person possessive pronoun in each text; and *Son* means male offspring. The words are the same, and the individual meanings of the words are also the same, but something has happened between Hosea and Matthew. The text no longer means quite what it meant. Something magical has happened between, so that the same words in the same order mean differently. Can we account for this magic?

Meaning can describe what is done with words. Umberto Eco recalls the moment in 1985 when President Ronald Reagan tested a microphone by saying, "In a few minutes I'll push the red button and I'll start bombing the Soviet Union." When challenged, Reagan claimed he was horsing around. Did he mean it or not? According to the intention of the work—the sense of the words themselves—he did say, "In a few minutes I'll push the red button." But according to the authorial intention, "he only *pretended* to say so." Eco takes this as an example of the commonsensical

conclusion that sentence meaning and intended authorial meaning do not always coincide.[18] Reagan was justified in protesting,
in response to reporters who suspected he was an aggressive war-
monger who really did mean what he said, "No, I didn't mean it. I
was only joking." He was not fudging on the word mean.

Put to a different use in different circumstances, the same set
of words in the same sequence would have a different meaning.
They could constitute a genuine threat: "In a few minutes, I'm
going to push the red button," says Reagan to Gorbachev over the
red phone. Uttered by Harrison Ford in a Clancy-inspired Cold War
film, the same set of words would be a pretended threat. Repeated
as a quotation from a movie by someone preparing to push the red
button on a lawn mower, the same set of words again becomes a
joke, but with a different texture than Reagan's.[19] "I do" could be
a promise of lifelong commitment, a lie, a pretense (if uttered in a
stage wedding), or a joke. Perhaps Matthew is *doing* something different with "out of Egypt I called My Son" than Hosea did.

But there are other options. Meaning also has to do with what
a text tells us to do.[20] "If your hand offends you, cut if off," says a
preacher, and the next Sunday, half the congregation comes back
mutilated. "I didn't mean *that*," he protests. "What I meant was
that you should deal forcefully with temptation and sinful habits."
Did he mean it? If we attend only to the sense of the words, then he
meant it. If we attend to what he wanted the congregation to do as
a result of his sermon, he did not mean it. After another sermon, a
church member says, "This means I'm going to have to change my
life." That is a perfectly sensible use of mean. "Can you sweep the
kitchen?" a mother asks, and when she finds the kitchen unswept,
she says, with exasperation, "I meant you should *do* it."

Meaning also has to do with personal significance. Grandma's
ivory comb does not mean much when she first gives it to the six-
year-old you, but over the years, it acquires more meaning. After
her death, it becomes a treasure: "I'll never part with it. It means
so much to me." Textual meaning can be enriched in similar
ways. *Macbeth* may mean little when you are forced to read it in
high school, but once you begin a political career, Shakespeare's
cautionary tale of unbridled ambition gives you the insight and

critical distance to make your way in Washington without losing your soul. This is part of the phenomenon of second reading, and third and fourth. Read by a young teenager, *Pride and Prejudice* may seem dreamily romantic—"Ooh, that Darcy!" Several years later, after some romantic disappointments, you might be especially moved by the painfulness of Bingley's breakup with Jane. If you read it again as an adult, you will notice the icy subtlety of Austen's wit. The book becomes more meaningful, differently meaningful, as it is reread in new circumstances.[21] "*Pride and Prejudice* means something new every time I read it" is a perfectly sensible sentence. We know what it means.

More examples could be given to suggest different nuances of the word meaning, but these should suffice to establish that, in various senses of the word, meaning changes over time. How could it be otherwise? Authors and readers are, in Eugen Rosenstock-Huessy's phrase, not contemporaries but "distemporaries," inhabitants of different times.[22] The "present" of reading, interpretation, and meaning is always the product of the meeting of distemporaneous authors, texts, and readers. It is a fundamental error of interpretation to think that the reader can or should be made a contemporary of the author. As Hans-Georg Gadamer points out, no matter how hard we try to inhabit the past or how good we get at it, it is still the present-tense *we* who inhabit it.

Readers cannot shed their own prejudices, strip off the clothing of intervening history, and embrace the author naked, as it were. Readers inhabit a particular time, are heirs to a particular history, share in a particular cultural tradition. No reader ever approaches any text in complete innocence, with a blank slate. We come to a text in our native language with a prior knowledge of that language, at least the language as used by our contemporaries. We also have certain preconceptions and prejudices[23] concerning all sorts of things: the nature of reality, the value of texts, the way the world works, what words mean, what beauty is, and so on and on. Many of these prejudices may be unconscious, but they exist nonetheless. Many of them may be false or misleading, but many may be quite accurate. The Enlightenment ideal of complete emancipation from prejudice is illusory.

Passion precedes reason. Why pick up a book at all unless you have an interest in its subject matter (or someone with authority and a big paddle tells you that you ought to have an interest in the subject matter)? Why do you pick up the spy novel at the used bookshop instead of the handbook on lawn mower maintenance (or vice versa)? Why do you skip over the book written in Castilian and pick up the one in French? Perhaps because you read French and not Castilian? What makes your eye stop at one and not the other? What is that but personal, familial, educational, cultural prejudice? A completely unprejudiced reader would be a nonreader, lacking all motivation to take up and read in the first place. Why read John's gospel unless you already have some interest—be it purely academic—in Jesus?

A reader without prejudgments is also a reader who lacks one of the basic tools for reading well. Reading a parody of a romance (say, *Northanger Abbey*) without some expectations of what we would find in a normal romance means we miss the point of the parody. We have to have some prejudgment about what the book will contain in order to grasp the author's purpose.[24]

With the Bible and some other books of major cultural importance, the role of prejudgments, as Coleridge noted, is even more complex, because we all, Christian or not, live in a world that has been profoundly formed by the Bible.[25] Slight turns of phrase—prodigal son, good Samaritan, do unto others—are drawn from the New Testament, and the Bible's view of things has been institutionalized in Western civilization in thorough ways. The God that Christopher Hitchens disbelieves is the God who is love, the God revealed in Jesus. Hitchens does not spend his time articulating his disbelief in Jove or Marduk. There are disputes about posting the Ten Commandments in courtrooms; there are no disputes about posting the Code of Hammurabi, because doing so would be of purely antiquarian interest. When we sit down to read the Bible, we read it as readers already preformed by the Bible.

In all these ways, we readers live in time, at a particular time, and our notions and prejudices are formed by the times we live in, the institutions and habits that make up our world.

The author lived in a particular time too, and his or her time is never exactly ours. Even a newspaper article hot off the press was written a few hours before, and if the story is still breaking, the circumstances of my reading might be quite different from the circumstances of its writing. Even a blog entry was composed at least a few seconds before it is read. When the time gap between author and reader expands, and we add differences in language, politics, and culture, the process of reading becomes much more complicated. Authors and readers are distemporaries who meet in the present through what Rosenstock-Huessy calls the "social energies" of faith, hope, and love.

In many respects, then, meaning changes with the times because texts and their meanings are like events in several respects. The original writing and publication of a text is an event; my reading of that text is an event, or a series of events, caused by the text; and public interpretation and discussion of a text is another event caused by the original text. Here, I focus on the latter two events of the text, and I aim to show that in these two senses, the text and its meaning change in various respects over time.

First, the time of reading makes meaning, and because it takes place over time, meaning changes as I go. As I read, the event of reading chapter 1 is brought into relation to the later events of reading chapters 2 and 5 and 8, and what happened as I read chapter 1 changes in the light of those later events. Chapter 1 takes on new properties and meanings as I progress. It takes on at least the property of being the beginning of the story that continues into the later chapters. Or we can put it this way: the events that the text records change as we read. The weak form of this thesis is that we do not fully know what happened in chapter 1 until we get to the later chapters; the stronger form is that the events of chapter 1 are themselves different events once the events of chapters 2 and 5 and 8 occur (in the narrative, in our reading of the narrative). Either version is strong enough to support typological reading.

Second, the passage of time and the events that occur between text and reader contribute to, and might change the meaning of, the text. A terrorist sends an e-mail to a subordinate instructing him to detonate a bomb at Heathrow. If the note is intercepted and the plot foiled, what happened when the terrorist sent the e-mail was a conspiracy to commit a terrorist act, but not itself a terrorist act. If the bomb goes off, the event of the text is a different event—not just incitement to terrorism but the initiation of a successful terrorist plot.

These lines of argument will finally help us to justify the ways of Matthew to men; they will unveil the mysterious way of an evangelist with a prophet.

THE EVENT OF READING

"Once," the storyteller says, and stops. We feel a lurch, and might suffer a kind of mental whiplash. "Once upon," he continues. But each new word both states itself and urges us beyond itself. Each word carries more semantic load than a note of music, but each word is musically straining beyond itself, and meaning cannot be had without that straining.[*]

Why do we do this? What makes us feel that something more must be coming? Here is our first musical feature of texts:[26] they take time.[*]

As Jeremy Begbie insists, this taking time is not a flaw in music, but a central part of what music has to teach us. We can take in a painting or a statue at a glance—not fully, of course, but we can get an impression of the whole. To get the full impact of either, we need to spend time staring, asking questions, looking again, noticing. But a first impression gives us a lot. A building is more spacious, and so we have to spend more time to take it all in. We can only see one perspective at a time. But we can still gain a good deal from the first glance: we can tell whether it is Gothic or classical or modern, we can determine colors and materials and shapes, and we might be able to gain some idea of its purpose and function.

We cannot take in music in a moment. A chord gives us several notes at once, but a chord is not music, or not much music. To hear the simplest melody, we need to listen for at least a few seconds. And more complex pieces of music can take an hour or more to experience. Notes follow notes, measures follow measures, movements follow movements. Music is not the kind of art that allows us to "get to it, man." If we are going to listen to music at all, we have to give it time to unfold.

Music, I said, teaches patience, but that formulation is too intellectualist, as if I am standing back, watching myself listen to music, and then concluding, "Ah, yes. I see that I am supposed to learn patience from the experience of listening to music." Much better to say that music trains us in patience. It trains us in moving through dissonance and tension toward resolution. It trains us in waiting for the climax, waiting for beauty to build and build. It trains us not to seize. Music trains us in good sex, sex that takes time.

Texts are musical in the fact that in both texts and music, meaning is temporally unfolded. We can take in a short lyric poem in a few moments, to be sure. If the poem is a pattern poem, we can gain some insight into its meaning. We notice the title "Easter Wings" above a Herbert poem that is shaped like butterfly wings, and without reading a word, we have a notion of what is happening. Without a word, Herbert has begun to fill our minds with chrysalises, metamorphoses, deaths, and rebirths. Of course, though, we have not really understood the poem at all if we treat it as a piece of visual art. If we want to know what Herbert's poem means, we need to start reading words, and even the fastest speed-reader has to take in a group of words at a time. And who would want to speed-read Herbert anyway?

Texts are musical in that they take time, and the time texts take is musical time. The time of music and the time of texts always involve reaching for the next moment. Music is always moving toward the next note, and we are always reading beyond the individual word. Each sentence compels us to move forward; each paragraph carries us along to the denouement.

From the viewpoint of music, we can critique our basic conceptions of motion and time, concepts that have their roots in classical Greece. Motion, Victor Zuckerkandl says, brought the Athenian enlightenment up short because the problem was never solved. Zuckerkandl suggests that Zeno's error was to conceive of the "between" of motion—what lay between the initial location of an object and its later location—as an "interspace." Greeks

assumed that the process of motion could be entirely comprehended in spatial data; in Bergson's language, they failed
to maintain the distinction between motion and its spatial
track, the path traveled. The contradictions and paradoxes
thus arrived at . . . merely show that motion cannot be
entirely comprehended in spatial-local data. It is precisely
the essential element of motion which slips through the
net of spatial relations—and the more surely, the tighter
the net is drawn. . . . Rightly understood, what Zeno's paradoxes teach is that the stage on which motion is enacted
cannot be—or cannot be only—the space of places. Motion
must be something else than things changing place;
it must also occur—and perhaps occur essentially—where
no more things change their places.[27]

This is precisely what motion means in music:

To hear a tone as a dynamic quality, as a direction, a pointing, means hearing at the same time beyond it, beyond it
in the direction of its will, and going toward the expected
next tone. Listening to music, then, we are not first *in* one
tone, the in the next and so forth. We are, rather, always
between tones, *on the way* from tone to tone; our hearing
does not remain with the tone, it reaches through it and
beyond it. . . . It is a process on two levels, on one of which,
the "lower," there is nothing but the pillars, tones of definite pitch [which, Zuckerkandl points out, are static]; on the
other, the "higher" nothing but the transition, the passing
over. And the motion we hear is not at all the "tone|tone" of
the lower level; it is the "between" of the upper level, pure
betweenness, pure passing over. . . . the investigation of
seen motion and the investigation of heard motion coincide
in their end result. . . . The only difference lies in the fact
that, in the motion of things, the core of pure dynamism is
well concealed and had to be isolated artificially, whereas
in tonal motion barely anything is perceived but the purely
dynamic. . . . Not unjustifiably may we say that musical
motion is at the core of every motion; that every experience
of motion is, finally, a musical experience.[28]

The motion of a text is a "betweenness," and the time of reading
is always a time, to paraphrase Zuckerkandl, on the way from
word to word.

This does not appeal to us. We are often impatient with music, and we are impatient with texts. A writer lingers, and we want to grab him by the throat and say, "Get to the point, man!" Evangelicals would reverently refrain from throttling an apostle, but the demand for practical Bible teaching often has this threatening subtext. "Don't give me all these names, lists, genealogies, stories. Tell me what to do. Tell me about Jesus."

God in his infinite wisdom decided to give us a book, a very long book, and not a portrait or an aphorism. God reveals himself in his image, Jesus, but we come to know that image by reading, and that takes time. God wants to transform us into the image of his image, and one of the key ways he does that is by leading us through the text. If we short-circuit that process by getting to the practical application, we are not going to be transformed in the ways God wants us to be transformed. "Get to the point" will not do because part of the point is to lead us through the labyrinth of the text itself. There is treasure at the center of the labyrinth, but with texts, the journey really is as important as the destination. "Get to the point, man" is the slogan of the liberal theologian; it is a demand for the kernel without the annoying distraction of the husky twists and turns of the text itself.

We cannot get the meaning of a text without taking time. And as the text takes time, the meanings of earlier texts shift with the introduction of later texts. The meanings of the text emerge through the time of reading.

Grand Disappointments

Because it takes time, reading involves us in a process of searching, guessing at the next direction in the text, making judgments and misjudgments. Stanley Fish points out that readers do not come to the text "empty," and they do not simply extract what was "in" the text. Reading is—obviously, when one steps back and thinks about it—an interactive process between a text and a reader preprogrammed with all sorts of expectations and assumptions, not least about what the text is going to say. Fish writes that readers

are ignored because the text is taken to be self-sufficient—everything is *in* it—and they are devalued because when they are thought of at all, they are thought of as the disposable machinery of extraction. In the procedures I would urge, the reader's activities are at the center of attention, where they are regarded not as leading to meaning but as *having* meaning. The meaning they have is a consequence of their not being empty; for they include the making and revising of assumptions, the rendering and regretting of judgments, the coming to and abandoning of conclusions, the giving and withdrawing of approval, the specifying of causes, the asking of questions, the supplying of answers, the solving of puzzles. In a word, these activities are interpretive—rather than being preliminary to questions of value, they are at every moment settling and resettling questions of value—and because they are interpretive, a description of them will also be, and without any additional step, an interpretation, not after the fact but of the fact (of experiencing).

He adds, "Everything depends on the temporal dimension."[29] Exactly right. Everything depends on the temporal dimension.

The point can be illustrated with two recent literary "disappointments": Ian McEwan's *Atonement* and Cormac McCarthy's *No Country for Old Men*. In calling these disappointments, I do not mean that the novels fail to achieve their aims. They achieve their aims powerfully, but the aim of each is to create hopes in the readers that the author intends to dash in the end. The authors create tensions, compelling readers to move through the story in hopes of resolution, only to have their hopes ultimately disappointed. Dissonances in the plot leave us begging for resolutions that do not come. That movement of hope and despair is what the novels mean.

Atonement's effects arise from an erotic scene early in the novel, when thirteen-year-old Briony Tallis walks in the library to find her sister Cecilia making love to Robbie Turner, son of the Tallis housekeeper. Briony had already concluded, through a series of misinterpretations of events in the house, that Robbie was a sex maniac. She watched from a distance as Cecilia had an altercation with Robbie near the fountain in the yard, during which Cecilia stripped to her underwear and jumped in the fountain. Briony could not see that Robbie had accidentally broken a valuable vase, and Cecilia was retrieving the handle from the water. Later, Robbie asks Briony to deliver a note of apology to Cecilia, but too late he recalls that he had put a crude note in the envelope instead of his actual apology. Briony peeks at the note and is frightened; when Cecilia gets the note, she is aroused, and invites Robbie into the library when he arrives for dinner.

When Briony's cousins disappear from the house that same evening, the dinner guests fan out to search for them. Her girl cousin, Lola, is attacked and raped in the dark, and Briony comes to her just in time to see a tuxedoed figure running away. Despite the darkness and the fact that she never got a clear look, Briony convinces herself that she saw Robbie leaving Lola. Robbie is convicted of assault on the basis of Briony's false testimony, spends three years in prison, and is released only to enter the army to fight in World War II.

The interrupted romance of Robbie and Cecilia hangs over the rest of the novel, as we follow Robbie to Dunkirk and Briony to London, where she works as a nurse during the war. Finally, Briony finds Cecilia and Robbie living together in London, and they have a brutal, intense exchange. Briony now knows that Robbie did not assault Lola, and she promises to make atonement for the wrong she did.

In the final section of the novel, McEwan takes this slight gesture toward a happy ending from us. Briony reveals herself as the narrator of the whole tale, and admits that she never saw her sister:

> It is only in this last version that my lovers end well, standing side by side on a South London pavement as I walk away. All the preceding drafts were pitiless. But now I can no longer think what purpose would be served if, say, I tried to persuade my reader, by direct or indirect means, that Robbie Turner died of septicemia at Bray Dunes on 1 June 1940, or that Cecilia was killed in September of the same year by the bomb that destroyed Balham Underground station. That I never saw them in that year. That my walk across London ended at the church in Clapham Common, and that a cowardly Briony limped back to the hospital,

unable to confront her recently bereaved sister. . . . How could that constitute an ending? What sense or hope or satisfaction could a reader draw from such an account? Who would want to believe that they never met again, never fulfilled their love? Who would want to believe that, except in the service of the bleakest realism?[30]

Briony (McEwan) ends the novel wondering what sort of atonement is available for a novelist with her "Godlike" powers to determine outcomes.

Atonement is a brilliantly rendered novel on many levels, but I have two main points here concerning the temporality of reading and meaning. First, the meaning is not the timeless summary of the text (which is not strictly timeless anyway); it unfolds through the reading. McEwan makes Robbie so thoroughly appealing that we protest the injustice of his ruin; we feel all his indignation.[31] And he makes the attraction between Robbie and Cecilia so palpable that the novel is filled with an expectancy, a breathless hope, that the two young lovers will someday reunite. This is certainly part of the reader's experience of the novel, and the scene where Briony sees them together brings relief, touched by melancholy. But this is not only part of the experience of reading; it is the meaning of the novel, as McEwan makes clear in his metanarrative closing. The meaning arises from hoping, thinking we see our hopes realized, and then watching those hopes slip away. The meaning is disclosed only by taking the time that the text takes.

Second, the early events of the novel themselves change as we are given different endings. We can describe what happened in the library in a skeletal fashion: Robbie and Cecilia were having sex; Briony walked in; they stopped. That event happened, and its happening is a crucial fixed event of the story. But we do not know yet that this event is grounds for Briony's misapprehension (or lie), that it is the beginning of Robbie's tragedy, or that it is the beginning of a frustrated romance. So we do not yet know fully what happened in the library, because what happened in the library has not played itself out. We cannot know any of that until we get to the end of the story, and the end of the story changes not only what we thought happened but what did happen. McEwan's double ending makes the point very effectively: for a brief moment, we feel the satisfaction of Robbie and Cecilia's reunion, and the library scene and Briony's lie are a cross borne with patience and eventually overcome. Then McEwan withdraws his atoning ending, and the earlier events become different events right before our eyes. Briony stepping into the library was the end of Robbie and Cecilia's romance.

No Country for Old Men differs in nearly every respect from *Atonement*. McCarthy's prose is as arid and empty as the Texas landscape it depicts,[32] while McEwan writes lushly, with a formality that mimics the social standing of his characters. McEwan's novel takes us onto the field of World War II, but never achieves anything close to the terror and intense violence of McCarthy's "peacetime" novel.

What they share is a (sadistic?) effectiveness in arousing and dashing readers' expectations. In McCarthy's case, the expectations are not of romantic fulfillment but of justice. His villain, Chigurh (ironically pronounced something like "sugar"), is a brutal, relentless, conscienceless killer. A couple of pages into the novel, he chokes a deputy to death with the chains binding his hands, and then he steals a police car and stops the first motorist he finds. He walks to the car, still covered in the deputy's blood, carrying a loaded cattle gun and an air compressor, and puts a nail through the driver's head.

When Llewelyn Moss finds a case full of money from a busted drug deal, the dealers send Chigurh to get the money back. Sheriff Bell is after Moss too, as much to protect him as to force him to give up the money. The novel is a complex chase, with a growing body count as Chigurh dispenses with one after another of the counter–hit men sent to stop him, and anyone else unfortunate enough to get in his way. There are few novels that provide a villain so utterly evil, a villain that every reader wants stopped.

But he is not. Sheriff Bell is nearing retirement, and is, as a friend put it, not so much a relic of the Old West as a son of a relic.[33] He is not up to the task, and he knows it. In italicized meditations scattered throughout the book, Bell muses on his life in law enforcement, the increased violence of the world, and his own inability to handle the new challenges. The country he lives in is no country for old men, and at the end of the novel, Chigurh is still at large, limping away from a car accident shortly after killing Moss' wife. The book rouses all the indignation it can against this cold-blooded, amoral man, and then lets him go.

What the novel does to us is central to its meaning. McCarthy's title comes from Yeats' poem "Sailing to Byzantium," but the thematics of the novel are closer to Yeats' "The Second Coming."[34] Bell lives in a world where "the best lack all conviction / and the worst are full of passionate intensity." Chigurh is a rough beast to be sure, slouching toward Bethlehem to be born, a true and living prophet of destruction, as Bell calls him. If a reader is not caught up with a desire to see Chigurh get the justice he deserves, he has not gotten the point of the book. The novel means "Chigurh is one nasty customer whom you hope gets punished but he gets away."

John in Real Time

It takes time to read John 9, as it takes time to read any text. What happens as we take time to move through the labyrinth of John 9? How does the event of reading verse 1 change when the event of reading verse 15 happens? How do the events recorded in verse 5 become different events when we move later in the story? There is a great deal to say here, but I will highlight only a few aspects.

For a reader with some inkling of who Jesus is, the appearance of a blind man within Jesus' range of vision sets up expectations about what will happen next. Jesus is the One who gives sight to the blind and hearing to the deaf and makes the lame to skip like the gazelle. We suspect it is going to be a miracle story. As soon as we move to verse 2, the path of the text turns in a different direction. Instead of a simple "Jesus saw a blind man; the blind man asked for help; Jesus helped him" story, the disciples intervene with a question about the relation between the man's blindness and sin. We have expectations about where the text is taking us, and further expectations about what the text is going to teach us when we read Jesus' words about sickness and

[handwritten margin notes: How previous scripture events are meant to build [anticipation] of events in real time.]

sin in verses 3-5. But then those expectations are brought up short with Jesus' unusual actions in verse 6. Here is a blind man waiting to be healed, and Jesus is playing and spitting in the dirt like a schoolboy. We eventually get to a miraculous healing in verse 7, but the odd delay leaves us with questions that we hope John will answer—why clay? Why spit? Why "anoint" the man's eyes? What is going on?

Before there is any answer to these questions, the story veers in a different direction with the appearance of the inquisitive neighbors. The exchange between the blind man and his neighbors opens up yet another pathway through this text. These verses initiate another melody line with the question, "Where is He?" Jesus is nowhere to be found. Though we probably had not noticed, the question suddenly becomes the reader's question: "Yes, exactly, where did Jesus go?" Last we saw him, he was instructing the blind man to wash, but the man came back not to Jesus but to curious neighbors. And the question also makes us wonder what is actually going to happen to the blind man. He does not know where Jesus is either. Will he ever meet Jesus? Is he going to remain in darkness even after he has seen the light? Will he ever see the "light of the world" (v. 5)? What we suspected was becoming a testimony or a conversion story takes a twist, rouses expectations but delays satisfaction. Perhaps this is not even the story of the blind man's conversion, much less that of his neighbors.

The neighbors are surprised and confused, but not necessarily suspicious or skeptical. But John is not done adding to the cast of characters, and the next entry into the drama—the characters hiding around the next bend in the path of the text—are Pharisees. If our reader knows something about Jesus, the introduction of the Pharisees will send a chill through the story (v. 13). Since the neighbors bring the formerly blind man to the Pharisees, perhaps they are not as innocent as we thought. No sooner have we learned that the Pharisees have gotten involved than we find that it is a Sabbath day (v. 14), a crucial piece of information tucked away a third of the way through the chapter. The coming of the Pharisees, combined with the information that there is a legal dispute in the offing, intensifies the drama of the story. With sweeping capes and twirling handlebar moustaches, the villains enter stage left.

Here we get to the point of this excursion. John 9 is, in a sense, moving us through the experience of the first-century Jews themselves. Jesus appears, speaks, and heals, leaving confusion in his wake. We do not know what to think about this zephyr that blows through Israel (cf. John 3:8). When the surprise of the healing has worn off, the Jews—and we—realize that there is something potentially shady about this Jesus. He does things on the Sabbath that Jews strictly forbid. We, like the Jews, are forced to confront the question of Jesus' own sin, of his own lawbreaking. The disciples' question, "Did this man sin or his parents?" turns into "Is this man called Jesus a sinner?"

Throughout the blind man's confrontation with the Pharisees, the severity of the Pharisees' accusations increases, and so does the blind man's boldness. His Christology becomes increasingly high. As readers, we sympathize and root for the blind man. We already know that the Pharisees are villains, and we admire the blind man, as bold as he is ignorant. We do not know what happened earlier in the chapter, when he received his sight. We thought Jesus was only giving him eyes to see the world. We realize later that this is not all that happened; we realize that in giving sight, Jesus gave insight as well.

If we are looking for practical applications, we have one here. The blind man is a bold witness for a Jesus he barely knows, even when faced with highly trained Torah experts, even when bullied and browbeaten, even when threatened with expulsion from the synagogue. But it does not work to skip the story and say, "Be a bold witness for Jesus." The story gives us some idea of what it feels like to be a bold witness for Jesus. It enables us to feel the exasperation of trying to convince Pharisees of self-evident truth. We feel their cruelty and their blindness.

That question, "Where is He?" still lingers in the background. Indeed, where is he? Where did he go? And, more importantly, why is he not where he is supposed to be, that is, at the side of the blind man, defending and protecting and vindicating him? We know that Jesus can scatter a self-righteous crowd with a single sentence, and that he can corner them into murderous silence. He has just done that at the beginning and end of chapter 8. He was there to protect the woman taken in adultery, and he did not drift away while he was debating the Pharisees. But he is not around to help the blind man. Here, again, the meaning of earlier events of the text comes clear only later. We probably did not even realize Jesus had slipped away from the story until everyone started asking about him. What happened, and the meaning of what happened, changes as that earlier event comes into relation to later events. Jesus' departure takes on the property of "Jesus leaves the man undefended before a Pharisaic assault."

The story is not only a story of abandonment; it leads us through the experience of abandonment. Having come to light but not yet to Light, the blind man has to face his enemies without Jesus. Jesus does not return until it is too late: he comes back after "they put [the blind man] out" (v. 34). If only he had shown up earlier, the formerly blind man might have been able to remain in the synagogue.

But why would he have wanted to? The narrative makes it clear that as long as the blind man remains in the synagogue, he is not with Jesus. As soon as he steps across the threshold, he finds his Lord. Who would want to be in a synagogue that does not have Jesus in it?

All this is the meaning of the story. The narrative leads us here, turns us around, raises this question and then that, introduces new characters, and puts us with the blind man in the middle of a pack of Pharisees, teeth bared. If we do not share the blind man's joyful relief when he finds Jesus, we do not know what the story means. It does these things, though, only so long as we take time to pick our way through the labyrinth. What the text means to us emerges only as we follow the time of the text, as one event in the text is modified by the later events, as one event of our reading changes as we read on.

Writing and Reading Promises

John wrote the story of the blind man in such a way that we have to follow the twists and turns of the plot in order to see how the meanings of blindness and sight change. He knew when the story began that the man's literal blindness would be transposed into a different key by the end of the story, and he intended that deeper, or inverted, meaning from the beginning. Typology is deliberate foreshadowing, and the change in meaning from expectation to conclusion is the change from promise to fulfillment. The original text changes meaning when brought into relation to other texts.[34]

In this process, the original sense of the statement is not lost. It has to be retained to make sense of the fulfillment. As Eco points out, *pig* could never come to connote *filthy person* unless *dirty* and *stinky* were semantic adjuncts of pig.[35] Pointing to a barnyard animal and saying "pig" and describing a person as a pig is not just a matter of repeating the same sound in a different setting. The content of the word is carried along into the new usage, or the metaphorical use means nothing. Similarly, when "out of Egypt I called My Son" transfers from Hosea to Matthew, the original sense remains. Hosea is alluding (at least) to the "out of" of the exodus, to the Egypt of oppression, to Israel as Yahweh's near kin, his "son" (Exod 4:23).

As I understand Matthew, he is talking about Jesus' flight from Herodian Israel. If nothing else, the placement of the Hosea quotation links it more directly with Jesus' flight from Israel than with Jesus' return from Egypt. If this is the case, then the major terms of Hosea 11:1 have come under the shadow of ironic quotation marks. Jesus is fleeing not from Egypt but from "Egypt," and it is not Israel-the-son who escapes but Jesus-the-Son. The words have taken on a new meaning in this new setting, but a new meaning foreshadowed in Exodus and in Hosea. And Matthew's use of Hosea would not make sense unless his ironic "Egypt" still retained its connection with the original, literal Egypt. That is, the meaning of the quotation is lost unless we see that Herod is acting like Pharaoh, killing Israelite children; that his court trembles at the announcement of Jesus' birth, as Pharaoh's court was in fear of the plagues; that Herod consults his court magicians, as Pharaoh did. We miss the meaning of Matthew's application of "Son" to Jesus if we fail to see its connection with Israel the son. Jesus is the miracle child born from the seed of Abraham, who escapes from Pharaoh, who passes through the sea, who ascends a mountain to teach the law, et cetera. Even in Matthew, Egypt depends on Hosea's Egypt, and Matthew's Son depends on retaining Hosea's son.

I have suggested that Hosea 11:1 should be read as a foreshadowing type of Jesus' escape from Herod, analogous to the novelistic devices that evoke our anticipation of an approaching climax. That seems, however, to depend on a double-author theory rather than on the factor of time. After all, Hosea surely could not have known that he was writing of Jesus, and could not have intended the meaning Matthew attributes to him. While that is true (he surely did not know the names of Herod or Jesus or Joseph, and did not have the magic in mind), it is only part of the truth. Texts are sometimes interpreted as if their authors were interested only in speaking to the ears they can see, but many writers write for the ages, imagining future generations of readers.[36] Thucydides wanted his history to be a "possession for all time," and it has been. He would be delighted, but not surprised, to find college students still sweating over his text and professors still discovering new depths to, and applications of, his insights. It is just what he intended.

Hosea too. He was not only an author who hoped that future generations would listen, but was, besides, an Israelite prophet, living out of the achieved reality of the exodus and hoping against hope for a greater exodus to come. He surely did not think that the exodus from Egypt was the final word in Yahweh's salvation. How could he? He spends much of his prophecy castigating the idolatries of Ephraim, the northern kingdom. Surely, Israel in Hosea's time was just as much in need of escape as the Hebrews in the time of Moses. Like all faithful Israelites, he hoped for a redemption far beyond what Israel had already experienced. Like Isaiah, he could look back to the exodus from Egypt as a pattern for a future deliverance from a future Pharaoh. Matthew gives new meaning to Hosea, but the meaning he gives does not violate Hosea's original meaning. The meaning changes as Hosea's prediction comes to fulfillment, but the change is consistent with the original sense.

helpful Shown the exodus of Jesus and the even greater exodus of the cross and resurrection, Hosea would have nodded: "Yes, this is just what I was hoping for."

Thinking of types as foreshadowing gets us some way to recognizing the typological character of texts, but it is not the whole way. In addition, we need to consider what happens to texts after they seem to be finished.

TEXTS AND THEIR AFTERLIVES

How can each detail of Scripture is like a brilliant unfolding detective story

Historian David Steinmetz has suggested that apostolic readings of the Old Testament can be compared to readings of double narratives such as detective stories. Detective novels tell two stories at once: the story on the surface and the real story unveiled to the gathered suspects in the final chapter. Once the detective gives his solution to the crime, the reader cannot go back to the first narrative; the second completely overshadows it, and suddenly, conversations between characters that seemed on first reading to be of no very great significance now appear to be charged with unmistakable importance. How could I, the reader wonders, have overlooked the Irish wool cap in the closet, the old newspapers on the front steps, the half-smoked cigar in the ashtray, or the chipped vase on the side table?" Earlier, the story seemed "an almost random succession of events," but now it appears as "a complex and intelligible narrative guided unerringly to its destined end by the secret hand of its author. Under the circumstances, reading backwards is not merely a preferred reading strategy; it is the only sensible course of action for a reasonable person."[37]

Steinmetz is a historian, and is suggesting an analogy between detective fiction and the process of historical explanation, not merely literary explanation. Historians are faced with a welter of facts, and from that they construct a second narrative that attempts to "save the appearances" by accounting for all the relevant data. Historians must necessarily write from their own perspective, in which the story presents itself as a finished product: "It would, of course, be anachronistic to ascribe to the characters in a story a knowledge of how things would turn out as the events themselves were unfolding. But it is not anachronistic for historians to write history in the light of their knowledge, not only of how it unfolded, but also of how it ended."[38]

Thus, for instance, Steinmetz does not believe that "Second Isaiah" (who is really just plain old Isaiah) "had an explicit knowledge of the crucifixion of Jesus of Nazareth" when he wrote the servant songs:

> Like many of the characters in a mystery novel, Isaiah had something else on his mind. But the meaning of his work cannot be limited to the narrow boundaries of his explicit intention. Viewed from the perspective of the way things turned out, his oracles were revealed to have added dimensions of significance that no one could have guessed at the time. It is not anachronistic to believe such added dimensions of meaning exist. It is only good exegesis.[39]

Texts must be read in the light of "the way things turned out."[40]

Meaning, in short, is not only personally variable but culturally mutable. It depends on the way things turned out. Like events, texts not only can but must be read in relation to later events and texts. The original text and its meaning change with time, and our understanding of it must change accordingly.

Pride and Prejudice has a different cultural meaning in an age of casual dating, living together, hooking up, shacking up, getting down, premarital sex, and feminism than it did when Austen wrote it, or during the Victorian era.[41] For some, the changed circumstances lend *Pride and Prejudice* a halo of nostalgia that it certainly did not have for Austen: "Oh, for the simple clarities of gentry life" is a twenty-first-century sentiment not shared by the author. For others today, *Pride and Prejudice* is a stumbling block, a symbol of the oppression and repression from which, in the course of human events, we have happily been liberated. For still others, *Pride and Prejudice*, authored after all by a sheltered female, is part of that liberation, however much Austen might have played the Straussian and dressed her own feminist agenda in the patriarchal garb of her day. While we can establish more or less the cultural significance of Austen's novel to her and her original readers, that is certainly not what it means for us. The intervening history has given the novel a different meaning.

If novels are too complex in themselves and in their reception to make the point clearly, we can do it with simpler utterances. When first spoken, the sentence "Not even God can sink the Titanic" was not a wry joke. It already expressed the hubris of modern industrial man, but the hubris of the sentence is inflected today with an irony that it did not have in its original context. If we miss the irony, we do not know what the sentence means. Ditto for the statement, uttered at the beginning of the nineteenth century, "Everything that can be invented has been invented." History has a way of subverting pride against the intentions of the proud, and if we miss the subversion, we have missed the meaning of the sentence. Texts, we will learn in chapter 4, are jokes, and humor is often unintended by the author and unnoticed by the first hearers. We all stand in danger of being ironized by the course of time. We all stand in danger of being judged, not only by what we say, but by the fruits of what we say.

Texts and Their Fruits

This is true of many types of texts, not merely literary ones. Texts are events, and as events change their properties because of subsequent events, texts change their properties as they cause readers to say and do things.

Take Darwin: should Darwin be read in the light of what Darwinians have done with his theories? Do his texts mean something different now than they did then?

One of the most popular Darwinian biologists in nineteenth-century Germany was Ernest Haeckel. Darwin admiringly quotes Haeckel a number of times in his own work, and Haeckel's books were among the most popular nonfiction books in nineteenth-century and early twentieth-century Germany.[42] He was an avowed Darwinian who pressed the social and political implications of Darwinism more vigorously than Darwin himself. Societies, he insisted, could not rely on natural selection, but had to engage in artificial selection to ensure the health and fitness of the nation:

> In the same way as by careful rooting out of weeds, light, air, and ground is gained for good and useful plants, in like manner, by the indiscriminate destruction of all incorrigible criminals, not only would the struggle for life among

the better portion of mankind be made easier, but also an advantageous artificial process of selection would be set in practice, since the possibility of transmitting their injurious qualities by inheritance would be taken from those degenerate outcasts.[43]

This is chilling, and it is hard to read this without thinking of National Socialism. In fact, there is no evidence that Hitler read Haeckel, but Hitler's statements about struggle among nations, the need for "weeding" the garden of the *Volk* to ensure that the fit survive, and racial superiority are reminiscent of statements from Haeckel and other Darwinians. In a 1923 speech, Hitler said,

Decisive [in history] is the power that the peoples (*Volker*) have within them; it turns out that the stronger before God and the world has the right to impose its will. From history one sees that the *right* by itself is completely useless, if a mighty power does not stand behind it. Right alone is of no use to whomever does not have the power to impose his right. The strong has always triumphed. . . . All of nature is a constant struggle between power and weakness, a constant triumph of the strong over the weak.[44]

And from *Mein Kampf*:

A stronger race will supplant the weaker, since the drive for life in its final form will decimate every ridiculous fetter of the so-called humaneness of individuals, in order to make place for the humaneness of nature, which destroys the weak to make place for the strong.[45]

And from a 1928 manuscript:

While nature only allows the few most healthy and resistant out of a large number of living organisms to survive in the struggle for life, people restrict the number of births and then try to keep alive what has been born, without consideration of its real value and its inner merit. Humaneness is therefore only the slave of weakness and thereby in truth the most cruel destroyer of human existence.[46]

Lining up abstracted, contextless quotations may seem unfair, but historical connections exist and have been made by a number of historians, most notably Richard Weikart.

My point, however, is hermeneutical. Assuming that we can make the historical connections, is it eisegesis to read Darwin in the light of the Darwinian echoes in Haeckel and Hitler? Is it legitimate to interpret Darwin in the light of these later statements and movements? Is it legitimate to interpret Darwin's texts as seeds of Nazism and the Holocaust? Is it fair to read old texts in the light of newer ones, or of later events? Can we say of texts, "By their fruits you shall know them"?

Of course, it is not always possible to determine the character of the tree from the fruits. Traditions of interpretation can be traditions of misinterpretation. The fact that some Christians have used John 8–9 as justification for pogroms does not necessarily make those interpretations properly part of the text's unfolding meaning. This is where our first explorations of textual meaning are crucial. The text is fixed in the sense that the same words stand in the same order, and the original sense of the text can be fixed (or approximated) by historical study. An interpretive tradition can belie its source, and the tradition should be tested against the source text. Readers may misconstrue a text and read it in a way that not only goes beyond the author's intention but also directly contradicts the text and its author. Misreadings happen, and are not to be celebrated.[47]

So the echoes of Darwinian language force us back to the source text. Have Haeckel and Hitler misinterpreted Darwin? Did he repudiate these implications?

In this case, the original does not belie the interpretive tradition but confirms it. Examined in the aftermath of the Nazi regime, Darwin's notorious comments on breeding, human evolution, and racial/national superiority are horrifying. The first is from *On the Origin of Species* and the other two are from *The Descent of Man*:

> In each well-stocked country natural selection acts through the competition of the inhabitants, and consequently leads to success in the battle for life, only in accordance with the standard of that particular country. Hence the inhabitants of one country, generally the smaller one, often yield to the inhabitants of another and generally the larger coun-

try. For in the larger country there will have existed more individuals and more diversified forms, and the competition will have been severer, and thus the standard of perfection will have been rendered higher.[48]

At some future period, not very distant as measured by centuries, the civilized races of man will almost certainly exterminate, and replace, the savage races throughout the world. At the same time the anthropomorphous apes . . . will no doubt be exterminated. The break between man and his nearest allies will then be wider, for it will intervene between man in a more civilized state, as we may hope, even than the Caucasian, and some ape as low as a baboon, instead of as now between the negro or Australian and the gorilla.[49]

With savages, the weak in body or mind are soon eliminated; and those that survive commonly exhibit a vigorous state of health. We civilized men, on the other hand, do our utmost to check the process of elimination; we build asylums for the imbecile, the maimed, and the sick; we institute poor laws; and our medical men exert their utmost skill to save the life of everyone to the last moment. There is reason to believe that vaccination has preserved thousands who from a weak constitution would formerly have succumbed to smallpox. Thus the weak members of civilized society propagate their kind. No one who has attended to the breeding of domestic animals will doubt that this must be highly injurious to the race of man. It is surprising how soon a want of care, or care wrongly directed, leads to the degeneration of a domestic race; but excepting in the case of man himself, hardly anyone is so ignorant as to allow his worst animals to breed.[50]

These passages might have frightened some of their original readers. Some, however, nodded vigorously and got to work implementing Darwin's proposals. If, in the light of subsequent history, we fail to feel the chill, fail to hear the rap of the jackboot and sense the pressure of the Gulag, we do not understand what Darwin means.

John 9 as Fruit

John 9 takes time to read, and the meaning emerges as we do so. John 9, though, is part of a much larger text, and its meanings depend on its relation to earlier texts, just as the meanings of those earlier texts become what they are because of the event of John 9. In the following chapters, I will be examining different aspects of the typology of John 9, but we can make a beginning now.

Jesus says, "I am the light of the world" (9:5), a statement that alludes back to John's prologue (1:4-5) and ultimately to the first day of creation. Yahweh spoke and light shone out of darkness, and he spoke again in the incarnation to shine light into the darkness. In between, too, Yahweh promises again and again to give light. He gives light to Israel in the darkness of Egypt (Exod 10:23) and the night of the wilderness (Exod 14:23). He *is* David's light (Ps 27:1), his word a guiding light (Ps 119:105). Isaiah promises that one day Yahweh will shed a great light on all who are in darkness (9:2) and set up Israel itself as a light (42:6) to which the kings of the nations will repair (60:1-3). The God who created light at the beginning will bring in everlasting light, with no shadow of night (60:20).

Once we reread that account with John 1 and 9 in mind, we realize that the speaking of light on day one of the world was a promise of another speaking of another light. Genesis 1 moves us toward a future light, and once that light comes in the form of Jesus, we cannot read Genesis 1 in the same way. Genesis 1 and all the promises of light from Genesis to John take on a new dimension of meaning in the light of how things turned out.

Jesus makes clay and heals the blind man with clay, an allusion to the creation of Adam in Genesis 2. Again, John 9 teases out new meaning from Genesis. Adam was created from dust, and part of the curse is that he will return to that dust. But Genesis 2 leaves us with the hope that a God who made man from dust at the beginning will be able to raise him again from that dust. Hints of this hope are a major thread of Old Testament history—Isaac born from Sarah's dead womb, Israel reborn from the grave of Egypt and the death waters of the sea, David rescued from one mortal threat after another, Jehoiachin taken from prison and placed at the table of Merodach of Babylon, Israel's bones called from Babylon. All of these come to fruition in the story of John 9, as well as other episodes of the Gospels and Acts. Jesus is the One who fulfills all the hopes of Israel, the One who brings new life from the dead clay with breath and water from his mouth.

John 9 is also reminiscent of the story of Elisha and Naaman (2 Kgs 5). John Wesley notes that the blind man

> believed, and obeyed, and found a blessing. Had he been wise in his own eyes, and reasoned, like Naaman, on the impropriety of the means, he had justly been left in darkness. Lord, may our proud hearts be subdued to the methods of thy recovering grace! May we leave thee to choose how thou wilt bestow favours, which it is our highest interest to receive on any terms.[51]

John Chrysostom sees the same connection and, like Wesley, praises the blind man's faith:

> For it was likely that he would have considered with himself, and have said, What is this? He made clay, and anointed my eyes, and said to me, "Go, wash;" could he not have healed me, and then have sent me to Siloam? Often have I washed there with many others, and have gained no good; had he possessed any power, he would while present have healed me. Just as Naaman spoke respecting Elisha; for he too being commanded to go wash in Jordan, believed not, and this too when there was such a fame abroad concerning Elisha (2 Kings 5:11). But the blind man neither disbelieved, nor contradicted, nor reasoned with himself, What is this? Ought he to have put on clay? This is rather to blind one the more: who ever recovered sight so? But he used no such reasonings. Do you see his steadfast faith and zeal?[52]

This gives fresh insight into John 9, for it means that Jesus is the greater Elisha, performing signs like the great prophet of the divided kingdom. But it also works the other way: John 9 sheds light on the ministry of Elisha, whose very name ("My God saves") anticipates the name of the greater prophet, Yeshua of Nazareth.

CONCLUSION

At first blush, typology looks strange, a holy way of reading with little to teach us about reading in general. Once we realize that typology is merely a way of reading that acknowledges the fundamental temporality of writing, reading, communication, and interpretation, it ceases to be a biblical oddity and gives us insight into the nature of language and history.

The apostles teach us to recognize that "how it turned out" exposes dimensions of the original event or text that may not have been apparent, and perhaps were not even there, until it turned out as it did. Typological reading is simply reading of earlier texts in the light of later texts and events. Reading Hosea in the light of the event of Jesus is, in principle, just as ordinary as reading Darwin in the light of Nazism, *The Descent of Man* in the light of *Mein Kampf*. The event of Darwin's text becomes a different event, with a new meaning, in the aftermath of Nazism. Prior to Hitler, Darwin's text did not have the property of "providing the theoretical foundations for National Socialism." After Hitler, it did.

Similarly, "Out of Egypt I called My Son" takes on new properties, new meanings, as Jesus flees from the Egypt of Herodian Israel. "God spoke and there was light" takes on new meaning once we hear Jesus say, "I am the light of the world." Yahweh forming Adam from the dust is a different event once Jesus bends down outside the temple to make clay from dust and spittle.

Three

Words Are Players

Semantics

[handwritten: How modern linguistics tend to a "husk" philosophy of Scripture translation]

Let us use words to talk about words. I begin with several representative quotations from contemporary hermeneutics texts. The first is from Eugene Nida:

> This process of maximizing the context is fully in accord with the soundest principles of communication science. As has been clearly demonstrated by mathematical techniques in decoding, the correct meaning of any term is that which contributes least to the total context, or in other terms, that which fits the context most perfectly.[1]

Moisés Silva warns against reliance on word histories, derivations, or etymologies, since most speakers are aware only of current usage:

> We must accept the obvious fact that the speakers of a language simply know next to nothing about its development; and this certainly was the case with the writers and immediate readers of Scripture two millennia ago. More than likely, even a knowledge of that development is not bound to affect the speaker's daily conversation: the English professor who knows that *nice* comes from Latin *nescius*, "ignorant," does not for that reason refrain from using the term in a complimentary way. It follows that our real interest is the significance of Greek or Hebrew *in the consciousness of the biblical writers*; to put it baldly, "historical considerations are irrelevant to the investigation" of the state of the Koine at the time of Christ.[2]

Peter Cotterell and Max Turner agree with Silva, but are sterner: "Appeal to etymology, and to word formation, is . . . *always* dangerous."[3] Behind these comments stands Ferdinand de Saussure's distinction between diachronic and synchronic linguistics, the first devoted to tracing the historical background of language and the second to analyzing the relations within a language at a particular time. Cotterell and Turner think that synchronicity is all the rage:

> Only word studies based on a *synchronic* analysis of the language should be allowed to inform interpretation; that is, only a study of the senses of a word known to be current at the time of the writing of the discourse is of primary relevance to its interpretation.[4]

Finally, Anthony Thiselton warns that interest in isolated words is retro:

> A consideration of the issues discussed in the remainder of this essay . . . will show that a "mechanical" emphasis on verbal and propositional forms is not only pre-critical in terms of Biblical studies, it is also obsolete in terms of *semantics*, violating virtually every modern insight into the nature of meanings.[5]

All these writers have points, and important ones. Cotterell and Turner are correct to note, for example, that not all compound terms are as transparent as *watchdog* and *afterlife*. Butterflies fly, but have little to do with churned dairy products. Pineapples are fruity like apples and spiny like pinecones, but they do not really resemble a combination of pines and apples. Though resurrection men like Jerry Cruncher exist, most undertakers leave rather than take what is under.[6] Silva has a ball imagining misuses of etymology:

> I have mistrusted ranchers ever since I met a few who seemed mentally unbalanced. It is probably not a pure accident that English *ranch* . . . is etymologically related to *deranged*.[7]

> Dancing is forbidden to Christians. Isn't it suggestive that the word *ballet* comes from the Greek *ballo*, which is also the origin of *diabolos*, "devil"?[8]

Words change meaning, and it is not the case that the original meaning is more pure, more right, or more meaningful than what a word means now. As many have pointed out, *nice* does not really mean ignorant, nor *glamorous*, witchy.

James Barr, whose *Semantics of Biblical Language* has deeply influenced contemporary evangelical hermeneutics, is also quite right to warn against what he calls "illegitimate totality transfer." He acknowledges that there is some use in compiling the different senses of biblical terms, and agrees that this compiled concept may be described as the biblical meaning. The biblical concept of *ekklesia* is the combined product of biblical statements about the church: the church is body and bride of Christ, the people of God, and so on. Yet it is illegitimate to take that combined meaning and plug it into any particular use of *ekklesia* in the New Testament: "The semantic indication given by 'the Church' is [in particular texts] something much less than 'the NT conception of the Church.'" An illegitimate totality transfer occurs when "the 'meaning' of a word (understood as the total series of relations in which it is used in the literature) is read into a particular case as its sense and implication there."[9]

So they do all have points. Yet I am suspicious.

MODERNITY AND LINGUISTICS

I am most suspicious of Thiselton, not least because his statement is stuffed with implicit put-downs, moral passion, and, dare I say, bullying. Why is it a problem to be "pre-critical"? He does not say, but he makes it clear that pre-critical is not something any self-respecting interpreter will want to be. The claim that biblical studies needs to catch up with the development of semantics presumes, among other things, that there is some consensus among linguists on the nature of meaning. That this is manifestly not the case is evident from the essays on the meaning of meaning that keep flowing from the pens of philosophers and interpreters. The final clause that accuses certain biblical interpreters of "violating" modern insight is where the moral passion is at its highest pitch. In the course of his sentence, the insights of modern semantics assume normative force. Their dictates can be violated like divine commands.[10] How did that happen? How can insights be imperatives?

Put aside Thiselton's rhetoric, and I am still left with this question: why should I attempt to conform to modern insight about the nature of meaning? We saw in chapter 1 that modern treatments of the meaning of the Bible are destructive of the Bible's authority and power. Why should I now trust the conclusions of contemporary semanticists about how biblical words mean?

Call me hypersuspicious, but I even hear faint reverberations of the liberal dichotomy of form and content, of husk and kernel, in contemporary linguistic discussions. Cotterell and Turner give nine sentences illustrating the variety of meanings of the verb *run*, and conclude, "Any attempt to find some single overarching 'meaning' for run here would not only be subjective, but bound to fail. It is the *lexical form* which is held in common, not any major component of sense."[11] If we are thinking of constructing a dictionary, they again have an important point. By all means, lexicographers must keep those various runs from running into each other. But does the fact that these various senses share a lexical form not mean something?

Give those nine sentences to a poet or a comedian, and suddenly they will be jostling over the page—running noses and running engines and running colors and stories run in the *New York Times* and leases that have run for two years already and still have a year to go. The fact that the same unit, run, is used in diverse ways opens up linguistic and intellectual possibilities not available in a language that uses different words. The fact that the form is the same opens the possibility of linking sense, as we begin to imagine noses with small churning legs and pumping arms, engines dripping mucus, puffing overweight leases, newspaper stories that will not keep still on the page.

As a matter of linguistic principle, though, Cotterell and Turner want us to separate the form of the word from its sense. The fact that "moving by rapidly moving the legs" and "standing as a candidate for Congress" are marked by the same English verb is irrelevant. To my ear, this sounds a lot like husk and kernel, operating now not at the level of dogmatic formulation but at the more subtle and fundamental level of verbal meaning. Have evangelicals adopted Kantian assumptions about meaning into their core beliefs about language?

Nida's translation theory of "dynamic equivalence" sounds suspiciously as if it partakes of the same Kantian assumptions. According to Nida, the aim of translation is to produce "in the receptor language the closest natural equivalent to the message of the source language, first in meaning and secondly in style." First and second here enumerate translators' priorities: faced with a choice, "the meaning must have priority over the stylistic forms."[12] Style can never be rendered exactly in translation. Translating Greek to English is translating from an inflected language to one where word order is the primary carrier of syntax. Yet Nida's principle does not only apply to inevitable discontinuities of this order. Paul's use of the Greek *sarx* (flesh) does not communicate in the receptor language, modern English, and instead is rendered as "sinful nature." "Dying you shall die" is not an English idiom, so it is changed to "you shall surely die." We can render God's word in a vocabulary and style of contemporary English, because the original style is detritus.

We get the word atonement creative invention via neologism?

As I noted in chapter 1, this is a major departure from the procedure of earlier translators. The Septuagint created a new form of Greek by incorporating Hebraic forms into Greek. Even individual Greek words took on new nuances and connotations under the pressure of this translation.[13] Earlier English translations enriched English style, by rendering Hebraisms as directly as possible into English, and vocabulary, with neologisms like atonement.

I am also wary of Nida's claim that the correct meaning of any word is that which contributes least to its context. Cotterell and Turner agree:

> The use of a word restricts the possibilities of what may follow; sometimes to a lesser extent ("good" could be followed by a wide variety of nouns and participles), usually to a greater (only certain nouns could fill the blank in "he smashed his head in with a _____"). A word

> may even be utterly specific in its collocates: what is "ran-
> cid" other than butter, what can be "addled" other than
> eggs (or, figuratively, brains); what licks but a tongue? The
> point is that there is a sense relation between (e.g.) "kick"
> and "feet" which makes it *inappropriate* to continue an
> utterance beginning (say) "he kicked him. . ." by the words
> "with his fingers." . . . There is something to the claim
> that you can tell the sense of a word from the company it
> keeps.[14]

In many uses of language, this is perfectly sensible. If I want to
report earnings to the Board of Trustees or write a computer manual or bark out instructions to the nurse assisting me in surgery,
I want words to communicate without confusion. I am not trying
to be poetic. But some writers do want to be poetic. Poets, for
instance.

Or, we may ask, what if a word begins to keep new company? We all know that bad company corrupts good morals,
and words that keep company with new companions are likely
to be changed in the process. Many uses of language—the most
interesting ones—are strictly inappropriate. It is easy enough to
imagine rancid things other than butter: a marriage, a landscape,
Congress. Flame licks, and cold, wintry wind licks more slop-
pily than a beagle. Anyone with a bit of imagination can fill in
the blank in the quotation above with any number of nouns—
syllogism, lilac, violin concerto, another shot of brandy, and so
on. And why stop at nouns? "He smashed his head in with blue"
is odd, but in a certain context, it could make vibrant sense. Cotterell and Turner would no doubt object that my examples range
from the metaphorical (wind does not actually lick) to the nonsensical (even the sturdiest lilac cannot smash a human skull).
That is just the point. They are surprising because they do not
conform to normal expectations. Why say anything if we just say
what everyone expects? Who says that we cannot use words met-
aphorically? Cotterell and Turner construct a theory that scorns
linguistic surprise.[15]

Cotterell and Turner's theory is fundamentally classicist.
That is, they want texts to function in a single register. (Or, what
could be worse, they think that all texts actually *do* function in

a single register.) Authors should employ the words we expect in the places we expect them. They want epic poetry to sound epic, the Bible to sound biblical, and they certainly do not want people smashing in heads with lilacs or concertos. As James Wood has pointed out, by contrast, much of the human effect of modern prose writing (not to mention poetry) is produced by changes of register. When Philip Roth uses "tit" and "cunt" in the same sentence with *"uberare"* in a reference to Tintoretto's painting of Juno, his style "incarnate[s] the meaning," which is "all about the scandal of equalizing different registers." Even a "classicist" writer like Jane Austen achieves her effects by combining different registers in a single, surprising phrase. Going strawberry-picking, the imperious Mrs. Elton equips herself with an "apparatus of happiness" (*Emma*). Wood's brief analysis of the phrase makes it clear that the unexpected combination of words does not destroy meaning but multiples it:

> Suggestive of technical efficiency, the word [apparatus] belongs to a scientific register that puts it at odds with "of happiness." An apparatus of happiness sounds more like an inverted torture machine than a bonnet and basket, and it promises a kind of doggedness, a persistence, that fits Mrs Elton's character, and which makes the heart sink.[16]

One could try Cotterell and Turner's test on Austen's phrase. Fill in the blanks: "_____ of happiness" or "apparatus of _____." Few besides Austen would have conceived "apparatus of happiness," and we should all be grateful that she was perfectly willing to violate every modern notion of meaning.

Austen's phrase does not just give us new content. It enriches our language, as well as our moral imagination, because it juxtaposes words in a new way. Each word has its particular history, sense, and normal contexts of use, but putting them in the same beaker creates a new compound.

Stephen Prickett's primary and most damning complaint against Nida's theory (and also against structuralism and poststructuralism) is that it neutralizes the possibility of saying something new. Translation theories that depend on the husk/kernel dichotomy make it impossible for God's word to say anything that we have not already heard. The receptor language will always determine what the source text is allowed to say. Cotterell and Turner's linguistic theory likewise pushes inventiveness to the margins. In their defense, they would confess that a text can say something new, but would qualify their confession by saying that the newness comes in the content of what is said and not in the form of expression or in new (or renewed) vocabulary. But that is just to fall back into the old husk/kernel dichotomy all over again.

Words, I will argue, are stage players, and first of all they are players in this sense: the best players surprise us. They do the unexpected, or do the expected in unexpected ways. Was Heath Ledger's performance in *The Dark Knight* appropriate? Probably not. But would we have wanted it any other way?

POETIC WORDS

introducing new meaning is the point of good news

In a sense, the linguists discussed above are claiming much less than they appear to be. Many of the principles they enunciate have to do with determining lexical or dictionary meanings of terms, not the meanings of terms in particular context. Linguists all acknowledge that alongside lexical meaning there is discourse meaning, or what Owen Barfield and C. S. Lewis described as "speaker's meaning." Cotterell and Turner point out:

> We simply have to take the caution: not all contextual senses and usages are actually lexical meanings. We need to distinguish between usages which are *conventional* (at least to a group), and so an established "sense" of a word (for that group, or more widely), and those which are not.[17]

In a story where a bicycle has been identified as "Uncle George's old red one," the word *bike* itself takes on the character of "oldness, redness, and to-Uncle-George-belongingness."[18] These would not be part of the lexical but of the discourse meaning of bike. One would not list "an old, red device for transportation belonging to Uncle George" as one of the dictionary meanings of bicycle. Discourse meaning comes about because "the situational and semantic context modulates the sense of included lexical units, highlighting some components of the meaning of a lexical unit and backgrounding others."[19]

At the end of a long and mainly illuminating chapter on lexical semantics, they even admit, sheepishly (or so I take it):

> In the light of the distinction just made between lexical senses and discourse concepts, it is not unlikely that many interpreters will conclude that it is actually the broader *discourse concepts*, rather than the lexical, contextual or specialized word sense, with which they are primarily concerned![20]

Just so. Preachers and commentators, people who lead Bible studies and Sunday school classes, are not writing dictionaries. They are concerned with words in particular texts, and with the way the text brings some features of a word to the foreground and leaves others in the background. Cotterell and Turner are happy for them to do just that. But that leaves one slightly mystified about the balance of their discussion, which, according to their book's title, is an effort to apply linguistics to biblical interpretation. Why spend such a large portion of a chapter in a book on biblical interpretation telling us how to write a dictionary?

Most linguistically oriented Bible scholars not only recognize the phenomenon of speaker's meaning but recognize also, as Lewis pointed out, that speaker's meaning plays a role in semantic development. Once upon a time, *chip* had no association with *computer*, and neither did *terminal* (which, as a noun, denoted airports and, as an adjective, described illnesses). Now they do. Somebody invented those uses, in one epoch-making conversation or piece of writing or advertisement. Prior to that invention, and the general spread of that innovative use, the combination of *silicon* and *chip* was strictly inappropriate. It became appropriate.[21] Once it became standard usage, it opened up a whole new range of linguistic experimentation:

"What do programmers bring to parties?"
"Silicon chips."

"Why is that programmer so angry?"
"I don't know. He's always got a chip on his shoulder."

"What do you call a programmer's son?"
"A chip off the old block."

Barr acknowledges this process, though he is ambiguous about it. In *Semantics of Biblical Language,* he dismisses Bruce Metzger's claims about the transforming effects that Christianity had on the Greek language. According to Metzger, Christianity "let loose in the world a transforming energy which made itself felt in all domains, including that of language." Because of Christianity, "old worn-out expressions were rejuvenated and given new luster," and in some cases "new words and phrases were coined." Terms that "expressed servility, ignominy and sin were washed clean, elevated, and baptized with new meaning," while other words were revealed to be "even more somber and wicked in their significance than had been previously realized."[22] To Barr, this is nothing more than "romanticization" and a "linguistic allegory" that arises from an illegitimate "transfer to the sphere of linguistic change of the soteriological effects which Christianity claims to have made in life in general."[23]

Yet Barr knows that word meanings change over time (this point is central to his whole argument), and that they change as they are used in actual utterances by the users of the language: "The use of words is often deeply influenced by their past history of use," he concedes in a discussion of etymology.[24] He even concedes that the Christian use of common Greek words might well have caused some semantic changes in those words. While emphasizing that the uniqueness of the Christian message resides not in a unique vocabulary but in the statements made with common Greek vocabulary, he says that "the use of a word might come in due course to be specially stamped by its frequent recurrence in sentences of a particular kind, and so undergo a semantic change."[25] The frequent recurrence of the Greek *theos* in statements like "God is love" or "God was in Christ reconciling the world to Himself" has the potential to give new meaning to the Greek word itself. Having conceded so much, how is it that he can find Metzger guilty of romanticization?

More crucially, Barr's criticisms of Metzger help to display the limits of lexical semantics. Barr is well aware of those limitations, as are other scholars whose work is based on his. Moisés Silva makes the obvious but illuminating point that lexicographers arrive at their conclusions from earlier dictionaries and ultimately from earlier exegesis,[26] and Silva argues that context does not merely color meaning but *"makes* meaning."[27] Context enables us to determine which of several meanings is in play in a particular text. The verb in "I see" means something quite different if uttered by a formerly blind man healed with spittle and dust, by a student who has just received an extended explanation of a difficult mathematical theorem, or by a skeptical wife whose husband offers a lame explanation for the lipstick on his collar. In the first context, *see* refers to physical sight, while in the latter two it refers to understanding, and in the last it could hardly be said without a heap of sarcasm.

Silva, however, limits his discussion to words that have "multiple meanings," presumably multiple lexical meanings. With such words, context serves not to enrich meaning but to "eliminate multiple meanings."[28] This might well apply to certain kinds of texts, as noted above. If I am writing a prescription, I do not want to revel in the rich possibilities of meaning. I want to heal and not kill the patient, and ambiguity might be deadly. But is that true of every kind of text? Are there texts where lexical meanings are not paramount, and where we examine context not mainly to pare away meanings but to enrich them?

Here, again, words are players. Like the best stage characters, words are complex entities. Words are, in E. M. Forster's often-discredited phrase, "rounded" characters. Because they are rounded, we cannot see them all at once, but have to view them from different angles in different scenes. Lear is imperious father and king in some scenes, a babbling madman on the heath, and in the end almost a suckling child wanting to snuggle up with Cordelia. Lear is all of these all the time, but only certain aspects of his character are evident at any one time. If words are players, context limits meaning. Lear is not going to undo his button and stand unaccommodated during the opening scene. He is distributing his inheritance, and that dramatic context limits his range of action.

Yet, and here is the crucial point, when we see the play a second time, we can already see the suckling child just under the surface of the imperious father (he is desperate for Cordelia's love already in the first scene), and the stripped madman is always threatening to break out into the open. Once we have seen the whole play, we realize that Lear begins shedding his "accommodations" in act 1.

So too words, I shall argue. Words are round characters. Many words have a variety of meanings, and even those that have only a single lexical meaning have a variety of associations and connotations. These dimensions might not be connected to one another in any obvious way. A running nose and a running engine have little in common, except that each puts out a form of refuse. In many English sentences, talk of a running nose would not be remotely related to a running engine. But in some contexts, running might bring both associations to mind: "Whenever the engine was running, a thick, oily mucus dripped to the ground." When we read a text, especially one with a high level of craftsmanship, we should be alert to the possibility that a covert sense is lurking just under the surface of the overt. We should realize that the madman of the heath is already lurking there as Lear divides up his kingdom.

Poetic Meaning

Scripture is a multi-dynamic play that is meant to shape and make a life, not content to it [handwritten marginalia]

Poets know that words are rounded players (though not just poets—think Flaubert), and they want to get as much of the character on stage as they can. Poets are often interested in the evocative power of a word's connotations as much as in the precision of its denotation. In a classic modern text on poetry, *How Does a Poem Mean?*, John Ciardi and Miller Williams devote a very long chapter to "the words of poetry." For poets, words are not just labels for things, but are themselves things that evoke feelings, bodies, and history, and present a picture. The denotation of *rat* is "a rodent that resembles a mouse but is larger and marked by a different sort of tooth structure," but when a gangster calls someone a "dirty rat," he "does not mean that his accomplice is a rodent resembling a mouse but larger and having a different tooth structure."[29] Because of the thing that the word rat names, the word takes on the feeling of the object. Since "most people think of rats as despicable, vicious, and filthy," the word absorbs the character, and gives off some of the aroma, of the object itself.

Word and world do not correspond in a one-to-one fashion. There are many objects in the world for which we have inadequate language, and there are also many different words and descriptive phrases that can be used to describe a particular object or event. Each of these descriptions is not only an effort to describe but an effort to persuade: "we are often less concerned with identifying a thing than we are with expressing a feeling toward it." If we describe a certain "Alderman John J. McGinnis" as "that thieving skunk," we are clearly trying to persuade our audience to take a certain stance toward the alderman.[30] Word choice is not just semantic but rhetorical.

Consider the word *lamb*. Assuming that the word is a noun (which is not necessarily the case), it can be defined by reference to a dictionary as (1) "a young sheep," (2) the "meat of a young sheep," (3) a "gentle, meek, innocent" person, (4) "a person who is easily cheated or outsmarted," or (5) a reference to Christ, the Lamb of God (all from Dictionary.com). Barr and Silva are correct that the context disambiguates the ambiguous word. If we add *chops* to lamb, we are clearly dealing with the second definition, while if the context makes it clear that the lamb is a human being, we know that we are in the realm of the third or fourth definition. The "first thought" meaning of the word in isolation will depend on a host of factors—whether or not you grew up on a farm, how close it is to dinner, who used the word and in what setting. If I call somebody a lamb, I clearly do not mean that person is a wooly young ovine. In any scene, the player *lamb* might be limited to one or the other meaning.

Even while context eliminates certain possible meanings, it is bringing others to the fore. When John the Baptist calls Jesus the "Lamb of God, who takes away the sin of the world," we are, lexically speaking, working with the fifth definition, but to leave it at that is to leave it at nothing. Lamb in that context brings forward the whole of the sacrificial system, in which lambs were offered for sin, and specifically the lamb of the Passover, whose blood, spread on the doorposts of Israelite homes, turned away the angel of death. In sheer semantic terms, the word lamb means lamb, but that does not tell us very much.

Put the word lamb into a poem, and even if we do not know any of the other words or phrases of the poem, we begin to have some suspicions about what the word might connote. We might think about Blake's "Little lamb, who made thee?" We might instinctively put the lamb in a full-blown pastoral setting.

Suppose we add the word *white* to lamb, producing the unusual locution *lamb-white*. Here we have a small bit of context that both narrows and broadens the meaning of the word. Most people know that most lambs are white, but their whiteness is not part of the lexical meaning, since lambs are not always white and a lamb's whiteness does not help to distinguish it from other things—from white snow or white picket fences or white-hot iron. White narrows lamb to the first dictionary definition, since lamb chops are not white and since African Americans and Koreans might be as lamblike as Caucasians. Even more dramatically, by adding white, we are abstracting one feature of the lamb to focus on, its color. If we had been thinking pastorally, suddenly we are confronted with a patch of wooly whiteness.

At the same time, however, white enriches lamb, and the meaning of the combination expands beyond the meaning of either in isolation. This is partly a function of the originality of the phrase lamb-white. I have not investigated thoroughly, but I am fairly certain that even the 128-color box of Crayola crayons does not include a color named lamb-white. The phrase is arresting, in the original sense of the word: it stops us in mid-sentence and forces us to think, now what could that mean? And once we begin to think along those lines, the combination of lamb and white acts like a chemical reaction. Lamb itself can denote as well as connote an innocent or guileless person, but when the color word is added, that aspect of the word's lexical meaning slips out from behind the curtain to the front of the stage. Though the dictionary tells us that white describes a color—the all-color absence of color, as Melville knew—it has a host of associations that cling to it in various contexts. It connotes purity, cleanliness, and spirituality. Brides wear white, and so virginity is white. Whiteness is blankness, and so whiteness is the color before color, the color before one gets dirty or becomes sexually experienced. Most actual lambs in the field are not white, at least not pure white, but are covered with mud and dag. If a lamb is innocent, a white lamb is still more so: perfected innocence; original, unspotted innocence.

Now let us add a further substance to our test tube: lamb-white *days*. If lamb-white was arresting, adding days increases the strangeness of the phrase geometrically. Lambs are white, so "lamb-white," though unusual, is at least within the realm of our experience. We have all seen white, or nearly white, lambs. But days have color only in a metaphorical sense. We do speak of days that are blue or bright, but the day itself is a period of time, and time is not literally colored. Lamb-white was energetic, but it stayed within our daily experience, and could be interpreted in a straightforward, literal fashion. Even at this literal level, the words were reacting to one another to produce something more than literal. But we simply cannot stay at the literal level when we start talking about days that are white, much less lamb-white.

What has happened? We have already noticed that background connotations of lamb come to the surface in the presence of white, and when days is added, it confirms our suspicion that this phrase is doing something. If lamb-white suggests innocence and purity, then lamb-white days must be days of bright, sunlit innocence. Various aspects of the player *lamb* emerge and submerge depending on what other players share the stage.

None of this speculation on words should give rise to any fears that I have made the words mean whatever I want them to mean. There is no hint of linguistic relativism. I have not taken lamb as "nutria"; nor have I taken white to mean "slim and elongated." Instead, I argue only for recognition that words have rich connotations as well as denotations, and also that in certain kinds of texts, the connotations are as important as the denotations. I am not arguing that Lear is Hamlet is Shylock is Macbeth is Estragon. I am only arguing that Lear is round.

Lamb in Context

The phrase we have been considering is not original with me (how I wish it were), but comes from Dylan Thomas' poem "Fern Hill." Inspired by Thomas' childhood visit to his aunts' dairy farm in Carmarthenshire, "Fern Hill" is one of the most famous evocations of childhood happiness and the emerging consciousness of age and time in English poetry. Thomas depicts a fairy-tale world of childhood innocence: a "lilting house," where "once below a time" he was "prince of the apple towns"; a world where, under the young sun, he was "huntsman and herdsman," calling for his calves like a character from a nursery rhyme; a farm borne away by owls each night, only to awaken in the morning with the "cock on his shoulder." The narrator's heedless, carefree happiness is soon shadowed by time and its unshakable dominion. Our suspicions about the connotations of the phrase *lamb-white days* are perfectly suited to this context.[31] Now we have all the players assembled, and we can think further about the rounded character of lamb in the play of this poem.

Among the many striking features of Thomas' poem is his use of color terms. *Green* appears seven times in the poem's six stanzas, twice in combination with *golden* and five times by itself. Through most of the poem, green connotes freshness, youth, and vigor. "Young and easy under the apple boughs," the narrator is "happy as the grass is green" and "green and carefree." Golden is first introduced from the perspective of time, who "lets me play and be / Golden." Childhood is not merely fresh and green, but valuable, beyond decay and rust. Together, "green and golden" express the character of childhood that the poem celebrates— the happy ease and childish lordliness over the apples, the trees, the leaves. By the end of the poem, "green and golden" is haunted by the narrator's mature recognition that "time allows / In all his tuneful turning so few and such morning songs." Children "green and golden" will eventually follow time "out of grace," out of favor. Golden in the favor of time, the child is also growing out of time's favor, as time itself grows out of favor. By the end of the poem, green has become the color of decay and death: "Time held me green and dying," already while the child was "young and easy in the mercy of his means," even "though I sang in my chains like the sea." Time becomes a prison, an inevitable forward movement that, like each night, leaves the farm, the child, the horses, all that is green and golden behind.

As we had begun to suspect before we ever looked at the poem in its entirety, Thomas' striking "lamb white days" evokes precisely the innocence of childhood and the innocence of the world. The word white first appears in the fourth stanza, describing the waking of the farm after a night of nonexistence. The farm awakes, in Thomas' alliterative phrase, "like a wanderer white / with the dew." The dew is what makes this wanderer white, but the line break also suggests that "wanderer white" can stand, if ever so briefly, on its own. Morning wakes like a returning pilgrim, dressed in the color of purity and innocence, perhaps in the color of a bride. As the stanza continues, Thomas connects the rebirth of the farm after the death of night to the birth of the first farm, Eden, where "Adam and maiden" greeted the freshly created sun, newly born. When the word white reappears in the final stanza, these associations of Edenic innocence are still reverberating. All his childhood days are white days.

But lamb adds another note to the final stanza. Thomas' poem speaks of many different animals: calves, foxes, horses, and birds—nightjars, swallows, and the cock on the shoulder of the white-clad morning. And these animals and birds come with associated connotations, connotations that Thomas clearly wants us to catch. In the second stanza, he mentions calves and foxes—domestic cattle over against the foxes on the hills. Calves respond to the boy's horn, but foxes bark out in the wild. Owls are birds of the night, bearing the farm into darkness, while the cock announces the return of the wanderer white, the return of Edenic day. Given these associations, the connotations of lamb are unmistakable. The days are "lamb white" only in the final stanza, when the realization of time's passing has already moved like an afternoon cloud over the sun of childhood. Lamb white days are not only days of innocence but days of heedless, careless innocence, a time when the narrator was careless "that time would take me / Up to the swallow thronged loft by the shadow of my hand." During the lamb white days, the narrator did not care that he could hear time "fly with the high fields" or that he might "wake to the farm forever fled from the childless land."

What does lamb add to white in Thomas' description of childhood days? It adds a note of Passover, of the lamb led to the slaughter, of the innocent sinner Jesus slain, of all innocents chained to time eventually dying. Lamb white days are days of innocence that exist only to be slaughtered to times, only to "follow him out of grace."

Words Have a Past

What was Lear doing before the play started? Nothing, it seems, since he does not exist outside the play.[32] Yet, as we watch the play, we learn some things about his past and that of other characters, and we begin to suspect other things. We learn something about Gloucester's youthful indiscretions, and we begin to reconstruct an imaginative background for the interactions of the three daughters. Any actor of weight is going to think deeply about the past of his character. Even if the past never surfaces in express language or action, it is back there, motivating the action.

Words are players in this sense too. Above, I quoted Silva's claim that speakers know only the contemporary meanings of the words they use, and therefore that synchronic analysis of words is of primary relevance to interpretation. There is an important insight here (one which I am loath to "violate"). Obviously, a word cannot bear a meaning that was not available at the time. *Grass* in a fourteenth-century text cannot be a reference to marijuana; nor was Shakespeare joining ACT UP when he endorsed *gaiety*. This is an obvious point, but, as Lewis points out, one often forgotten in practice. When we meet a familiar word, "if it makes tolerable sense our tendency is to go merrily on. We are often deceived. In an old author the word may have meant something different."[33]

Biblical linguists' main concern is with the use of earlier, or original, senses of a word. They do not deny that a study of word histories is part of linguistics, and they may even admit that such a study might illuminate cultural, political, or philosophical history. They might be willing to say with Richard Trench that language is "fossil poetry," as well as "fossil ethics, or fossil history."[34] What they deny is that these histories are relevant to the interpretation of particular texts.

But if words are players, then their background affects their behavior, even if the background never comes to the foreground. We cannot understand characters without knowing something about their hidden past.

So I dispute Silva's claim, and dispute it first as a matter of fact. I asked my children, the oldest present being fourteen. With only slight prompting from me, they all immediately thought of the changes in the words *gay* and *buff*. Gay has moved from meaning "carefree and happy" to "homosexual," and buff from "naked" to "having a powerful physique." I can imagine my children doing wordplays with gay: "He's not gay," says one. "What made him sad?" says the other. I can definitely hear them giggling (maybe averting their eyes in mock-chastity) when their older brother boasts about how buff he has become. Older speakers of English would have many more examples. Old people do not evaporate when a new generation arrives, and neither do old uses of a word disappear when a new one happens by. People have memories. Some even read old books.

I also dispute it as a matter of philosophy. Language is historically formed, taking shape over the course of time. Language, like every other human institution, exists in a complex entwinement of past, present, and future. We never exist in a pure present. Psychologically, our present is inflected with memory; culturally, the present is organized by the institutions and achievements of the past. I do not make myself a new road every time I drive home from work. I use the road that is already there, that was there before I moved into my current house, possibly before I was born. Not all of the past persists to the present, of course. My house stands where it does because the trees that used to be here do not, and the road I take home cuts through what must have once been meadow or forest. But the past is present in the present; in fact, as Augustine knew, the only past we know is the "present of the past."

If present time as such is infused with the past, how can language escape the past's influence? How can a word be any less dinged, chipped, and scarred by its history than my lawn?

Linguists acknowledge that poets and other literary artists pay more attention to word histories than others, and the poets agree. Ciardi and Williams note that poets often revel in the histories of words, and enjoy tucking hidden and forgotten meanings into words that will be evident only to a few initiated readers. *Starve*, they point out, originally referred to "any slow death, as by exposure, torture, hunger, or thirst," and was narrowed down to death by hunger because of the use of starvation (in our sense) as a weapon of siege warfare. For some writers and readers, though,

> The old meaning is still there, still available for some situation in which it can enrich the total communication. "The starved thief of the wind and the hanging tree," is an invented example. Were it an authentic line of poetry, its effect would depend on many allusions. Nor does the writing demand full awareness of such allusions: the general sense of the line is suggestive even when its "meaning" has not been located. But certainly there is an added richness hidden away in "starved" and waiting for the reader who can unlock it. Many poets like to hide away such happy additions: they do not insist that every reader respond to them; it is enough that such touches delight the writer and are ready to delight the reader who is able to respond to them.[35]

In such cases, context does not narrow the meaning of a word, or at least does not do that only. Context can bring the hidden history of the word to the surface.

But let us suppose that even the best educated among us are unaware of the origins and history of most of the words we use. That does not relieve my suspicion entirely. Perhaps our ignorance is less an inherent property of language use and more a specific habit of modern language use. Perhaps we do not remember word histories because we have been trained to ignore them.[36] Is modern linguistics perhaps only a theoretical justification for how we do things, rather than a timeless description of how language works? This brings us to a place to begin.

Intriguing as the philosophical issues are, we can cut through a great deal of abstract theorizing by making a historical case. Whatever may be true of modern speakers and writers, even highly literate ones, ancient writers were very interested in word derivations, etymologies, and histories. Contra Silva, ancients did know earlier meanings of words, or at least thought they did. Theories differed, but nearly every ancient writer of note employed etymologies in their own writing, and looked for etymological clues when they interpreted the writings of another. We discover this interest in varying degrees and with varying purposes in writings from the Old Testament through the Renaissance and beyond. Socrates may or may not be in earnest about the etymologies he spins out in *Cratylus*, but even so, the dialogue is evidence that many Greeks were in earnest. Even sober Aristotle appeals to etymologies, and Ovid is veritably inebriated with them. Virgil, as we might expect, is more sensible than Ovid, as is Quintilian, but Virgil engages in etymological wordplay, and Quintilian thinks that argument according to name is an open rhetorical option. Closer to the New Testament, we find Philo indulging in creative etymologies of Hebrew words and names. Isidore of Seville's *Etymologies* was the key theoretical text, and interest in etymology persisted into the Renaissance, and was central to Coleridge's thought and to Hamann's writing and reading.[37]

Biblical writers fit right into the middle of this history. As a purely historical matter, aside from the theories of modern linguistics, we should expect the biblical writers to have shared these interests. In their historical context, we should expect them to have been curious about the histories of the linguistic players they assembled on the stage of their texts. The burden of proof is on those who think the biblical writers did not care about word histories.

We can do more than expect, though. The biblical writers display their etymological interest in names, personal and place names especially, on their sleeves. There are as many as eighty explicit etymologies in the Old Testament,[38] and many of these etymologies contribute substantially to the poetry and theology of biblical narratives. Lamech's etymology of the name Noah is not, linguistically, correct: he says that Noah will bring relief (*nacham*), but gives him a name (*noach*) that means "rest" (Gen 5:28-29). Inappropriate and ahistorical the etymology may be, but shards and fragments and puns on the name Noah splay out through the flood story. Sometimes the connection is palindromic: Noah (*nch*) finds grace (*chn*) in the eyes of Yahweh. More substantially, plays on Noah's name cluster toward the end of the flood narrative, when Noah is in fact giving rest (8:4, 9), and the "soothing" of the sacrifice contains another pun on the name (*hnychch*; 8:21). If Noah's name anticipates the Sabbath toward which the story moves, puns on the name of Ham prepare us for Ham's sin in that new morning of the world. As soon as Ham (*cham*) is introduced, the author records the violence (*chamas*) of men (6:11, 13) and the Lord is planning to blot out (*mchh*, another palindrome) the earth (6:7).[39]

Plays on names are also a feature of Homeric poetic style. *Hector* means shield or protector, and Homer is clearly aware of this link: "Hector, where has your strength gone, which you always held [*exeskes*] before? You said that you would hold [*exemen*] the city without the host or allies" (*Iliad* 5.472–73). When Andromache expresses her grief after Achilles has killed her father, she includes a multiple pun on her enemy's name: "Nor is there other consolation . . . but heartaches [*ache*]; nor do I have a father and honored mother. For Godlike Akhilleus [*achilleus*] killed my father" (*Iliad* 6.411–14). Elsewhere, Achilles brings pain to his own people, living up fully to his name—*achos* (affliction) plus *laos* (people). In 16.21–22, Patroclus makes this crystal clear, complaining of the evils (*achos*) come upon the Achaians (*achaion*) because of Achilles' absence from the field. The *Odyssey* includes a famous passage that provides an etymology for the hero's name, and fragments of the Greek words "man of sorrow" are sown throughout the poem, coming to a climax in Penelope's speech to Odysseus (19:560–65).[40]

Etymologies are not only found in ancient writings, and not only in literary texts. What would Heidegger be without etymologies? Not much. According to one study, Heidegger's etymological musings on Sinn, sinnen, senden, and sense provide a fundamental scaffolding for his understanding of thought as a *Denkweg*, a thought-path:

> The root of these words, *sent-*, means to head for, go; to take a direction; to look for a trail or scent. *Sinnen*, to think over, brood, goes back to the Old High German *sinnan*, which meant to aspire, in the sense of directing one's thoughts toward something, and, more originally, meant simply to go, travel. Old High German *sin*, *sind* meant way, course. The Old English doublet *sinnan* signified to care for, mind, heed, and *sand* denoted a sending, message, messenger. Herder's usage, in the essay of 1770, of *besonnen*, circumspect, to characterize the human creature, suggests, from a Heideggerian point of view, "on the track." Our apparently negligible phrase "in a sense" likewise reverberates with the idea of thought-path, *Denkweg*. . . . Primordially thought, a sentence is a scenting and sensing, a godsend consented to, a going and sending.[41]

In the end, we circle back to the poets.

Dylan Thomas' "Fern Hill" illustrated how words take on reverberations beyond their lexical meaning in particular texts, and several poems by Nobel laureate Seamus Heaney illustrate the continuation of ancient etymological interest in modern poets. In the collection *Wintering Out*, Heaney offers several etymological musings on Irish place names. One of the most evocative, and the most similar to "Fern Hill," is "Anahorish," describing memories of springs and winters past.[42] The Gaelic name means "place of clear water," and the etymology suggests a place of purity and innocence. Anahorish was near Heaney's childhood home in County Derry, and its association with his childhood modulates into an association with the childhood of the world. It is not merely his first hill, but "the first hill of the world." There, the water is "clear" and the grass "shiny" in the sun. As the poem moves, the clear water of Eden and childhood grows cloudy, and instead of washing down to the cobbles, it freezes in the well and needs to be broken up. We begin with running water and end with ice. We begin with clear water and end with dunghills. We begin with life and end with the refuse of life. Anahorish enters a wintry world, not the spring.

In between, Heaney puns on "barrows," describing the wheel-barrows going through the yards on winter evenings, but evoking also the mound-barrows in which Vikings are buried.[43] The people of Anahorish are mound-dwellers not only because they live on the hill but because they are nearly as dead as their ancestors in the barrows.

Heaney's meditation on the name Anahorish itself is not limited to its original sense, but includes an interest in its actual shape, the letters that constitute it. Anahorish—the word—is a landscape, a "soft gradient / of consonant" with its purring *n* and *h* and *r* and its final whispering (perhaps watery) *sh*, as well as a "vowel-meadow" of *a*'s, *o*, and *i*. If the "gradient" is a slope in the road, Heaney is thinking of the name as a union of meadow and highway, of nature and culture, as well as of consonants and vowels. Beyond what Heaney actually says about the word, the way he says it is notable. With a nod to the alliterative verse of Anglo-Saxon poetry (Heaney much later translated *Beowulf*), Heaney uses the kenning "vowel-meadow" to describe the word. Merely by using the form, Heaney discloses yet another historical layer to the place, for Anahorish was perhaps once a place where bards sang, on the "first hill in the world."

Henry Hart explains that Anahorish was "also the name of a 'mixed' Catholic and Protestant primary school which [Heaney] attended between 1945 and 1951."[44] This, too, has been lost, like the running water and the spring. What Hart describes as a "wistful lament" for childhood, Eden, and Irish unity piles up into, or is drawn out of, one haunting name. Heaney squeezes all this from an etymology of a single word.

"Toome," another poem from the same collection, follows some of the same pathways as the narrator searches for artifacts in a bog. Toome, Hart notes, is "a small townland in County Derry near Mossbawn, the farm where Heaney grew up," and is "one of the oldest inhabited areas of Ireland, the site of major archaeological finds."[45] Heaney is among the amateur archaeologists who hunt the ground for something "new" in ground that bears the castoffs of "a hundred centuries" of war, destruction, decay, and rubbish. For Toome is a tomb, and the whole poem depends on the pun.

Up to his arms in mud, Heaney is not just prospecting for musket-balls but digging for the roots and beginnings of life. He is a robber of Toome who hopes to discover something new to say in the earth of Ireland. In the opening stanza, his mouth is a cave, a hole, a tomb that "holds round" as it softly blasts the name Toome. By the same token, the digging site is a mouth, as Heaney pushes under the "slab of the tongue" into a subterranean treasure house. Toome has a tongue, and Heaney is the one whose mouth makes it speak, disclosing its hidden history.

Heaney's interest in wordplay, word derivations, and such is also evident in the complex mix of dialects that appear in the poem. *Souterrain* is a technical term from archaeology for an underground passage or grotto, and derives, obviously, from French. It sits oddly by the Saxon and Gaelic *loam* and *torc* and *bogwater*, perhaps suggesting that there is something foreign in the way Heaney records the treasures of Toome. Hart suggests a link with the "underground" of the Irish Nationalists of the eighteenth century, quoting a writer on the archaeology of Derry who says that "ancient souterrains were used as hiding places or deposits for 'dumps' of arms during the recent periods of fighting in Ireland."[46]

A torc is a collar or band of twisted metal, a true treasure. But it lies in the loam beside the fish-bones and shards of pottery. And that suggests another twist on torc, which puns with the absent French torque. Torque is rotation, or some mechanism that causes rotation, and the torc in the mud symbolizes the torque of history as well as the empty pedestal of "Ozymandius." The wheel turns and treasured ornaments are lost, to be picked up long after by a stranger "sleeved in / alluvial mud."

JOHN THE POET

That poets like to play with words as boys do with toads is not lost on Cotterell and Turner. Considering the possible wordplay in John 3:8, they suggest that "deliberate *double entendre*" is "the exception, not the rule." It is, however, "more common to some genres of literature than to others (to poetry more than to prose narrative)." With the Bible, we should suspect than an interpreter who finds too many double meanings "is simply fudging the exegesis."[47]

Let us try to forget Joyce and Pynchon, and the whole modernist movement in fiction that aimed to make fiction as poetic as poetry. Let us grant that poets make more use of wordplay than prose writers. But that merely begs one question and raises another. It begs the question, how do Cotterell and Turner know that the biblical writers write like prose narrative writers? Are we imposing our genre distinctions on biblical texts that resist them?

We can ask the same questions in a different idiom: are the biblical writers more like everyday modern speakers or more like the literate writers of Greece and Rome? From the historical review above, it seems we have some grounds for suspecting John of having poetic aspirations. The text confirms these suspicions.

John evidently has an interest in language, linguistic diversity, word histories, and etymologies. He includes translations of several terms in his gospel. He translates the Aramaic/Hebrew *Rabbi* as "Teacher" (1:38), and then uses rabbi (great one) without explanation throughout the remainder of the book, seven other times of Jesus (1:49; 3:2; 4:31; 6:25; 9:2; 11:8; the variant *Rabboni* in 20:16) and once of John the Baptist (3:26). He translates Andrew's confession of Jesus as "Messiah" into the Greek equivalent "Christ" (1:42), and Peter's Aramaic name "Cephas" into the Greek "Petros" (1:42). All of these might be explained by John's need to render Aramaic and Hebrew words unknown to his readers into familiar Greek. Messiah makes no sense in Greek, but Christos is a known quantity.

He includes another translation in chapter 9. After Jesus spreads his clay-and-spittle appliqué on the man's eyes, he sends the man off to wash in the pool of Siloam. John pauses to tell us that the word *Siloam* can be translated (awkwardly rendered, "hermeneuticized")[48] as "sent" (John 9:7). John's translation of Siloam in 9:7 is a different sort of thing from the other translations, however. In the other cases, John translates words that he will use frequently throughout the gospel, sometimes in the Aramaic form (rabbi) and sometimes in the Greek (Christ). Siloam is mentioned only in 9:7 and 11. And in 9:7, *translated* does not mean the same thing that it means elsewhere in the gospel. When

John says that "Messiah" is "translated" by "Christ," he means that the figure Hebrews call Messiah is Christ to the Greeks. But no one would call the pool of Siloam by the Greek equivalent John provides: the pool *Apestalmenos*. "Translated" does not mean translated, but interpreted or etymologized.

John could have told his story without any reference to the name of the pool, and it would have been perfectly possible for John to describe the incident without explaining the meaning of the pool's name. The context tells us clearly enough that Siloam is a pool somewhere in Jerusalem, close enough to the temple for a blind man with mud over his eyes to get there without losing his way. John does not feel the need to tell us what Bethsaida means (1:44), or Cana (2:1) or Galilee (2:1) or Capernaum (4:46), or any of the other places in the gospel. Siloam is unique. John wants us to know the derivation of the word Siloam.

Why? There is no exact Hebrew equivalent to Siloam, but most Bibles point readers to Isaiah 8:6 as a cross-reference. There, the prophet warns that Judah has "rejected the gently flowing waters of Shiloah, and rejoice in Rezin and the son of Remaliah," the heads of Syria and Israel respectively. In place of the gentle waters of Shiloah, Yahweh is going to bring the raging overflow of the Euphrates, "the king of Assyria and all his glory" (v. 7). Some also connect John's reference to Nehemiah 3:15, which mentions the "Pool of Shelah," located at "the king's garden as far as the steps that descend from the city of David." Bible dictionaries and commentators tell us that we can visit the pool Siloam to this day by walking through Hezekiah's tunnel until we get to the city of David. Shiloah and Shelah are close to the Greek word, and both seem to derive from the verb *shalach*, translated as "send" in most of its hundreds of uses in the Hebrew Bible.

Closer to John 9, sending is a hugely important theme in John's gospel. He uses the verb *apostello*, the root of his etymological translation of Siloam, nearly thirty times, and the near-synonym *pempo* even more. More important than these sheer statistics, John identifies Jesus by the fact that he is the One sent by the Father (5:23, 36, 37; 6:44, 57; 8:16, 18, 42; 12:49; 14:24, 26; 17:21, 25). Once in this very chapter, Jesus refers to the Father as "Him who sent me" (9:4). Because Jesus is the One sent by the Father, he is also the One who sends. He promises that the Father will send the Spirit in his name (14:26) and that he himself will send the Spirit from the Father to be with his disciples (15:26). Jesus also sends the disciples, breathing out the Spirit on them (20:21-22). Jesus is sent by the Father so that he can receive the Spirit, whom he then sends to be with his disciples when he sends them into the world. The fact that *apostello* is the etymological root of *apostolos* suggests that John is offering a double translation. Siloam equals sent, and sent links up with apostle. The blind man is being healed by the Sent One in the pool of sending, and thereby becomes one sent, a type of an apostle. He is plunged into the pool "Sent" by the One Sent, immersed in the Sent One's sending.

The Hebrew root can also be used in a negative way, to mean "send away," "expel" (Isa 16:2) or "dismiss" (Gen 44:3; Isa 27:10). It is the verb used in Genesis 3:23 when Adam and Eve are "sent out" from the garden, and the Septuagint translates with the related verb *exapostello*. The pool of Siloam is a pool of sending, connected to the Sent One, but also a pool of expulsion, foreshadowing the blind man's dismissal from the synagogue (v. 34). The two sendings go together: the blind man can be sent out by the Sent One only if he is willing to be sent out of the synagogue by those who reject the One whom God sent.[49]

As we shall see in subsequent chapters, the reference to Siloam as sent fits with the thrust of the story of the blind man in John 9, a story about discipleship as much as anything else. Here, I want to probe what John's translation of Siloam tells us about his intentions as a writer. If he wants us to recall the etymology of Siloam, is he hinting that we should look for etymological meanings behind other place names?

Several times, John identifies places by their Hebrew names, though he is aware that they also have Greek or Latin names. In 5:2, he identifies another pool by the Hebrew/Aramaic name Bethesda (some manuscripts spell it Bethsaida or Bethzatha), which has been etymologized as "house of mercy" or "house of pity" or "house of the fisherman." At the side of the pool are the "sick, blind, lame and withered," waiting, according to some manuscripts of John's gospel, for an angel to stir up the water so that they can be healed (vv. 3b-4). The pool is appropriately named as a place of mercy, and Jesus makes it even more so as he heals a man who has been paralyzed for thirty-eight years and has been lying at the poolside for a long time (vv. 5-9).

Later in the gospel, Pilate brings Jesus out before the Jews, and sits down (or, possibly, sits Jesus down) in the seat of judgment "at a place called The Pavement, but in Hebrew Gabbatha" (19:13). The Hebrew term is not a translation of the Greek *Lithotrotos*, but an alternative name for the place. The Greek word indicates a stone pavement, and echoes the temple dedication scene in the Septuagint of 2 Chronicles 7:3, but the Hebrew word means "high place" or "elevation," and possibly refers to an elevated platform in Pilate's praetorium.[50]

That place name fits neatly into the narrative and the theology of Jesus' trial and death. Jesus describes his crucifixion as a "lifting up," an elevation (3:14; 12:31-33), and John constructs his narrative to bring this out. Jesus is arrested in a garden that is associated with the Kidron Valley (18:1-3), rather than on the Mount of Olives (cf. Matt 26:30, 47). According to John, the arrest takes place in a "low" place, and afterward, the characters ascend.[51] First, Jesus is taken to Jerusalem, where he appears before the high priest on the mountains of the city. The location of Pilate's praetorium is uncertain, but it was certainly in the high districts of the city. As the soldiers mock Jesus, they parody a coronation scene, fixing a crown and a robe on Jesus and honoring him with "Hail" (19:1-3). At the climax of the trial scene, Jesus is brought to Gabbatha, a high place, an elevated platform where he appears in his ironic splendor as king of the Jews. The elevation continues as he is nailed to a cross and lifted up from the earth. John surely knows that not every one of his Greek readers will grasp the force of Gabbatha, but he places it there as one more hint that Jesus' trial, despite the appearances, is not a humiliation but an elevation. It is the lifting up of the Son of Man.

These examples suggest that John has some interest in place names, the derivations of words, and linguistic diversity. He uses some place names thematically, so that in their narrative contexts, a buried inflection in the place name is brought to the surface. He knows that Siloam and Bethesda are rounded characters, characters with submerged pasts, and he wants us to notice too.

John has an interest not only in the meanings of place names but also in the names of persons. This is evident from his introduction of Cephas, whose name he immediately renders in Greek as Peter (1:42). If he is interested in interpreting Cephas' name, he might also be interested in reminding us of the names of various other characters in the story. John is Johannas, the "Favor of Yah"; Nathanael is "Gift of God"; Philip is "Horse-lover."

In chapter 3, Nicodemus visits Jesus by night. Nicodemus is derived from two Greek words, *nike* (victory) and *demos* (people), so his name means, according to Thayer's *Lexicon*, "Conqueror of the people." This is an appropriate name for a man identified as "a ruler of the Jews," but there are a couple of additional dimensions. The Greek *demos* is used in the New Testament only in reference to non-Jewish peoples (Acts 12:22; 17:5; 19:30, 33). Nicodemus' name would thus imply that he is a conqueror of Gentiles, but John's description indicates that he is instead a ruler of the Jews. This might imply that Nicodemus represents an ascendant Israel that rules over the nations; alternatively, it might suggest that the Jews themselves have become just another *demos*, another Gentile nation. Jesus' assaults on the Jews throughout the gospel suggest that this is the case. He says that they are not children of Abraham but of their father the devil (John 8), and in various places, he speaks to Jews of "your law" or "their law" (8:17; 10:34; 15:25), as if he were not a Jew. As a ruler of the Jews, Nicodemus is in fact ruler of what is merely another nation.

This fits also with the conversation that Jesus has with Nicodemus. What astonishes Nicodemus has less to do with the conception of spiritual rebirth itself than with the demand that he, as a leader of the Jews, must be born again. Jesus is talking not merely about individual renewal but about the need for Israel itself to be born again, a fact indicated by his use of a plural pronoun in 3:7:[52] you all, you *Israel*, must be born again. Israel must pass again through the waters and under the cloud, baptized in the cloud and sea as they were in the exodus, if they are going to see and enter the kingdom of heaven. In their current condition, they are just a *demos;* they must be born again.

Nicodemus' next appearance in the gospel gives his name a further ironic twist. A council of Jewish officers meets to discuss what to do with Jesus. They are divided between those who admire Jesus and those who consider him a threat to the nation. None of the experts—none of the seminary professors—follow Jesus, so how can he possibly be legitimate? He is capable only of misleading the "accursed" multitude that "does not know the Law" (7:49). At this point, Nicodemus reminds the experts on the law what the law requires: "Our Law does not judge a man, unless it first hears from him and what he is doing, does it?" (7:50). Instead of responding with the law, they dismiss Nicodemus as a Galilean (7:51). The Pharisees who curse the ignorant multitudes are involved in a self-curse, since they prove that they are equally ignorant of the law. Nicodemus, that ruler of the Jews, finds that he is in a council that might as well be in Athens or Rome. The council has no more understanding of the Torah's demands than Gentiles. Though ruler of Jews, Nicodemus truly is Nike-demos.

So it appears that John's etymological and hermeneutical comment in 9:7 is not unique but characteristic. John is a writer who knows that words have pasts, even though those pasts are often suppressed. He wants those histories to come to the foreground as we read his gospel story. He wants us to know that the blind man is washing in a pool whose Aramaic/Hebrew name means sent, because the blind man is in fact being sent, just as Jesus was sent, just as the disciples were sent.

Minimal Meaning?

John's etymologies and translations suggest that he is as much a poet as an evangelist. He is not content to use the appropriate word, and does not want us to rest content with understanding the minimal meanings of the words he uses. Beyond the overt etymology, perhaps his word choices involve puns and other wordplays. Can we imagine that he took a poetic interest in the onomatopoetic *ptuo* and *ptusma* for "spit" and "spittle" (9:6)? It is unprovable but plausible.

His other word choices display the artistry of a poet. He uses the verb *epechrisen*, inexplicably translated as "applied" in the New American Standard Bible (NASB) of 9:6. The very same form of the very same verb is translated as "anoint" in the NASB of 9:11, which better captures the meaning. The verb contains the verb *chrio*, which means "anoint." In Greek, the verb can refer to rubbing or stroking part of the body, and it fittingly describes Jesus' action of putting the spittle-mud on the blind man's eyes. But there were other options in John's Greek. He uses *ballo* for "put" in 5:7 and 12:6, *tithemi* in 19:19, and variants of each in other places in his gospel. John, in short, knows that there are other verbs that express sheer placing. He even has another word for anoint, *aleipho*, used for Mary's anointing of Jesus (11:2; 12:3). In John 9, though, he uses a verb that contains the verb *chrio*, with all its massive aural interaction with *christos* (cf. 9:22; 10:24). The blind man comes to see after being anointed with mud by the Anointed One, and in being so anointed, he becomes an anointed disciple of the Anointed One. The verb choice puts us in the frame of mind to read the story as an allegory of discipleship. It suggests that the man who has been anointed is becoming Christlike, a suspicion that will be amply confirmed as we study the passage further. John's choice of verb also throws the Jews' questions into ironic relief. "Is he the Christ?" they ask about Jesus, while an anointed one is standing right in front of them with open eyes.

If we were writing a dictionary, we would want to list "apply" or "rub on" as one of the senses of *chrio*. In the discourse of John's gospel, however, the word has other properties, which it borrows from related words in the passage and the gospel as a whole.

Another of John's word choices is theologically pregnant. *Knowledge* is one of the key themes of John 9. In the NASB translation, the word is used over ten times in the chapter. In John's Greek, he had the option of using one of two verbs, *ginosko* and *oida*. In sheer lexical terms, the verbs are virtually synonymous, and little appears to motivate one choice or another. Throughout John 9, though, John uses *oida* and only *oida* (vv. 2, 20, 21 [2x], 24, 25 [2x], 29 [2x], 30, 31). Paul Duke suggests that this is because

John wants to establish a link between knowledge and sight, and *oida* is related to the verb *eidon*, "to see."[53] Through most of the chapter, John uses an alternative verb for seeing, *blepo* (vv. 7, 15, 19 [2x], 21 [2x], 25, 39 [3x], 41). At the beginning of the story, though, John records Jesus' first sight of the blind man using the verb *eiden* (v. 1).

This does not mean that, in general, Greeks believed that knowing was a kind of seeing, or seeing a kind of knowing. They might well have, but the linguistic evidence does not prove that by itself. But in John 9, the link between the two is not merely linguistic. The blind man comes to see, and as he does so, he gradually comes to know. Early on, he can only say, "I know not" (v. 12), but by the end of the story, he is astonished at the ignorance of the Pharisees (v. 29). He knows better than the teachers of Israel; he can see more than they see, because his eyes have been opened and theirs are still covered.

Chapter 9 is not the only place where John writes with a poet's attention to the variety of meanings, histories, and derivations of the words he uses. It is a truism of Johannine study that this evangelist is peculiarly fond of double entendres. He says that the light comes into the darkness, and the darkness cannot "comprehend" or "overcome" it—the verb means both, and both are important themes in the gospel. Both meanings are necessary to get the sense of John's statement: the darkness not only fails to understand but also becomes actively hostile. Jesus is "lifted up" on the cross, but the lifting up goes further to describe his ascent to the Father. Most dramatically, John uses a deliberate grammatical ambiguity in the trial scene, leaving us without clarity about who is seated on the "judgment seat" in Pilate's praetorium. The ambiguity is clearly intentional, and creates a double-level scene. On the one hand, there is the man Jesus, who is on trial before the Roman governor Pilate; hovering over that scene, or, better, injected into and permeating it, is the reality that Jesus has already announced: "Now is the judgment of this world." Pilate and especially the Jews are the ones on trial, not Jesus.[54]

Do not pigeonhole the text, let it come fully "on stage"

CONCLUSION

The evangelical scholars quoted at the beginning of this chapter do not want us to treat words as players, rounded characters with rich, perhaps contradictory personalities and behaviors and hidden but influential pasts. They want to reduce words to cardboard cutouts, one-dimensional characters. I do not believe that this is the Bible's own attitude toward words; it is not John's attitude. The Bible is closer to poetry than to a scientific manual, and the biblical writers' use of words is more like that of poets than of linguists or scientists.

If we were talking about poetry, it would be a tragedy to keep texts from surprising us, to tell Lear to be just one thing, to do as little as possible. The failure is much deeper when we are talking about translation of the word of God. Clive James' lament returns: translation and linguistic theories emasculate Scripture, depriving it of much of its linguistic, cultural, and political potency, and perhaps even its religious power: how can we hear good news as *news* if the Bible's words are not permitted to say anything new?

Talk to Tyler about this

Four

The Text Is a Joke

Intertextuality

"How did he get that from that text?" It is a common question, often framed as a complaint against critics and commentators who, it is charged, find things in texts that are not there.

Ask a literature professor what Melville's *Moby Dick* is about, and he will go on and on about the search for meaning and reality in a world of appearances, about how the whale represents a world that resists human mastery or a tyrannical God hostile to man, or about the moral courage of defying whatever it is that lurks behind the pasteboard mask of visible reality. Ask his students, and they will tell you that the book is about Captain Ahab's search for a whale, short on plot and more than a little boring. With special effects and a good soundtrack, it might make a watchable film, but it is an unreadable novel.

Suspicion that interpreters write expansive commentaries full of what is not in the text is one of the reasons why literature is so often seen as a subjective un-discipline, as students learn to free-associate on the text just as their professors do. And it is one of the reasons that students inclined to hardheaded scientific realism dislike, when they do not disdain, literature courses.

Fortunately, students of the Bible are usually inoculated against literary fancies early on in their training. The more expert they get, the more inoculated they become. In an effort to turn theologians and Bible students into hardheaded realists, professors of hermeneutics and their textbooks have pounded the distinction between exegesis and eisegesis into the students'

unsuspecting heads.[1] The first is a solidly scientific enterprise, employing proven methods to extract, like a coal miner, what is contained in the text; the second pretends to be creative but is actually muddlebrained, feathery as a cloud, and foolishly literary, as its practitioners pour into the text all kinds of unhealthy things that are not there and were never intended by the writer.

It is something of a shock for modern interpreters to turn to patristic literature and discover the Fathers, who bequeathed orthodoxy to the church, indulging the most fanciful forms of what appears for all the world to be eisegesis. Justin tries to convert the Jew Trypho by pointing to the identity of Jesus' name to that of Joshua, the conqueror of Canaan; by suggesting that Moses' outstretched arms during the battle against the Amalekites (Exod 17) was "a type of nothing but the cross"; by insisting that the red cord outside Rahab's window in the wall of Jericho was a "symbol of the blood of Christ." To the Jews, he argues that Joshua did not lead the people to the promised land; it took a Jesus to accomplish that.[2]

It is more than a shock when modern readers turn to the Bible itself and recognize that when the biblical writers use the Old Testament, they seem to be reading all kinds of things into the text as well. As we saw in chapter 2, the New Testament authors seem to find many things in the Old Testament that are not there. Was Hosea thinking of Jesus' escape from Herod when he wrote "out of Egypt I called My Son" (Matt 2:15, quoting Hos 11:1)? Did Moses know that the "Rock was Christ" (1 Cor 10:4)? If Paul can allegorize on the story of Abraham's two wives (Gal 4:21-31), can we allegorize on the story of Ruth's two (potential) husbands? Perhaps we can distance ourselves from Athanasius and Augustine and retain our Christian credentials. But Paul and Matthew?

The struggle against eisegesis is well motivated. As a simple matter of courtesy, we should refrain from stuffing words into the mouths of others. Especially when we are dealing with Scripture, the very word of God in the words of God, we should find no more than what is there.

On the other hand, we should find no less, either, and the surpassing failing of modern interpretation is not over-reading but drastically under-reading Scripture. Interpreters should aim for both accuracy and fullness. We want to hear as precisely as possible what is being said, but surely we also want to hear all that is being said.

What does it mean for something to be there in the text? Strictly speaking, all that is in the text are the words on the page, unless we count the spaces in between. We might think of interpretation as a reduction of sentences to algebra: let C = cat, M = mat, and ^ = the relation of "lying on." Interpreting "The cat lies on the mat" would be translating it to C^M. But interpretation is more than repeating the text; it is something more than barely disguised plagiarism, more than substituting near synonyms for the words on the page, as if the interpretation of "The cat lies on the mat" could be reduced to "A definite feline is pronely placed on a definite smallish floor covering."

Dale Allison is, I think, more accurate in saying of Matthew 1:1 that "The interpretation of this line can be nothing other than the unfolding of what is not stated."[3] What is not there? Lots. Allison is so good on this point that I cannot help quoting more:

> all the words in 1:1 derive from tradition, and to under-
> stand them aright we must know their itinerary. *Biblos
> geneseos* occurs in LXX Gen. 2:4 and 5:1 while "Genesis"
> came to be, in the Greek-speaking world, the title for the
> first book of Moses. As for *Christos*, it was firmly associ-
> ated with Jewish eschatological expectation. So too *huios
> David*. And *huios Abraam*, likewise a fixed expression,
> also had its own special connotations. Now all this, which
> was undoubtedly known to Matthew's Jewish-Christian
> audience, is fundamental for interpretation. But Matt.
> 1:1 directly conveys none of this information. Rather
> it assumes that the requisite sensibility will pass from
> the explicit to the implicit, that it will go beyond what the
> words directly denote to what they connote—which is
> why the more Matt. 1:1 is engaged, the more it evokes.
> Words and phrases . . . are not simple things; nor is lan-
> guage ever born anew: it is always old. A combination of
> words is like a moving trawler, whose dragnet, below the
> surface and out of sight, has taken catch and now pulls
> along so much. Just as it would be erroneous to equate

the function of the fishing vessel with what goes on in plain sight, so similarly can focus on what is explicit in a literary text lead one right past much meaning—above all in a book such as Matthew, beneath whose literary surface is the Jewish Bible, which is alluded to far more than expressly cited. . . . The truth is, our evangelist had no need to trumpet the manifest, and the allusions to Moses were . . . manifest enough to those who lived and moved and had their being in the Jewish tradition.[4]

One might be tempted to respond to the charge of eisegesis by insisting that everything is right there in the text. That is the wrong answer, and can only kill interpretation. It is not all there, and it should not be. In fact, it cannot be. Interpretation is all about tracing out the crucial missing elements that make the text mean what it does.

Anyone with a minimal facility with a language can read what is there. If interpretation is merely explaining what is on the page, why do we need interpreters? We should all pack up and go find real jobs. Yet the Bible shows that there are supposed to be teachers in the church. Teaching is in Paul's lists of spiritual gifts. If there are teachers, they must be doing something, and they must be doing something that not everyone has time or inclination to do. They must spend their time unfolding what is not stated.

Can we make sense of this? Can we offer a reasonable and responsible description of textual meaning and interpretation that can account for the offhanded way the New Testament writers read and quote the Old Testament? Can we account for their eisegesis without endorsing a hermeneutical free-for-all, where texts can be made to mean anything the interpreter damn well pleases? Practically, can we make sense of the biblical writers' use of the Old Testament without supporting what Umberto Eco calls "interpretive drift"?

Yes. We have made a start of this in chapter 2 by considering texts in time, but here, I am attacking a more specific problem from a different angle.

HERMENEUTICS OF HUMOR

First, let me tell some jokes.[5]

> A priest, a rabbi, a nun, a doctor, and a lawyer all walk into a bar. The bartender says, "What, is this a joke?"

A few years ago, several of my children asked me to explain this joke from *Reader's Digest*. This is always a delicate parental moment. Even when the source is as safe as *Reader's Digest*, it is still possible that one will be confronted with humor that would be difficult, if not illegal, to explain to children. Fortunately, the joke was clean.

But it was puzzling to my children. Why? They understood each of the words in the sentence and understood the sentences as sequences of words. Had I asked them to draw me a picture, the artsy ones could have. Some of them caught the frame-breaking humor of a bartender who knows he is in a joke. The older of them could have done an interpretation by substituting synonyms: "An indefinite Catholic minister, an indefinite Jewish pastor, an indefinite convent dweller, an indefinite physician, plus an indefinite barrister come into a pub. A definite man serving drinks asks, 'Are you trying to make me laugh?'" Even those who could have offered this kind of interpretation were puzzled because they did not understand why the bartender would draw that conclusion in the first place. They knew all the words, grasped the syntax of the sentence. But they did not *get* it.

The joke depends on a confluence of two joke traditions: jokes about diverse religious figures or professionals on the one hand, and jokes about barroom conversations on the other. The bartender, clearly well informed about these joke traditions, suspects what is happening.[6] My children lacked that information, and missed the point completely. Even at the most literal level, the meaning of the joke depends on all sorts of things that are not there, things from outside the text. An interpreter not only has to know something outside the text, but also has to know what information from outside the text is relevant. Knowing that rabbis study Hebrew, that some lawyers specialize in torts, or that nearly forty percent of bartenders are Irish[7] would not help anyone get the joke. What is remarkable is not that my children failed to understand the joke, but that thousands of readers do get it. How do they know what information is relevant when the writer of the joke has given no explicit indication? Or has he? That is a mystery that will bear some further attention below. For the moment, more jokes.

My insight, if such it is, into the workings of humor was reinforced and generalized when I watched *Shrek*, a movie that I now tell my students is a gold mine of hermeneutical insight. All the funny parts of that film assume that the viewer has information the movie does not provide, information from three main sources: nursery rhymes, fairy tales, and popular culture, especially other movies. During one scene, the evil Lord Farquaad is torturing the gingerbread man in his dungeon—dunking him in milk, breaking off his legs, threatening to remove his gumdrop buttons. Finally, he gets the gingerbread man to talk, and this exchange ensues:

> Gingerbread Man: Do you know the muffin man?
> Farquaad: The muffin man?
> Gingerbread Man: The muffin man.
> Farquaad: The muffin man who lives on Drury Lane?

Ha! you say. What made you laugh? How did you know it was a joke? It is a torture scene, for goodness' sake.

In another part of the film, Shrek fights his way into a castle tower to rescue the beautiful Princess Fiona, who is being held prisoner by a dragon. Shrek's commotion wakes the princess, who speaks in stilted fairly-tale English, wonders why she has not been kissed, and is horrified to learn that the dragon is still alive: "You haven't killed the dragon?" she asks. "It's on my to-do list," is Shrek's response. Now, what makes that funny?

When Shrek and Fiona are waylaid by a group of mincing merry men in the forest, we suddenly learn that Fiona has picked up some martial arts training. During the fight, she leaps into the air, and the action stops as the "camera" rotates slowly around the scene, an allusion to the film techniques of *The Matrix*.[8] At the end of the film, the wedding scene echoes that of the Disney film *Beauty and the Beast*. Fiona is under a curse that turns her into an ogress every night, but she hopes that when she receives true love's kiss, she will be released from the curse and remain a beautiful princess forever. When Shrek kisses her, she begins spinning and flies up into the air, raining sparks, just as the Beast does in the Disney film. When the Beast comes back down to earth, he has been transformed into a handsome prince. In one of the most delicious subversions in the film, when Fiona descends, she is still an ogress. I did not catch the *Beauty and the Beast* reference the first time I watched the movie. My kids had to point it out to me, repayment for that bar joke.

This is only a small sampling, but the point is clear: *Shrek* is impenetrable unless the viewer comes armed with a cache of nursery rhymes, fairy tales, and recollections from pop culture.[9] A viewer ignorant of these resources does not miss some marginal features of the film; he misses the entire meaning. He does not get it.

The same goes for a viewer who knows all the relevant information but does not realize it is relevant. Imagine a viewer who knows all the fairy tales in Grimm, has mastered every nursery rhyme in Mother Goose, and has watched every major feature film emanating from Hollywood during the past quarter century. Imagine, too, that this viewer watches *Shrek*, but never once is reminded of Grimm or Mother Goose or another film. Unlikely, but theoretically possible. What do we say about this kind of viewer? He is not ignorant, but he is a bad viewer. He does not get it. But what exactly does he not get? What did he miss? How was he supposed to know?

Like the jokes in *Shrek*, I submit, every text depends for its meaning on information lying outside the text. Every text is a joke, and a good interpreter is one with a good sense of humor, one with a broad knowledge and the wit to know what bits of knowledge are relevant. All interpretation is a matter of getting it. All texts mean the way jokes mean. Or, to put it more sharply. . .

THE TEXT IS A JOKE

How is this true? How are texts like jokes? And how is interpretation like getting a joke? First, it is true in the apparently trivial sense that no text defines all its terms for the reader. At the least, the reader must bring a basic understanding of the language of the text. No text can define every term without turning into a Borgesian infinite dictionary. Without a knowledge of Hebrew, no English speaker can begin to understand the original text of Genesis; it does not provide Hebrew-English equivalents along the way. A reader with less Greek than Shakespeare will be forced to say of Paul's letters, "'Twas all Greek to me."

This is, as I say, an apparently trivial point. It is trivial in the sense that everyone knows it, and in the sense that it is uncontroversial. But the hermeneutical import of the point is far from trivial. It means that every reader, no matter how literal-minded and scientific, no matter how committed to exegesis or hostile to eisegesis, is pouring stuff into the text that is not there, or, perhaps more accurately, siphoning off stuff that is not there. If he comes to the text with his mind a tabula rasa, the text will be as empty as his head. A Greek reader who reads about *sarx* in Paul knows what the word means because he learned it in grammar school, or saw it in another text, or heard it used in the meat market. It is nonsensical to object that no one can be sure that Paul means "flesh" when he writes *sarx* because Paul never defines it. Of course he does not define it. Parchment was not cheap, and he had better things to do than write a dictionary. He had a gospel to preach.

Even the most rigorously grammatical and historical exegesis of the Bible depends on connections between text and text, or text and speech, or text and extratextual reality. When a New Testament scholar plunders papyri to discover how a particular Pauline word was commonly deployed in the first century, he is seeking relevant information outside of Paul's text. Were one to ask, he would insist that this external information is indispensable to unraveling the meaning of Paul's letter. And it may well be. Historical information works the same way. When an Old Testament exegete tries to illuminate the brief account of Sennacherib's retreat from Jerusalem (2 Kgs 19:35-37) by poring over Assyrian texts, he is bringing extratextual information to bear on his text, in the hopes that the text will become clearer by reading it alongside relevant information that is not in it.

This phenomenon is sometimes described as *intertextuality*, but that term has its limitations.[10] The primary limitation is that relevant information may come, not from other texts, but from extratextual reality. Archaeologists decipher texts and inscriptions, but can also illuminate ancient texts by discovering nontextual artifacts and ruins. I had my suspicions about what "horns of the altar" looked like, but pictures of excavated horned altars clarified what I imagined.[11] Knowing the distance from Jericho to Gilgal illumines Joshua, and knowing the distance across the Sea of Galilee enhances the reader's grasp of John 6's story of Jesus walking on the water. This is Augustine's reason for encouraging pastors and teachers to be familiar with all the liberal arts.[12] The Bible speaks of animals, so some knowledge of zoology is useful; the Bible alludes to music, so the interpreter must know music; the Bible includes historical, geographical, and other sorts of information, so the better informed a reader is, the fuller and more accurate his reading will be.

In other words, even the most rigorously exegetical readers are eisegetical, or might be called so by someone more rigorously exegetical than thou. Everyone brings information to the text that is not in the text, and seeks to illuminate the text with light from outside. They fill in the gaps between words and sentences to produce a whole picture. That is perfectly fine and, I have been arguing, inescapable. What is not fine is the pretense that literal reading does not involve this process, the claim that a reading is doing nothing but getting what is there.

It is quite common, for instance, to suggest that the setting for John 9 is in the temple precincts, and that this narrative forms the climax to a series of incidents during the Feast of Tabernacles. This seems perfectly reasonable, and illuminates several details of John's account. But the fact is that John 9 nowhere says that Jesus is in the temple, or that it is the Feast of Booths. That has to be plucked up from the context and read into John 9. Such a procedure looks sleekly scientific, grammatical-historical, and literal. If one suggests that Jesus working with the clay should be read in the light of Old Testament potter-and-clay passages (as I will below), many would cry foul, or, more likely, "eisegete!"

In principle, though, there is no difference between reading the
Feast of Booths into John 9 and reading Jeremiah 18 into John 9.
The fact that one text is further away than the other appears to
make one literal and the other arbitrary. But in principle, it is the
same procedure, and Jeremiah 18 is no further from John than, say,
Homer is from Virgil. Certainly Jeremiah 18 is at least as close to
John as the Jamnia Council, that symbolic marker of the parting
of the ways of Jews and Christians, which is often proposed as the
master historical context for John's narrative. Studying historical
context, extrabiblical usage of words, archaeology—that all looks
scientific and scholarly, but it is just as much eisegesis as apostolic allegory.

The question I raised earlier—how does the reader know what
bits of his collection of knowledge are relevant?—is fairly easy to
answer in such cases. John talks about an overnight sea voyage
across Geneseret, and that either leads a reader to think, "Ah, I
know how far they went," or to ponder, "I wonder how far they
went." A good reader trying to imagine the size of the monumen-
tal pillars outside of Solomon's temple either knows how long a
cubit is or has the curiosity to find out.

A good reader not only brings knowledge of historical information and the vocabulary and grammar of the language to his reading but also brings knowledge of earlier portions of the text he is
interpreting, as well as knowledge of other texts, and these also
shed light on the particular text he is studying. Examples of this
sort of intertextuality abound in Western literature, because every
great writer, and many lesser ones, knew of other works in that
tradition and wrote against the background of that tradition. Virgil
knew Homer better than virtually any modern Homeric scholar,
and Homeric styles, scenes, characters, tropes, and allusions are so
deeply embedded in the *Aeneid* that Virgil almost appears to us as
a plagiarist. Dante had read Virgil who had read Homer, and Virgil
plays a major part in the *Comedy*. Eliot had read Dante who had
read Virgil who had read Homer, and as a result, Eliot's poetry is
several layers thick with allusion. Nor is this confined to what we
think of as high literary art. Kenneth Grahame's *Wind in the Wil-
lows* borrows from the *Odyssey* (suitor-like weasels take over Toad

Hall until the hero returns), and Fiver in Richard Adams' *Watership Down* is self-consciously based on Cassandra from Aeschylus' *Agamemnon*. The next time you watch *The Lion King*, keep a copy of *Hamlet* open on your lap.

And so on and on. Each of these stories and poems is coherent in itself. A reader innocent of Homer can still read Virgil with profit, and children who have never heard, and perhaps never will hear, of Aeschylus can enjoy Adams' novel. But an interpreter who wants to catch all that a writer throws at him will have to be alert to these echoes and allusions. A reader will get the poet's point fully only if he not only knows the prior text but also knows that he needs to know the prior text, and knows when to bring which part of the prior text into play. An interpreter is there to explain what is not in the text. And do we not want to hear everything God says in the Bible?

TEXTS IN TEXTS

Let us look at two more extended—I almost said more serious—examples. Robert Penn Warren once said that the most natural reading of a poem occurs not on the first or the tenth but on the hundredth reading. To get the poem, a reader has not only to remember what he has already read, but to remember the part of the poem he has not read yet. In other words, the first level of intertextual action is within a single text. To get all an author gives, one has to be alert to the network of connections within his or her text.

Though Shakespeare is often considered a secular writer in the humanist tradition, recent work has highlighted his use of the Bible, his references to Christian tradition, and his apparent use of the stage as a pulpit. Nowhere are the biblical references more explicit or abundant than in *The Merchant of Venice*.

Early in the play, Antonio, the merchant of the title, enters a loan agreement with the Jewish moneylender Shylock. The contract says that if Antonio defaults, Shylock will be able to cut out a pound of flesh from close to Antonio's heart. Antonio defaults (of course), and instead of giving up his claim, Shylock insists that the contract be enforced. The play's climax is a courtroom scene in which Shylock demands that the Duke of Venice decide in his favor and enforce the last letter of the law. Portia, disguised as a lawyer, enters to save the day by pointing out that the contract makes no mention of blood. Shylock can have his flesh, but if he sheds Antonio's blood, he will be charged with murder.

Contemporary readers, A. R. Braunmuller notes,[13] sometimes think of Portia's speech as a "setup that turns on a technicality" that "turns back on Shylock a legal rigidity he had been duped into demanding," but Elizabethan audiences would likely have taken the turnabout more favorably. For starters, "the blood/ flesh distinction that defeats Shylock's agreement with Antonio has ample biblical precedent: Genesis 9:4, Leviticus 7:26, Deuteronomy 12:32, Acts 15:29, among others. These Scriptural distinctions and prohibitions give rise to many important Judeo-Christian practices." Further, the court scene "exemplifies what folklorists might call 'the Biter Bit'—Shylock, seemingly in command of his enemies, himself becomes a victim through the very means he employed to gain that victory, now empty and reversed upon him." Though Braunmuller does not note it, this comic twist also has biblical precedent, in the stories of the wicked falling into pits they dig (think Haman in Esther) and the stories of Yahweh employing the lex talionis against Israel's enemies.

Read in the light of biblical references, Shylock's plot has a more precise significance. By seeking to take a "pound of flesh" from Antonio's side, "nearest the heart," Shylock is attempting to perform a macabre "heart circumcision" on the Christian (Rom 2). As Marjorie Garber puts it, the logic of the bond is premised on this allusion to the Christian notion of heart circumcision: Shylock says, in effect, "You Christians renounce circumcision of the foreskin, but talk about circumcision of the heart. Yet your conduct shows that your hearts are fleshly. Forfeiting the bond therefore will involve removal of the 'foreskin of the heart.'" Shylock wants to force Antonio's conversion to Judaism with a fleshly circumcision, but the plot doubles back on him so that he himself is forcibly converted to Christianity, the religion of heart circumcision.[14]

Finally, Braunmuller hears the echoes of Romans 11 in the conversion of Shylock:

to understand how an Elizabethan audience might have understood Shylock's forced conversion, we must remember that such conversions were regarded as beneficent. Only converted could a Jew hope for (Christian) salvation, and Christian belief held that the "conversion of the Jews" (Andrew Marvell's phrase) would precede the end of time and the world's final return to eternal joy.[15]

Portia's adoption of the name Baltassar is also significant, since this is the name of the prophet Daniel, though the Daniel in view is the sleuth-like Daniel of Bel and the Dragon or Susanna rather than the canonical Daniel.

Finally, at the climactic moment of reversal in the court scene in *The Merchant of Venice*, Portia tells Shylock, "This bond doth give thee here no jot of blood." "Jot" comes to English through the Greek *iota*, linked to the Hebrew *yod* through Jesus' usage in Matthew 5. At this juncture in the play, the word not only denotes "a whit" or "the smallest amount" but evokes Jesus' claims about his relation to the Law in the Sermon on the Mount. That allusion is doubly relevant: first, because Shylock is clearly an example of the false righteousness of scribes and Pharisees, who insist on the letter of the Law but fail to recognize that mercy is the heart of Torah; second, because the very point of the courtroom drama enacted in the play is that "not one jot or tittle of the law" shall be annulled. Shakespeare was a good New Testament scholar: Jesus comes not to abolish but to fulfill; the gospel does not annul the law, but confirms it. But we cannot quite see all that until we unfold what is not in the text. Once we do, we can see that *The Merchant of Venice* is a big joke.

Prufrock and Dante

So, too, Eliot's poetry is a joke. Eliot took the second epigraph of "The Love Song of J. Alfred Prufrock" from Dante's *Inferno* (27.61–66):

S'io credesse che mia risposta fosse
A persona che mai tornasse al mondo,
Questa fiamma staria senza piu scosse.

Ma perciocche giammai di questo fondo
Non torno vivo alcun, s'i'odo il vero,
Senza tema d'infamia ti rispondo.

Longfellow rendered the lines this way:

If I believed that my reply were made
To one who to the world would e'er return,
This flame without more flickering would stand still;

But inasmuch as never from this depth
Did any one return, if I hear true,
Without the fear of infamy I answer.

In the original, the speaker is Guido of Montefeltro, imprisoned
in the eighth circle of hell, where sinners are punished for fraud
against nature. Wrapped in flame, Guido is a false counselor
who identifies himself to Dante with the words quoted by Eliot,
"If I thought you were alive, I would not speak: since you will
never return to the world, I'll tell you." He goes on to explain
that he spent much of his life in deception and cunning: "I knew
each winding way, each covert earth, and used such art and cunning in deceit that to the ends of the world the sound went
forth." His deeds were the deeds of the fox, not those of the
lion. After a life of deceit, he tried to redeem himself by becoming a Franciscan friar, but he fell back into his old ways when
the Pope asked for advice in gaining support for a war against
other Christians. Guido advised the Pope to make promises that
he would never fulfill, and as a result of this advice, Guido is in
the depths of hell for counseling the Pope to act fraudulently.
What does this have to do with Prufrock, that feckless, modern
would-be lover?

At one level, Eliot's epigram recalls the infernal setting of
Guido's conversation with Dante, and sets Prufrock in a living hell. Dante does not show people being punished so much
as being delivered over to their sin. They receive in full whatever evils they have toyed with throughout their lives. Turns of
phrase and imagery in Eliot's poem show that the same holds for
Prufrock. The image of the sky as a "patient etherized upon a
table," mocked by C. S. Lewis, is not intended to be a description

of the evening so much as a description of the speaker and his perception of the evening. The speaker and Prufrock live in suspended animation (or inanimation). Elsewhere, Eliot claims that the evening is "sleeping peacefully," stretched on the floor like a housecat after tea and cakes. Again, the description is more about Prufrock's emotional and spiritual condition than an accurate or evocative description of the evening itself. Prufrock does not have strength to bring the moment to climax.

The reference to Lazarus in Eliot's poem reinforces these links with Dante. Whether the Lazarus is the Lazarus of Jesus' parable, resting in Abraham's bosom, or Lazarus the brother of Mary and Martha, the reference to him reappearing would be to a man coming back from the dead. Prufrock is like Lazarus in that he is in a state of death or near-death. He is at least etherized, and he realizes that any show of passion or decisiveness would be like Lazarus coming from the tomb. The undersea imagery of the final lines of the poem also plays in here. Until human voices wake him, Prufrock is asleep, suspended, dead. In all these ways, the epigraph resonates through the poem and sets up expectations for the contents of the poem. We get the epigraph and the poem only if we catch these resonances.

The connection may be even closer, though, if the "you" of Eliot's poem is to be understood as a Dante figure. Prufrock is speaking, since this is his love song, and if we press the analogy, he is in the position of Guido speaking to the poet, the Dantesque Eliot (or the poetic persona that Eliot adopts). Eliot said around 1949 in a letter that the "you" is "merely some friend or companion, presumably of the male sex, whom the speaker is at that moment addressing," but that friend becomes a Dante figure because he reports back to the reader what he hears from Prufrock, just as Dante reports his experiences in his poem. Prufrock is an evil counselor, like Guido; more specifically, he is an evil counselor who, like Guido, tells his friend that the way to get by in the world is to promise much but pay little. In short, the good reader of these texts must have, or acquire, the necessary information from the intertext in order to interpret the text. Earlier texts perichoretically indwell later texts.

One of the chief objections to the contemporary treatment of intertextuality is the way it tends to reduce writing and text production to an impersonal process.[16] Intertextuality seems to reduce Shakespeare and Eliot to funnels through which other languages speak, nothing more than nodes in a network of texts. The author and his or her intentions in writing are ignored, and the writer is turned into a plaything of language, or of some literary tradition. But the phenomenon I have described poses no challenge whatsoever to the notion of authorial intention. Virgil clearly intended to build his story on the pattern of the *Iliad* and *Odyssey*, and Eliot obviously wanted to bring Dante and his *Inferno*—in fact, a specific incident in that poem—to his reader's mind. The examples from Shakespeare may be less convincing, but would an Elizabethan audience have missed the echo of Matthew 5:17-20 in Portia's unusual use of the word jot, or the references to circumcision in Shylock's obsessions with flesh?

Every text is a joke, depending for its meaning on things that are left unsaid, but that is the way the jokester intends it to be. He or she wants the reader to think outside the text.

JOHANNINE JOKES

How does all this apply to our reading of Scripture? Scripture has the same literary properties as the texts we have been examining. Just as Eliot read Dante who read Virgil who read Homer, so Matthew had read Jeremiah, who knew Kings (or wrote it), and the writer of Kings had read the Hexateuch. Let us look at some examples. Let me tell some biblical jokes, again taken from John 9.

The nearest intertextual echoes are the ones that John has built into his joyous, humorous gospel. First, John 9 records the story of Jesus healing a blind man, and already in John's gospel, sight has become an important theme. "No one has seen God at any time," John tells us toward the end of his prologue (1:18), but John's comment that "the only-begotten God, who is in the bosom of the Father, He has explained" (v. 18) gives us some hope that with the Word's arrival in flesh, the unseen God will be seen. We are not disappointed: "He who has seen Me has seen the Father" (14:9). In contrast to the Synoptics, which use *duna-*

mis to refer to Jesus' miracles, John uses *semeion*, "sign," a word that emphasizes their visibility. Many "behold" Jesus' signs and believe (2:23; 6:2). To see the kingdom requires not just new eyes but a new birth by water and Spirit (3:3). Those who are not reborn may see the signs and the sign-giver, but do not believe (6:26, 36). Seeing and believing are closely linked in John (4:48; 6:30).

All this should be rumbling around in the reader's mind as he comes to chapter 9 and watches Jesus pass by a man blind from birth, that is, a man whose physical condition mirrors the spiritual malady of unbelief that Jesus has challenged on several occasions. The rumblings return at the end of the chapter, when Jesus announces that he has come to bring judgment, which takes the form of giving sight to the blind and blinding the seeing (9:39). The Pharisees demand to know whether Jesus considers them blind, but Jesus will not give them that excuse. Because they claim to see, because they have seen Jesus' works and refuse to believe, they are still in their sin (9:40-41). They see, but they are self-blinded, and, with the Pharisees standing in front of him, Jesus goes on to describe the conduct of blind shepherds (10:1-18).

Prior to 9:1, John has used the word *blind* only once, in 5:3. At the pool Bethesda beside the sheep gate is a "multitude of those who were sick, blind, lame, and withered." The connections between John 5 and 9 are extensive. In both chapters, Jesus heals a man who has been afflicted for a long time (5:5; 9:1). In both cases, there is a reference to healing water: the water of Bethesda that cannot heal the lame man because he cannot get to it, and the sight-giving waters of Siloam. Both pools are given Hebrew names. Both healings occur on the Sabbath (5:9; 9:14), a detail that John delays in both passages, and both healings provoke a vigorous, vicious response from the Jews. In both passages, Jesus talks about the works he performed, even on the Sabbath (5:17; 9:4). Both men are assaulted by the Jews.

The lame man of John 5 has been lame for thirty-eight years, and his recovery gives him new life. The blind man has been blind since birth (9:1), and gaining sight is like being born again. He is so different that neighbors are uncertain about his identity (9:8-9), though, fortunately, his parents still recognize him (9:20). John uses the noun *birth* (*genete*) only here, but the noun is linked with the verb *gennao* (1:13; 8:41; 16:21; 18:37). The verb is used most often in two chapters, John 3 (7x) and John 9 (5x), and this is only one verbal and conceptual link joining these chapters in intertextual codependence. To Nicodemus, Jesus speaks of the necessity of being born of "water and Spirit" (3:5), and the man blind from birth is reborn seeing when he washes in the pool (9:7). One of the effects of being born again is "seeing" the kingdom (3:3), a theme obviously picked up in John 9, where the man sees the embodied kingdom, the King Jesus. The blind man is among those who are born when old, who, by water and Spirit, see and eventually enter the kingdom of God.

Jesus says, "You must be born of water *and the Spirit*" (emphasis added). Is there any indication that the blind man has experienced this double rebirth? Is John 3 one of the texts that we should bring into play to get the joke of John 9?

Yes. We often remember Jesus saying that the Spirit is like the wind, but that is not exactly what he says. For starters, in John's Greek, Jesus says that the *pneuma* blows where it wills, and *pneuma* does double duty (like the Hebrew *ruach*) as "wind" and "spirit." John 3:8 could be translated as "The Spirit blows where He wills." It is another of John's characteristic double entendres. More importantly, though, Jesus does not compare the Spirit to wind. Rather, what is like the wind is "everyone who is born of the Spirit" (3:8). Those who are born of the Spirit become like the Spirit, wispy and elusive, though audible. Those born of the Spirit are hard to pin down: we "do not know where it comes from and where it goes." Jesus is the preeminent One born of the Spirit (1:33), and throughout John's gospel, the Jews puzzle about Jesus' origins and destination. "Where did He come from?" and "Where is He going?" are frequent questions. In John 9, we get a hint of that elusiveness, but in this case, it is the man rather than Jesus only who is elusive. Who is the man? his neighbors ask. Is this the one? Yes, no, maybe. The blind man who washed in water has become like one born of the Spirit.

John 9 contains another hint that the blind man is conformed to Jesus, the One born of the Spirit. In response to the questioning of his neighbors, the blind man insists that he is the one who "used to sit and beg" (vv. 8-9). Translators shrink back here, but John is bold as a lion. Is this the beggar? neighbors ask, and the blind man says not "I am the one" (NASB) but simply "I am" (*ego eimi*, v. 9). John is famous for his "I am" sayings. There is even one in this chapter (v. 5). Elsewhere, though, Jesus utters *ego eimi* (6:35, 41, 48, 58; 7:29; 8:12, 18, 23-24, 28, 58; 10:7, 9, 11, 14, 36; 11:25; 15:1, 5; 18:5). Even John, greatest of the prophets, inserts the crucial negative: *ego ouk eimi*, "I am not" (1:20-21; 3:28). The most that John is willing to say is that he is the promised voice (1:23). Having washed in the pool, though, the blind man can declare, "I am." He is Christ's witness, and becomes a kind of replacement of Christ.[17]

Jesus says to his disciples, "We must work the works of Him who sent Me, as long as it is day; night is coming, when no man can work" (9:4). In this, he incorporates the disciples into his work, and specifically into his work as the "light of the world," laboring in the presence of the light, anticipating the removal of light, which is the departure of Jesus.[18] The disciples are going to carry on Jesus' illuminating work, and the blind man, illuminated and seeing, is a type of what they will experience when night arrives, when light departs.

Jesus has said "I am the light of the world" once before, in 8:12, where he declares before the Pharisees that "he who follows Me shall not walk in the darkness, but shall have the light of life." The Pharisees immediately reject Jesus' claims, charging him with bearing witness to himself. The Pharisees are the darkness that does not understand Jesus and cannot overcome him. Jesus instead shines his light on a blind man, bringing him sight and giving him the "light of life."

Jesus' identification of himself as light of the world is contextually appropriate, coming as it does during the Feast of Booths (7:2; and no major change of setting until 10:22).[19] Gary Burge summarizes the evidence from the Mishnah on Tabernacles:

> [It] provides lavish descriptions of both the water and light ceremonies and explains that whoever has not seen these things has never seen a wonder in his or her life! Four large

stands each held four golden bowls; these were places in the heavily-used Court of the Women. These sixteen golden bowls (reached by ladders) were filled with oil and used the worn undergarments of the priests for wicks. When they were lit at night (so the rabbis said), all Jerusalem was illumined. In a world that did not have public lighting after dusk, this light shining from Jerusalem's yellow limestone walls must have been spectacular.[20]

That is, "In the very court where the lightening ceremony takes place, Jesus stands beneath lit bowls of oil and says that he is not only the true light of Jerusalem, but of the whole world!" Burge mentions water rites at Booths as well, which brought together the seasonal need for rain with the memory of God's provision of water from the rock.

We are getting away from ourselves. We are moving beyond internal Johannine jokes to jokes that depend on texts outside John's gospel. But that is the nature of humor; once you start with a joke, you cannot tell where it is going to end.

example of an "inside joke"

Clay and Potter

John 1 begins with an overt, unmistakable allusion to Genesis 1: "In the beginning." As the prologue develops, John extends the parallels between the creation of the world and the coming of Jesus. On day one of creation, God creates light and separates it from darkness; John tells us that Jesus is light shining in darkness (1:4-5). John identifies Jesus, the true light, as the one through whom the world was made (1:3, 10). The light/darkness contrast in John 1, then, is, as we have seen, an intertextual allusion to Genesis, and when John recovers the threads of that imagery in John 9, the echoes of Genesis are still reverberating in the background. The man born blind is born again to see the light of the first day of creation, the uncreated light that created all things. His rebirth to sight is an entry into new creation. He is in Christ, and whoever is in Christ—behold a new creation (2 Cor 5:17).

Genesis haunts John 9 even further, however. Jesus goes to odd lengths to heal the blind man. He could have simply spoken and given sight; he could have sent the man to Siloam to wash in the pool. Instead, he goes through this elaborate process, first concocting spittle-mud, then anointing the man's eyes, and finally sending him off to the pool for washing. Why the clay appliqué? We get a hint from verse 5, where Jesus identifies himself as the light of the world, an allusion at one remove to the light of creation. Jesus is enacting a creation scene. Consider:

> Yahweh God formed man of dust from the ground, and breathed into his nostrils the breath of life; and man became a living soul. (Gen 2:7)
>
> When [Jesus] had said this, He spat on the ground, and made clay of the spittle, and applied the clay to his eyes. (John 9:6)

There are certainly differences here, but the similarities are striking. Especially given the theme of rebirth that resonates throughout John 9, Jesus working in the mud to give the sightless man a new, seeing life replicates the creation of Adam. Yahweh breathed life into Adam; Jesus combines breath and water to make the clay that renews the blind man, born of water and Spirit. The blind man is with Christ, and whoever is with Christ—behold a new Adam.

John 9 also jokes with passages in Isaiah, which are themselves linked with the creation narrative. According to Isaiah, giving sight to the blind will be one of the Messiah's characteristic projects. He will dispel the darkness in which the blind live (Isa 29:18), and he will restore the deaf, mute, blind, and lame to wholeness (35:5-6), pouring out water to turn the wilderness to garden in the process (35:7). Opening the eyes of the blind is like bringing prisoners from the dungeon, in a reenactment of the exodus (42:7), and once the eyes of the blind are open, Jesus will be able to lead them in new paths (42:16). Behind Isaiah's prophecies is the Torah's prohibition of the blind and the lame from ministering in Yahweh's house (Lev 21:18). Giving sight to the blind is part of Jesus' formation of a new priestly nation. Perhaps this is why Jesus uses the unusual method of washing to open the blind man's eyes. Washing normally removes uncleanness, and blindness is here pictured as a kind of defilement that falls like scales. The notion that blindness is analogous to uncleanness is stronger if, with many commentators, we hear echoes of the cleansing of Namaan, the Aramean leper (2 Kgs 5).[21]

Clay takes us in other directions as well. Within the New Testament, the noun for clay, *pelos*, is used only here (vv. 6 [2x], 11, 14, 15) and in Romans 9:21. It is used over twenty times in the Septuagint, and several of these are neatly linked to John 9. In Psalm 40, David praises God with a new song, something of a taunt song, because Yahweh has taken him from the pit of Sheol and the miry clay (*pelos*) and set him on a rock. The whole psalm might be the song of the man born blind, especially in the final half:

> I have proclaimed glad tidings of righteousness in the
> great congregation;
> Behold, I will not restrain my lips,
> O LORD, You know.
> I have not hidden Your righteousness within my heart;
> I have spoken of Your faithfulness and Your salvation;
> I have not concealed Your lovingkindness and Your truth
> from the great congregation.
> You, O LORD, will not withhold Your compassion from me;
> Your lovingkindness and Your truth will continually
> preserve me.
> For evils beyond number have surrounded me;
> My iniquities have overtaken me, so that I am not able
> to see;
> They are more numerous than the hairs of my head,
> And my heart has failed me.
> Be pleased, O LORD, to deliver me;
> Make haste, O LORD, to help me.
> Let those be ashamed and humiliated together
> Who seek my life to destroy it;
> Let those be turned back and dishonored
> Who delight in my hurt.
> Let those be appalled because of their shame
> Who say to me, "Aha, aha!"
> Let all who seek You rejoice and be glad in You;
> Let those who love Your salvation say continually,
> The LORD be magnified! (vv. 9-16)

Like David, the blind man is surrounded by evils, yet he does not close his mouth in the great congregation. He is finally vindicated against those who seek his life, and he knows what it means to see his enemies turned back in shame.

Isaiah 29 is an even closer match, linked to John 9 not only by the word *pelos* but by the themes of blindness, sight, confusion, and illiteracy. Other evangelists quote the words of Isaiah 29:13, applying them to the Jewish leaders (Matt 15:8-9; Mark 7:6-7). John does not quote the passage, but he depicts what Isaiah prophesies and implicitly issues Isaiah's warning:

> Then the Lord said, "Because this people draw near with their words and honor Me with their lip service, but they remove their hearts far from Me, and their reverence for Me consists of tradition learned by rote. Therefore behold, I will once again deal marvelously with this people, wondrously marvelous; and the wisdom of their wise men will perish, and the discernment of their discerning men will be concealed." (Isa 29:13-14)

Isaiah plays with the very same light/darkness motifs found throughout John's gospel, and links darkness with the clay's betrayal of its potter:

> Woe to those who deeply hide their plans from the LORD, and whose deeds are done in a dark place, and they say, "Who sees us?" or "Who knows us?" You turn things around! Shall the potter be considered as equal with the clay, that what is made would say to its maker, "He did not make me"; or what is formed say to him who formed it, "He has no understanding"? (vv. 15-16)

Few passages of the New Testament come closer to Isaiah's prophecy of judgment on Israel's ignorance than John 9:

> The entire vision will be to you like the words of a sealed book, which when they give it to the one who is literate, saying, "Please read this," he will say, "I cannot, for it is sealed." . . . For the ruthless will come to an end and the scorner will be finished, indeed all who are intent on doing evil will be cut off; who cause a person to be indicted by a word, and ensnare him who adjudicates at the gate, and defraud the one in the right with meaningless arguments. (vv. 11, 20-21)

Once we see Isaiah 29 lurking within John 9, the latter takes on a threatening tone we might otherwise have ignored.

Jeremiah 18 is the most famous of the clay passages of the Old Testament, largely due to Paul's apparent allusion to it in Romans 9. Jeremiah's prophecy about the potter and clay also inheres in John 9. Jeremiah warns that a potter will discard a misconceived pot and begin again, breaking the bad pot in the process. So also Israel is clay in Yahweh's hands, and he might discard them and begin again. In Jeremiah's day, and through Jeremiah's prophecies, Yahweh is preparing calamity, but if Israel turns, Yahweh will also turn. When Jesus, the incarnate Yahweh, bends to make clay to give sight to the blind man, he is making a new Israel, but he is simultaneously issuing a warning to the Pharisees: if they do not turn, they will be broken like a potter's vessel.

HOW CAN WE KNOW?

John 9 has taken us all over John's gospel, chasing connections. And then it took us back to Genesis 1 and Genesis 3, Isaiah and Jeremiah. Who knows where else it might take us if we had infinite time? But how can we be sure we have gotten the joke, and not read unintended humor in a serious text? How can we know we are laughing at the right things?

I read John 1:1 and I hear echoes of Genesis 1:1, and I begin to suspect that John wants to teach that the gospel story is a story of new creation. That conclusion does not rest simply on the phrase "in the beginning," but the phrase is certainly a pointer in that direction. I read about the ark of Moses, and I think of analogies between Moses and Noah. I read about Luke's description of Stephen's ministry, and see him as a second Christ; then I read Stephen's sermon and see that Moses came twice too. I read the early chapters of Matthew, and I think Matthew is telling the story of Jesus to bring out analogies with the history of Israel; I conclude that Matthew thinks Jesus is the new, the true, Israel.

How do I know all that? How can I be sure I am not stuffing words into God's mouth? What do I say to someone who reads the same passage and does not hear Genesis 1, or who hears Genesis 1 but draws a different conclusion?

Questions like these often make it appear that literary interpretation is arbitrary, subjective, and unprovable—in contrast, of course, to scientific or historical interpretations, which are taken to rest on solid evidence. But how does explanation take place? How do historians and scientists come to their conclusions?

It is sometimes assumed popularly that explanation in these "harder" disciplines rests either on a sheer accumulation of facts or on logical deduction from first principles or axioms. Scientists and historians, however, go through essentially the same process as literary interpreters. Or, to put it the other way around, literary interpretation is a kind of theory formation or hypothesizing.

While every explanation attempts to encompass all the known facts in as elegant a manner as possible, there is always an imaginative leap involved in forming a hypothesis that puts the facts into a coherent narrative. N. T. Wright offers this example:

> I have frequently asked my students why Rome was especially interested in the Middle East. Few of them come up with (what seems to me) the right answer: that the capital needed a constant supply of corn; that one of the prime sources of corn was Egypt; and that anything which threatened that supply, such as disturbances in neighbouring countries, might result in serious difficulties at home. (It is the more surprising that this story does not come readily to mind, considering the obvious analogies with late-twentieth-century politics: substitute oil for corn, certain other countries for Rome on the one hand and Egypt on the other, and the equation still works.) But this account of how things were—of why, for instance, someone like Pontius Pilate was in Palestine in the first place—is not read off the surface of any one particular text. It is a story told by historians to explain the smaller stories they do find on the surface of their texts. Reaching even so simple a story requires controlled and disciplined imagination, but imagination none the less.[22]

If grain does not take your fancy, think of gunpowder.

Gunpowder obviously changed the face of war, but this set off a chain reaction that had far-reaching social, political, economic, and architectural consequences. Gunpowder equalized warfare, so that an indifferently trained commoner could fight as effectively as a highly trained and richly equipped knight. That, in

turn, pulled out one of the central props holding up the aristocracy's social position—if they were not specialists in war, what
exactly was the basis for all the social privileges they enjoyed?
An aristocracy of refinement replaced the medieval aristocracy
of military prowess. Castles built in the old style could not with-
stand cannonballs, and one result was that brickmaking became
big business.

Theodore Rabb makes a very compelling case for this scenario,[23]
but nowhere does he cite a piece of conclusive documentation supporting his hypothesis. Nowhere is there a document that laments
how the world has changed since the introduction of gunpowder.
Nowhere is there a smoking gun (sorry).[24] It is difficult even to
imagine what kind of conclusive evidence could be cited in support
of this story line. The hypothesis is compelling because of the overall coherence of the story, which encompasses many established
facts but which goes beyond that mere collection of facts.

More generally, Wright points out that on a positivist model
of explanation, "hypotheses are constructed out of the sense-data
received, and then go in search of more sense-evidence which will
either confirm, modify or destroy the hypothesis thus created."
He finds this misleading, and says that "no reflective thinker in
any field imagines that this is the case." Rather,

> One needs a larger framework on which to draw, a larger
> set of stories about things that are likely to happen in the
> world. There must always be a leap, made by the imagi-
> nation that has been attuned sympathetically to the sub-
> ject-matter, from the (in principle) random observation of
> phenomena to the hypothesis of a pattern.[25]

Scientific theorizing moves along the same tracks. One
accumulates data, and the theory that one forms, the scientific
hypothesis, is an attempt to account for all the data. But theorizing always involves not only amassing data but telling a story
that gives the data coherence. There is an imaginative leap from
the data in Newton's gravitational theory, Einstein's relativity,
quantum physics, chaos theory, and Darwinian evolution. Theorizing is a joke too. It is a matter of gathering all the data, and
suddenly, joyously, getting it.

Literary explanation functions the same way, and the proof of a literary hypothesis is similar to that in history and science. The data in a literary interpretation is the text itself, these particular words on the page in this particular arrangement. We assume that these words did not appear randomly on the page, but were placed there by some intelligent being. The goal of interpretation is to account for this data.

In certain kinds of texts, the author makes his intention or the logic of his arrangement explicit. But in poetry, fiction, and more literarily minded nonfiction, this is not the case. So the interpreter attempts to discern the logic of the pattern of words on the page from the words on the page, bringing into play his or her knowledge of the author, the historical period of the writing, other literature, and so on. Coming to an interpretation of the text is not, however, simply an accumulation of the data, but involves the same kind of imaginative leap that historical explanation requires. From the data of Acts 7, the Christian interpreter concludes that Luke is showing that, through the Spirit, Stephen is a second coming of Christ, and that the Jews' rejection of Jesus and his Spirit continues their habit of rejecting deliverers. There are "proof texts" that point in this direction, but they are not absolutely conclusive. The interpretation involves a move beyond the gathering of data to a construction that explains the pattern of the data. Does this still seem too arbitrary? Think of the alternative.

Should we be satisfied with interpreters who refuse to offer such global hypotheses about the data? Would we be satisfied with a historical explanation that, taking note of Rome's interest in the Middle East or the coincidence of gunpowder warfare with the transformation of European society, simply said, "that's just the way it is"? Would we be satisfied with a scientist who presented data without any attempt to demonstrate a pattern in the carpet? We expect more from historical and scientific explanation. But when it comes to literary explanation, many abandon this expectation and are satisfied with a "that's the way it is" explanation. This is not interpretation, and it is not good reading.

Texts Are Cinematic

There are constraints on interpretive freedom. Authors draw other texts into their own texts, and want readers to get the joke. But they do not leave us orphans. They do not leave us simply to figure out those connections for ourselves. In all the examples from John 9 above, I worked from the words and phrases and images of John 9, which themselves directed me to other related texts, the texts that John wanted to bring into play. I followed a few of the uses of clay in the Septuagint, and found that several shed light on John 9. Getting the joke depended on careful attention to the letter. *watch the Subtitles!*

Further, historical context limits interpretation. When Isaiah promises that the Lord will "give a garland instead of ashes" (Isa 61), the context is the return from exile, and the "garland" connotes a scene of festivity, victory, and return that will take the place of the mourning, defeat, and exile suggested by "ashes." Interpreting John 9 in the light of Isaiah 29 makes sense when we consider the threat to Israel during the first century, a threat that becomes explicit at several points in John's gospel (11:47-48).

Conventions provide another constraint.[26] A joke begins with people walking into a bar, and the knowledgeable reader or hearer is immediately oriented toward certain kinds of results. Jesus comes across a blind man, and then the Pharisees creep up, and we have a path. We know what kind of joke is being told.

Imagine the opening scene of a movie: a dusty road, with a tangle of tumbleweed somersaulting across the screen. The camera moves to a doorway, and the door creaks open. Who is going to emerge? Probably the marshal; perhaps a bandit or a whore. But we have a limited number of possibilities, given the setup of the opening scene.

Or imagine a nighttime scene of a Victorian house. A sliver of moon rises behind the turret as a bat flies out the chimney. An owl hoots, and a shutter creaks in the night wind. What happens next? Let me give you a hint: this is not the opening scene of a Western, at least not a conventional one, and probably not a romantic comedy, at least not a conventional one.

You knew that. But how did you know? Was it rational for you to assume that you were going to spend the next two hours getting spooked out of your skull? Of course it was. You instinctively read the scene in the light of what was not there. You have a good sense of cinematic humor.

Imagine the first shot again: dusty road, tumbleweed, creaking door, but this time Stephen Hawking comes through the door in his wheelchair. That would be a shock, but why? It is a shock because the scene has encouraged certain expectations about the film, and the appearance of Stephen Hawking, a disabled English physics professor, is entirely out of place in the scene. We would know instantly that the filmmaker was up to something, and we would settle in for a wild ride, a film where virtually anything might happen, where a scary Victorian house might be the site of a Western or a romantic comedy.

The biblical writers also have their conventions, their standard archetypal scenes to draw on, to evoke, and to subvert. Entire scenes and story lines can be evoked by an object or two, by a gesture or a single line stroke. A tree by a river of water evokes Eden, and suggests that the righteous man is like a new Adam, whose surroundings are a recovery of Eden. A jackal and a thorn bush are sufficient to evoke a ruined city or a wilderness. "The cedar has fallen" (Zech 11:2) suggests the ruin of the temple, constructed from cedars of Lebanon. Abram leaves the land and returns enriched; then Jacob also leaves the land and returns enriched; by the time Jacob is taking his household down to Egypt, the sight of Hebrews leaving the land of promise has become as conventional as the dusty road and the tumbleweed: we know that sooner or later there is going to be an exodus, and that Israel is going to come out carrying the plunder of Egypt.

Not just any hypothesis will do. It must encompass the data, and it must operate within the constraints of historical setting and biblical conventions. But an interpreter familiar with the historical setting, biblical conventions, and intertextual connections is capable of getting it.

⚓ Conclusion: Jokes, Interpretation, and the Interpreter

If texts function like jokes, then texts require certain kinds of interpreters. What kind of interpreters? Funny ones? That would not be a bad start.

Interpreters must be well informed about the subject matter of the text. A reader of Virgil who is innocent of Homer will not get it, and a reader of Eliot who is not familiar with Dante, and Dante's readings of the Latin literary tradition, will not understand what Eliot is up to. The interpreter must have the relevant information at hand to get the joke, or, when he does not have that information, he must be able to find it. Of course, the best interpreters of jokes are the ones who have the relevant information at their fingertips, and do not have to do research to discover what the jokester intends to call to mind.

For interpreters of Scripture, as Augustine and Origen knew, this means that a good interpreter will have a wide range of knowledge at hand—knowledge about history and geography, about the languages of Scripture, about the flora and fauna to which the Bible makes reference. Above all, the good interpreter of Scripture must have Scripture at his fingertips, because Scripture itself provides the first context for interpreting any particular portion of Scripture. Though 1–2 Samuel is an ancient text that needs to be understood in the context of the ancient world, it is fundamentally a scriptural text that must be interpreted in the light of the Pentateuch, the history of the monarchy, the exile and return, and the culmination of Israel's history in Jesus.

There is no foolproof method for achieving such mastery of Scripture. Patristic commentators had Scripture at their fingertips because they read and copied Scripture; they heard it read; they chanted the Psalms and many had the Psalter memorized; they ate, drank, and breathed Scripture. And as a result, any single Scripture was not a single Scripture but brought a dozen other Scriptures immediately to mind. Method is a way of making up for the failure to master Scripture.

Yet it has been clear throughout this discussion that information is not sufficient. My children had a lot of information relevant to that *Reader's Digest* joke, but they did not get it. They lacked crucial information. More, they lacked the wisdom to know what information was relevant. They lacked the hermeneutical equivalent to a good sense of humor.

Modern hermeneutics has often aspired to a kind of scientific objectivity in interpretation, one that goes along with the obsession with method. If interpretation is a scientific or quasi-scientific enterprise, it does not depend on any character development or religious commitment in the interpreter. A Muslim can plug the numbers into the calculator as well as a Christian and get the same result. A pedophile can run the same experiment as the purest virgin, and both will reach the same conclusion.

If interpretation is more like getting a joke than it is like dissecting a frog, then only certain kinds of people will be good interpreters.

If texts are jokes, no strictly procedural hermeneutics will do. Rather, a "humorneutical" approach emphasizes instead the character of the interpreter. What, after all, can one do with someone who has no sense of humor? Analysis and teaching might improve things marginally, but that person's main problem is not a technical but a spiritual one: somebody without a sense of humor suffers from a contracted soul, and the only real solution is conversion. Interpretive skills can be taught and improved, but only the glad of heart make good readers.

Analyzing the experience of humor is, finally, a helpful angle from which to explore the experience of interpretation. For both the interpreter and the reader of interpretations, the commentator and the reader of commentaries, the experience of a good interpretation is very like the experience of a good joke. An exegete pores over a text, and finally, and often suddenly, a dozen pieces fall into place; the experience is one of sudden release (sex would also be a good analogy). The exegete might actually laugh: "Now I get it," he would say.

Five

Texts Are Music

Structure

What is John 9 about? It is a story about Jesus. Jesus performs a sign, revealing himself as the One sent by the Father, as the Creator of new Adams, as the light of the world. He is the Son of Man, the eschatological judge of Daniel 7, who comes into the world to blind those who see and to give sight to the blind.

It is also a story about a blind man healed by Jesus.[1] The blind man has never seen the light of day, and spends his pathetic life begging outside the temple. One day, a man named Jesus stops and talks with his disciples, puts some clay on the blind man's eyes, and sends him off to wash in Siloam. When he returns, he can see, but he cannot see Jesus because Jesus is gone. His neighbors and friends are befuddled, but since it is a Sabbath day, they turn to the Pharisees for a legal judgment. The Pharisees interrogate the man and come to a dead end: they do not want to endorse Jesus, but they cannot deny that the man can see. They turn to his parents, but that interview too ends in frustration. When they come back to the man, they try to bully him with threats and unfounded declarations about Jesus' sinfulness. Something is happening to the man who was once blind. He started out knowing only Jesus' name, but when the Pharisees ask him what he thinks of Jesus, he says that Jesus is a prophet. When they come back for a second interrogation, he has gotten bolder, doggedly pointing to the fact that he can see and asking how a sinner could do such a sign. In his boldness, he turns ironic: "Do you want to be His disciple too?" It is the Pharisees again who push him along in his commitment to Jesus: "We are disciples of Moses; you are His disciple." Finally, they expel him from the synagogue, and as soon as he steps over the threshold, Jesus is waiting outside for him. The blind man has deepening sight. He knows Jesus' name, then confesses him as prophet, then confesses he has come from God, and finally confesses him as Lord and Son of God and prostrates himself before Jesus.

Not so obviously, it is also a story of exodus. Early on, John links Jesus with Moses (1:17), and he tells a story of Jesus performing signs that correspond in detail with the signs performed by Moses in Egypt.[2] Moses turns water to blood; Jesus turns water to wine. Moses brings hail and lightning to Egypt; Jesus calms a storm. In Egypt, locusts eat all the grain, but Jesus feeds five thousand people. Moses brings darkness to Egypt, while Jesus brings a blind man from darkness to light. The specific plot of John 9 also retells the story of exodus. Jesus, the prophet greater than Moses, delivers the man from the Egypt of darkness and sends him through the waters. The man enters a wilderness of trial, temptation, and threat, where the leaders of Israel insist that this new Moses cannot be from God, but the blind man is a faithful Joshua or Caleb, who confesses Jesus with boldness in the face of the giants of the land.

Not so obviously, John 9 is also a story of Genesis. We have already noted that Jesus makes clay to make a man new, and reveals himself as the eternal light whose light came into the world on the first day and who became incarnate in these last days. Jesus is also the Lord who opens the eyes of the blind man, just as Adam and Eve's eyes were opened at the tree.

It is also a story about the Pharisees, a story about Israel's reaction to Jesus, a story about the man's parents, and a story about discipleship. And we could go on.

So the same words tell several stories at the same time. Does that not lend itself to arbitrariness and free play with texts, the evils of postmodern deconstruction? Is it not safer to stay on the surface and make sure that we do not put words into God's mouth?

Safer, yes. But caution is not the only hermeneutical virtue. At the same time we are making sure that we do not hear God say things he did not say, we want to make sure that we do not miss anything either. If God is telling us more than one story at the same time, do we not want to hear them all?

MULTIPLE STRUCTURE

Like intertextuality, multiple structure is virtually inescapable, especially in narratives and poetry. We can imagine a narrative that has only a surface structure, a text in which the only structure is the arrangement of individual words on the page. It would read something like this:

Johnny got up.
Johnny stretched.
Johnny went to the bathroom.
Johnny splashed water on his face.
Johnny went downstairs for breakfast.

And so on. This narrative has no connectives, and no subordinate clauses are allowed. As soon as we write, "When Johnny had splashed water on his face, he went downstairs for breakfast," we have subordinated the splashing to the breakfast. We have broken the surface, and put one action under the surface. We have put something in the foreground and something in the background, and that immediately creates something like a double structure. Subordinate clauses indicate subordination, and inevitably multilayer the text.

In fact, though, even this example does not count as a text with only a surface structure. The author of such a work still has to select from the infinite details he might record (about, for instance, Johnny's heart rate or respiration as he awakes, or the distance from the mattress to the floor, or the chemical additives in the water he splashes on his face) to decide to tell the story in an unimaginative fashion. He has to decide what words to put it what order. Besides, he cannot help arranging the words into groups, breaking the sheer sequence of words with periodic periods.[3] He cannot help verging on music with the recurring rhythm of simple declarative sentences and the repetition of "Johnny . . . Johnny . . . Johnny. . . ." Just possibly, we can imagine a text without layers, but can we imagine wanting to read it, much less write a commentary on it?

Happily, the Bible is not written this way, and few other texts are. Biblical writers are sensibly complicated, happy to tell several stories simultaneously and arrange their texts in three or four ways at once, just like normal people.

We saw in chapter 4 that texts are jokes. In this chapter, I argue that texts are musical jokes. Many of the points made in chapter 4 could, in fact, be reframed in terms of the musicality of texts. A good interpreter has a good sense of textual humor, and he must also develop an ear for the multiple melodies, not to mention the complex rhythms, of texts. A good interpreter must bring a body of knowledge to the text, or he will find nothing there, and he must learn to hear more and more by repeated, disciplined listening. Blind readers will accuse a good interpreter of finding what is not there, just as the tone-deaf accuse good listeners of hearing things. Fortunately, we have a Savior who comes to open eyes and unstop ears.

NON-IDENTICAL REPETITION

Are texts like music? Not everyone thinks so.[4] Musical philosopher Victor Zuckerkandl argues that music is unique in reveling in repetition. Transferring musical repetitions into other art forms leads to "nonsense" and "idiocy":

> A theme, a melody, is a definite statement in tones—and apparently music can never have enough of saying over again what has already been said, not once or twice, but dozens of times; hardly does a section, which consists largely of repetitions, come to an end before the whole story is happily retold over again. How is it that a procedure which, in any other form of expression, would produce sheer nonsense proves, in the language of music, to be thoroughly sensible—to such an extent that rehearing what has already been heard is one of the chief sources—for many, the chief source—of the pleasure given by music?[5]

And again:

> Innumerable compositions proceed according to a basic plan in accordance with which their often quite extensive first part is first repeated note for note, only to reappear

again in a slightly altered version after an interlude that is often very short. Imagine a play of which the first scene should be played twice and which, after the second scene, should begin at the beginning again! But the situation is even more paradoxical. In many compositions this interlude follows the pattern of a process of gradual intensification leading to a climax; and what appears at the climax, the event for which we looked with such tension and which actually forms the culmination of the entire development, is nothing but the repetition of the story we have already heard twice through. What would be sheer idiocy in a narrative, a drama, a poem—this beginning all over again—in music conveys the most powerful effects.[6]

While Zuckerkandl is correct that few narratives or dramas repeat the beginning over and over verbatim, some texts, and the biblical text in particular, do in fact begin again and again. Narratives often come to a climax that replicates the beginning. Ezra-Nehemiah tells the story of the exodus and conquest again, with variations. John begins Genesis again with "in the beginning," and then does it yet again at the beginning of his first epistle (1 John 1:1). So does Matthew, with his book of generations (1:1), and Luke cannot seem to think of a creative way to begin Acts, but relies on the old introductory address to Theophilus (Luke 1:1; Acts 1:1). Revelation 21–22 repeats much of Genesis 1–2, John apparently indulging in the very idiocy that Zuckerkandl condemns. Nor is this unique to the biblical story.

The Robinson Crusoe-esque film *Cast Away* begins and ends with scenes at a crossroads as a delivery truck rolls up a dusty Texas road, and the alarm clock scene(s) in *Groundhog Day* go on and on. At the other end of the literary spectrum, the orally based poetry of Homer employs repetitions in a variety of ways and for a variety of reasons. Achilles is frequently "swift-footed" or "swift-footed, godlike" Achilles. Descriptions of battles in the *Iliad* and of meals in the *Odyssey* are sung with very similar notes—victims commonly get smashed in the "brain pan," and everyone who sits to eat in the *Odyssey* "lays his hands on the good things." Poets commonly use refrains, which repeat the same words at regular intervals throughout a poem. Spenser's "Epithalamion" returns again and again to some form of "The woods shall to me answer, and my eccho ring," and the beautiful lines "Against the Bridal day, which was not long: / Sweet Thames! Run softly till I end my song" run through his "Prothalamion."

The French writer Raymond Roussel, who inspired better-known postmodern thinkers like Foucault, once wrote a story called "Parmi les noirs" ("Among the Blacks"). The final phrase of the story is virtually identical to the first line:

> Les lettres du blanc sur les bandes du vieux billard. [First line: The chalk letters on the sides of the old billiard table.]

> Les lettres du blanc sur les bandes du vieux pillard. [Last line: The white man's letters about the old plunderer's gangs.]

A single letter changes, and the whole sense changes. The sense changes not only because of the change in the last word but because of the story that comes between these two sentences. Virtually the same sentence means different things in different contexts.[7] The repetition can have the feel of a homecoming (as in a chiastically organized text, or in a simple inclusio) or the repeated words can have an ironic relation to the original use, since the situation has been wholly reversed and inverted by the intervening development. We can push the question the other way: is musical repetition identical repetition? Not really.

A composer may repeat precisely the same tones in different parts of a composition, but the second occurrence of a theme is different precisely because it is second. Individual notes, though acoustically identical, do not mean the same thing when repeated in different places in a piece or in different pieces, even if they are repeated right after one another. The melody of Bach's little Minuet in G (see appendix A) ends, not surprisingly, on G, while the bass plays a descending series of notes that are part of the G-major chord: G, D, and G. With the G, and the fragments of the chord, the minuet comes to rest. The next to last note in the melody of the hymn "Come Thou Almighty King" is also a G, but the G in the hymn does not bring rest and resolution; it sounds incomplete without the following F. The difference in the two Gs, of course, has to do with context: the immediate context of the surrounding notes and, more generally, what Jeremy Begbie calls the "dynamic field" of key. The very same note sounds different, is experienced differently, in a different melodic and harmonic context. Despite their acoustical identity, no two Gs mean exactly the same.

The more important forms of musical repetition are repetitions of melodic themes and rhythmic patterns. We can again turn to Bach's Minuet, which is constructed of multiple overlapping repetitions. Most obviously, there is the repeated rhythm of the beat (in ¾ time). Some melodic phrases are almost exactly repeated. The first phrase, consisting of eight measures, is repeated in the second phrase of two lines, the only difference being minor changes in the bass. Then this whole sequence is repeated again, exactly the same notes in the same order. But the same notes in the same sequence do not mean the same thing. The second statement of the theme evokes memory in a way that the first cannot. While the notes may be identical, the impact and the musical meaning of the second occurrence must be different from the first. When the music comes back to the opening theme, it is a return to familiar territory after a brief departure. As Kierkegaard knew, there is no such thing as identical repetition.[8]

The following three measures display a different sort of repetition. The notes are not repeated exactly. Instead, there is a rhythmic repetition (a quarter note followed by a series of four eighth notes) and a similarity in the shape of the melodic phrase. The repeated phrases move down step-by-step with each repetition. At one level, this can be called the same phrase, but the repetition is not in the notes but elsewhere. The second phrase is shadowed by the first.

Texts have analogous forms of repetition. Since Shakespeare has become nearly as integrated into the consciousness of the English-speaking world as the Bible, his plays are sources for other authors, from the Reduced Shakespeare Company (the parodic RSC) to the Tom Stoppard of *Rosencrantz and Guildenstern are Dead* and *Shakespeare in Love*. In the latter film, when

Shakespeare (Joseph Fiennes) warns his lover (Gwyneth Paltrow) that their love cannot work because he is married, she replies with something like, "We need no wife come from Stratford to tell us this." This is clearly an allusion to Horatio, who answers Hamlet's "There's never a villain dwelling in all Denmark / But he's an arrant knave" with "There needs no ghost, my lord, come from the grave / To tell us this" (1.5.121–24).

But how does it evoke Horatio's words? Few words are shared by the two sentences. Where Shakespeare has "ghost," the film has "wife"; the film replaces Shakespeare's "grave" with "Stratford." The "to tell us this" is a giveaway, but the film's allusion actually works because of the entire rhythm of the sentence. The arrangement and rhythm of the words in Shakespeare's sentence haunts the sentence from the film.

Even when no words are shared, intertextual relations can be achieved through repetitions of rhythms. Henry Beard's inventive *Poetry for Cats* is full of examples, like the poem "The Mongrel," which begins:

> Mongrel! Mongrel! Barking blight,
> Bane upon my yard at night;
> What infernal hand or eye,
> Could frame thy vile anatomy?[9]

Now, if you had to guess, what famous poet's cat wrote those lines? How did you guess? How did you get it? Intertextual music can be as ghostly as shared syntax, a shared meter, a shared rhyme scheme. There I go telling jokes again, after I had promised to be serious for awhile. Let us get back to the higher plane of music.

ARRANGEMENT

We have cleared some ground. Texts can have repetitions like the repetitions in music. Repetitions are never identical, either in texts or in music, and they can occur at various levels in both. Beyond that, I want to examine two other musical features of texts. First, music and texts both depend for their meaning on arrangement of notes/words, phrases/sentences, and movements/chapters. Second, music and texts both can have multiple structures without becoming incoherent.

Let us begin with arrangement. If we change the sequence of notes, phrases, or repetitions in a musical composition, we have a different musical composition. Mozart's famous minuet from *Don Giovanni*, for instance, has a simple form (see appendix B). The main theme runs through several measures and then repeats exactly. A second theme follows and is again repeated identically, and the piece ends with a double repetition of the main melodic theme.

Obviously, changing the sequence of notes in the melodic theme would change the melodic theme. Equally, changing the sequence of melodic repetitions and the departure-and-return sequence of theme, variation, and return theme would change the piece. In Mozart's piece, the completion of one melodic arc is signaled by a return to the beginning and the repetition of the same theme. So the first important subunit of the minuet is the statement of the melodic theme, or perhaps the double statement of the theme. The whole can be analyzed in the same fashion: AABBAA. It is not Mozart's minuet if the structure of the piece is different. The meaning and impact of Mozart's piece depends on this specific arrangement. If it were arranged as BBAAAA, it would not be the same piece of music.

Textual meaning, like musical meaning, arises not only from the words, phrases, sentences, and paragraphs—episodes taken in isolation—but also from the arrangement of words, phrases, sentences, paragraphs, and episodes. There are differences between music and texts, of course. The same story can be told differently, and a paraphrase of a sermon can communicate the same content as the sermon. One cannot paraphrase (though one can abridge) a musical composition in the way that one can paraphrase a text.

Still, the analogy holds. Music is not inflexible. Orchestration can be changed. Liszt transcribes Beethoven symphonies for piano; is it the same piece of music? Yes and no, just as a summary both is and is not a novel, a map both is and is not the territory. Rhythms can be changed. A classical piece can be made over into jazz or disco or rap, and it remains the same piece of music in some respects.

Coming from the other direction, texts have a certain degree of fixity. Fiddle with them enough and they become different texts. Asked to explain the meaning of *The Waste Land*, T. S. Eliot famously began reciting the poem. No paraphrase will do justice to "April is the cruelest month, breeding / Lilacs out of the dead land, mixing / Memory and desire, stirring / Dull roots with spring rain" because the meaning and impact of the poem depends on a particular sequence of words, particular rhythms and rhymes, particular combinations of sound and sound as well as sound and sense. Poetry is a concentrated excess of speech—concentrated because it expresses much in few words, excessive because the words do not serve any function. One could write a commentary on the first lines of *The Waste Land*, explaining the connotations of April, the strange juxtaposition of hopeful spring with cruelty, the odd notion of lilac breeding, the resurrection imagery of flowers from the dead land, and the connections between memory and desire and among April, memory, and desire. But that commentary would not mean the same thing as the poem, because the poem expresses the same things without all the intervening explanation. The poem works differently, and works on the reader differently. Map is not territory.

Poetry is the music of language, almost completely dependent on organizing the notes, the melodic themes, and the rhythms in a particular pattern. Even narrative, however, is similar to music in this regard. We can tell the same story differently, but the same story told differently becomes, in important ways, a different story.

Every text is a joke because it depends for its meaning on information outside the text, whether from other texts or from the world around us. Texts are jokes also because the force of the text depends, like a joke, on the order of presentation.

One more joke. The last one:[10]

> I met a farmer once who had a pig with three legs. I asked him about the pig, and he said, "Why, that's the greatest pig in the world. When we had a fire in the house, the pig squealed so loud he woke us up. When the tractor turned over on my leg, he ran up to the house and got help. That's some pig."
>
> "Yes," I said, "but why does the pig have only three legs?"
>
> "Well, a pig like that you don't eat all at once."

Consider this joke told in a different order:

> A farmer and his wife had a wonderful pig that saved
> their lives several times.
> They ate one leg of a pig and left the rest.
> One day, I asked him why the pig had only three legs.
> "Well," the farmer said, "a pig like that you don't eat all
> at once."

The first story, if it rises to the level of humor at all, does
so only because it withholds crucial information until the end of
the story. If that information is disclosed too early, the impact
of the story is changed. It is no longer funny; it is macabre.

Consider the classic story of *The Three Little Pigs*, which is
normally told, like many children's stories and fairy tales, in a
cyclical pattern.[11] The same sequence of events occurs several
times, with a crucial twist the last time around. Children's stories are told this way because, as Chesterton observed, children
share the heavenly Father's love of repetition. But that is not
all. Without this structure, the story loses much of its point.
Think of a story exclusively about the experience of the third
little pig:

> A pig bought bricks and built a house.
> A big bad wolf came to the door and threatened to blow
> down the house.
> The wolf was unsuccessful, and the pig lived happily
> ever after in his comfortable exurban home.

Perhaps this story holds some interest, but it holds far less interest than a story where the outcome of the third little pig's construction project is put into grave doubt by the experience of his
two brothers.

And the point of the whole story—insofar as there is a point,
beyond the sheer delight of the storytelling—depends on the
triple structure. Two lazy and improvident little pigs build inse-
cure homes that are quickly destroyed; in some versions, the lazy
and improvident little pigs meet an appropriately gruesome end
in the belly of the big bad wolf. So much for sloth and careless-
ness. The third little pig, who knows something about building materials and refuses to buy on impulse, fends off the wolf's

assault, survives, and prospers. Robbed of the first two sequences, the story lacks moral import.

Told as the climax of a series, the third pig's story is an initiation into the Protestant spirit of inner-worldly asceticism that Weber thought was the foundation of capitalism. It is designed to turn id-dominated terrors into little Puritans. All to the good, I say.

The emotional impact of the story likewise depends on the structure. The first two cycles end tragically, and when the third cycle begins in the same way as the first two, the reader immediately expects the worst. As soon as we read, "So the little pig finished his house of bricks," we breathlessly wait for "Then the big bad wolf knocked at the door." If we know about the hardy qualities of brick houses, we anticipate that the wolf will fail in his attack on the third pig, and the anticipation of a comic ending for the third pig after the double tragedy is central to the impact of the story. It is part of what the story means. If we miss how the structure works, we will not quite get it.

Moving from folk to high culture, one could retell the story of the *Odyssey* without the temporal twists and turns of Homer's story. A chronological retelling would begin with Odysseus' departure from Troy, tell of his adventures in sequence, and perhaps turn to Ithaca to update us on the fortunes of Penelope and Telemachus before bringing us to the climactic house-cleansing sacrifice. Homer's *Odyssey* begins in Ithaca with Telemachus and Penelope, moves backward in time to catch up with Odysseus in book 5, and devotes several books to Odysseus' retrospective account of his adventures since the end of the Trojan War. The text zigs and zags through time, replicating in its narrative structure the character of the hero, well known for his feints, false starts, disguises, and lies. The man of twists and turns gets an epic full of twists and turns.

Moreover, Odysseus is a famously hidden hero. Helen tells Telemachus that Odysseus once slipped into Troy during the war disguised as a beggar; only Helen recognized him. The Phaeacians bathe, feed, and entertain him long before he reveals himself by weeping over a song of Troy. He is a man of sorrows, known by his tears. When he arrives home in Ithaca, Athena helpfully disguises him again as a beggar, so he can sneak into his own house and plot with Telemachus against the suitors. Just as the order of the story mimics the hero described in the translation of the late Robert Fagles as the "man of twists and turns," so the order of the story hides the hidden hero. Odysseus is not named until the end of the proem, in contrast to Achilles, who impatiently bursts into the text in the first line of the *Iliad*. Odysseus does not appear in his own epic until book 5. Homer has hidden the hidden hero within his text; structure and character, structure and theme, match each other perfectly. Odysseus is famous for delaying his self-identification, as when he pretends to be "Nobody" until he has poked out the eye of Polyphemus. Homer writes the epic the way Odysseus would have liked, delaying the identification of the hero numerous times within the text.

Again, it would be possible to tell the same story without hiding Odysseus, without delaying his identification. But it would not be the same story. It would have a different melody, a different rhythm.

A biblical example: 1 Samuel tells the story of the capture of the ark in a chronological sequence. Israel is at war (4:1-3); Israel sends for the ark (4:4); the ark arrives (4:5); the Philistines fear Yahweh but encourage themselves (4:6-9); the Philistines defeat Israel (4:10-11); a man of Benjamin reports to Eli (4:12-18); Phineas' wife gives birth (4:19-22); Philistines capture the ark and place it in Dagon's temple, where Yahweh repeatedly topples Dagon (5:1-5); Yahweh strikes the Philistines with plagues (5:6-12); and the Philistines finally send the ark back to Israel (6:1-18). This is a fairly straightforward narrative. But we can imagine the story told differently. The writer could have given more emphasis to the death of Eli or refrained from quoting the words of the Philistines when they hear the shout from Israel. But the story would have been different; it would have had a different music.

MULTIPLE STRUCTURE IN MUSIC

The second analogy between music and texts is that both are arranged by multiple structures. In music, recognition of multiple structures is a standard part of musical analysis.

What, for instance, is the structure of Bach's Cantata no. 140 (*Wachet auf*)? On the one hand, the structure is obvious, more obvious than anything in the Bible. Bach has helpfully provided movements, seven of them, and we can say that the structure is this sequence of seven movements, which is true enough.

But there is more, much more, to be said. The movements are arranged in a fairly neat chiastic structure:[12]

> A. Chorale in E-flat major
>> B[1]. Recitative in C minor
>> B[2]. Duet in C minor
>>> A'. Chorale trio in E-flat major
>> B[1]. Recitative in B-flat major
>> B[2]. Duet in B-flat major
> A''. Four-part chorale in E-flat major

Chorales begin and end the cantata, and another chorale stands in the middle, while the middle chorale is surrounded by a recitative-duet sequence on either side. The corresponding sections are not exactly the same. The first recitative is by a tenor, and the second by a bass. In both duets, though, the bass sings with the soprano.

This formal structure is complicated by an overlapping narrative structure. Bach drew from a preexisting chorale that sings the story of the arrival of the bridegroom, and he used the recitatives and duets to fill out that story, all of which builds from the gospel reading, the parable of the virgins in Matthew 25. First, the watchmen awake Jerusalem, announcing at midnight that the bridegroom is coming. The first tenor recitative is the voice of a herald, an evangelist, who picks up the announcement of the watchmen: "Er kommt, er kommt" (He comes, he comes). The first duet is a dialogue between the bride (or soul) and Jesus, the soul questioning, "Wann kommst du?" (When are you coming?), and the bassist Jesus giving assurance: "Ich komme" (I come). The central chorale celebrates the bridegroom's arrival, as the watchmen follow Jesus into the hall. The bassist bridegroom in the second recitative invites the bride to enter the bridal chamber, and closes with a promise to kiss her (as in the Song of Songs). In the second duet, the bridegroom and the bridal soul are

together, and the final chorale, the seventh, looks to the eschatological banquet, in a city with gates of pearl where the angels
praise God around his throne. The cantata ends with the never-
ending song of the redeemer: "Ewig in dulci jubilo" (Eternal in
sweet jubilation). The cantata tells the story of the coming of
the bridegroom for his bride and the consummation of an eternal
marriage. It is a divine epithalamion.

Even this double structure does not capture the complexity of
the arrangement of the cantata. The contrasts between the corresponding sections are as important as the correspondences. There
are two duets, with the same singers, but the duets differ not only
in their tone and lyrics but in the way the two voices interact. In
the first duet, the soprano and bass are broken. Only once do they
sing in unison, on the line "zum himlischen Mahl" (to the heavenly meal). Bride and groom, though moving toward one another,
are not yet one, not yet united in voice and spirit. In fact, each
voice is broken within itself. At times, the soul/bride's first line is
broken in two; "Wann kommst du" is separated from "mein Heil"
(When do you come . . . my salvation?), and so too the bass/bride-
groom's "Ich komme" and "dein Teil" (I come . . . your own). This
brings *Heil* and *Teil* into rhyming proximity, but also musically
depicts the anxious and as yet unrealized longing of the bride and
groom for one another. Yet the fact that the two voices combine,
albeit briefly, in their anticipation of the heavenly banquet hints
at the resolution of the division between them. They are not yet
one, but they can anticipate being one in the eschatological city
with its bridal banquet.

The second duet is calmer. There is no anxious waiting and
no fragmented voices, as the bride sings confidently, "Mein Fre-
und ist mein" (My friend is mine), while Jesus replies with a
declaration of mutual ownership: "Und ich bin sein" (And I am
yours). Fittingly, in the second duet, the voices entwine around
each other in their mutual declaration of love, and combine often,
appropriately, on "Die Liebe soll nichts scheiden" (our love shall
nothing sever), on the "weiden" (feed) in a line expressing their
desire to feed together on the roses of heaven, and on the line "Da
Freude die Fulle" (there joy to the full).

We have a complex structure already, and we have not even begun to talk about the music. Calvin Stapert explains how the instrumental ritornello of the opening movement depicts the growing excitement of the watchmen as they see the approach of the bridegroom:

> It begins with four measures of dotted rhythms character-istic of the French overture. The French overture . . . was associated with royal pomp and splendor and, by exten-sion, all stately ceremonial occasions—in this case the wedding of Christ and his bride, the church. In the next four measures the upper instruments increase their rhyth-mic activity to sixteenth notes interrupted by ties while the dotted rhythms move down to the continuo. Both parts hint at the opening notes of the chorale melody. Finally, in the third section, the first violins break into uninterrupted sixteenth notes and the continuo into interrupted eighth notes bringing the rhythmic animation and the sense of eager anticipation to its peak.[13]

After the opening instrumental section, the sopranos sing the original chorale in fairly straightforward fashion, while the other voices elaborate on phrases from the choral, providing a kind of "commentary" on the watchmen's announcement (Stapert's term). Through the first six phrases of the chorale, the com-mentary remains behind, but by the sixth phrase it is coming in simultaneously with the soprano voices, and from then on it is "running ahead" of the watchmen: "In phrases 7 and 8 the lower voices precede the chorale by one measure. Then in phrase 9 [the alleluia] they jump ahead of the chorale entrance by fourteen measures!"[14]

Books might be, and have been, written on Bach's Cantata 140. I am not writing another, but I cannot let go without one last comment from Stapert, on the most familiar portion of the cantata, the fourth movement. Bach arranged the same theme for organ and also included it among his chorale preludes. In the cantata, the instrumental music provides a counterpoint to the second verse of the chorale, sung not in all four but in three (sub-eschatological) voices. Stapert describes the effect:

In the cantata the tenor soloist (or tenor section of the choir) sings the chorale unadorned except for some modest cadential ornamentation. Below the chorale the basso continuo moves in steady quarter notes that increase in speed to eighth notes as the music approaches cadences. Its steady, unhurried movement gives the music a processional character fitting for the next to last line of the text—"Wir folgen all zum Freudensaal" [We follow all to the joyful hall]. But it is the obbligato instrumental part above the chorale that dominates the piece and is mainly responsible for its overall affect. It adds something of the sway of a dance to the processional march of the continuo. Its movement is graceful, at once light and grave. It expresses great joy but in a measured way fitting the dignity of the occasion.[15]

After all this, what is the structure of Bach's Cantata? Is it the structure of the progression of individual notes and chords? Is it the structure of measures, or the structure provided by the meter? Is it the structure of the repeating phrases, fragments of the chorale that appears in movements 1, 4, and 7? Is it the obvious structure of seven movements? The chiastic structure linked to the singers in each movement? The narrative flow that follows the story of the first and second advents? Or is the structure a matter of pace or key signature, of instrumentation and the historical associations of different musical genres?

Yes. To all of them. Clearly, there are many overlapping, interpenetrating, simultaneous structures, depending on whether we are attending to musical features, the words of the chorale and libretto, the arrangement of voices, or whatever.

Just as clearly, these multiple structures do not render the music incoherent. On the contrary, they make the cantata almost unbearably rich. At any one time, a dozen or more different things are happening in the music together, and at any moment, the listener is at the intersection of a dozen or more different structures.

Telling Two Stories at Once

Many literary texts have the same kind of complexity. Certainly, not all texts do. All texts have structure, and that structure is always more than simply the sequence of letters and words and sentences. Paragraph divisions provide a kind of structure to even the most prosaic of prose.

But many texts, and almost all texts of enduring literary value, have multiple structures. Few literary texts are as simple in their structural design as *The Three Little Pigs*, but even *The Three Little Pigs* has a more complex structure than might be apparent. On the surface, the story moves forward in linear fashion from the experience of the first pig, to the second, to the third. Even the most naïve reader or hearer, however, will quickly recognize the repetition within each pig's story. Each pig's story begins with a purchase, moves through a construction project, includes a conflict between the big bad wolf and the little pig, and ends with a happy or unhappy outcome for the pig. This story, simple as it is, operates with at least two patterns of events—one a linear, Aristotelian movement from beginning to middle to end, and the other a cyclical, Polybian movement of nonidentical repetition.

In the witty and wise, and wittily wise, article I cited in chapter 4, historian David Steinmetz defends patristic typology, a form of double narrative, by reference to detective fiction, which, Steinmetz points out, always tells two stories at the same time:

> The first is a sprawling, ramshackle narrative that does not seem to be leading any place in particular. It is filled with clues, false leads, imaginative hypotheses, and characters who frequently seem overmatched by what appear to be quite ordinary criminal minds. . . . No one knows for certain where this apparently rudderless ship is drifting, not even (for several chapters, at least) the persons charged with bringing the ship safely to harbor. The principal characters, like the readers of the story (of whom they are oblivious), are often in deep puzzlement.[16]

Intertwined with this story is a second narrative, offered by the detective in the final chapter. By contrast with the first narrative, this one is "crisp and clear and explains in considerable detail what was really occurring while the larger narrative was unfolding." This is not a subplot, but instead "the disclosure of the architectonic structure of the whole story," a "compelling and persuasive disclosure of what the story was about all along."

Joyce's Music

James Joyce's *Ulysses* is not a detective story, but it announces its double-narrativity in its title and chapter headings. On the surface (but where is the surface in *Ulysses*?), the novel follows the intersecting journeys of Leopold Bloom and Stephen Daedalus over about a twenty-hour period on what has come to be known as Bloomsday. Each chapter also bears the title of an episode from the *Odyssey*, and the complexity and interest of the novel arise from the interaction of the Dublin story and the *Odyssey* story. What does it mean for the chapter in which Bloom fixes his breakfast to be called "Calypso"? Who is Calypso? Is she Bloom's wife, Molly? And why is Stephen's debate about Shakespeare in the library in a chapter entitled "Scylla and Charybdis"? And this double narrative hardly begins to penetrate the multiple layers of Joyce's story, which is also following narratives from Shakespeare and which begins with a quotation from the Latin Mass, intoned by plump Buck Mulligan.[17]

Joyce's *Portrait of the Artist as a Young Man* appears to be much more straightforward. It is divided into five chapters that trace Stephen Daedalus' progress toward his artistic vocation. After an initial chapter about his childhood and his formative experiences with other schoolboys, priests, and parents, chapter 2 describes Stephen's first sexual experience, with a prostitute in Cork, where he goes with his father, who is pawning the family furniture to pay for debts. In chapter 3, guilty from his sexual sin, Stephen goes on Catholic retreat, where he is brought to repentance by a series of terrifying speeches on hell from a very effective fire-and-brimstone priest. Stephen decides that he is called to the priesthood. The chapter ends with communion, and despite the conversion in the chapter, there is a hint that Stephen will ultimately reject the clerical vocation. This suspicion is fulfilled in chapter 4, where Stephen makes a definitive decision to refuse the priesthood, partly because he refuses to give up his sexual experiences. The chapter ends with a beatific vision of a young woman at the seaside, which inspires the young artist to abandon the church, and then his family and nations, and pursue an artistic vocation. In the final chapter, Stephen lays out his artistic credo, which borrows its terminology, though not its substance, from Aquinas. The book ends with Stephen intent on leaving Ireland.

At the same time, the book is organized in a cyclical pattern. Each chapter leads up to what is usually a secular epiphany, often described in mystical or theological terms: Stephen's triumph after going to the headmaster about an abusive priest (chapter 1), his sexual liaison with the prostitute (chapter 2), communion at the Catholic retreat (chapter 3), the bird girl at the beach (chapter 4), his decision to leave Ireland (chapter 5). Each of these soarings is immediately followed by some revelation that brings him down to earth. His complaint against the priest, he learns, was treated like a joke by the headmaster; his sexual encounter is followed by a humdrum meal back at school, which threatens to reduce his sexual ecstasy to animal desire; communion is followed by doubts about his ability to resist temptation; after the vision of the girl, he returns to the squalor of his parents' house.

This could be taken as a sign of the vanity of artistic aspirations, but it seems instead to express Joyce's view of artistic life. Of the girl on the beach, Stephen says,

> Her eyes had called him and his soul had leaped at his call. To live, to err, to fall, to triumph, to recreate life out of life! A wild angel had appeared to him, the angel of mortal youth and beauty, an envoy from the fair courts of life, to throw open before him in an instant of ecstasy the gates of all the ways of error and glory. On and on and on and on! (New York: Viking, 1968, p. 172)

Life is error and falling as well as soaring triumph, and the true artist, the true artistic priest, embraces the one with the other. The true artist embraces the transcendent delights of sex, but knows that sex involves comically designed organs and actions and is, in one sense, to use the current vulgarity, an exchange of fluids; he delights in the smells and tastes of food, but knows that the food will take its passage through his intestines and then, as Jesus said, go out in the latrine (Mark 7:19).

Stephen is well, if incompletely, named. He is Daedalus soaring. He is also Icarus falling. *Portrait of the Artist* has (at least) a double structure, and yet it is a coherent story. Perhaps the Bible is the same way.

THE MUSIC OF JOHN 9

What is the structure of John 9? G. R. Beasley-Murray says that, after the initial miracle story (vv. 1-7), the structure is "obvious":[18]

vv. 8-12   Blind man questioned by his neighbors
vv. 13-17 Interrogation by the Pharisees
vv. 18-23 Interrogation of the man's parents by the Pharisees
vv. 24-34 Further interrogation of the man by the Pharisees
vv. 35-38 Jesus seeks him and leads him to full confession of faith
vv. 39-41 Aftermath of the sign: Jesus declares the purpose of his coming

That seems obvious enough to Beasley-Murray for him to move on quickly to other things and leave the structure behind.

Is he wrong? Not at all. That outline of the chapter is clearly there. John tells the story like an archaic Greek playwright, each scene consisting of dialogue between no more than two characters:

Scene 1: Man and neighbors
Scene 2: Man and Pharisees
Scene 3: Pharisees and parents
Scene 4: Man and Pharisees
Scene 5: Jesus and man
Scene 6: Jesus and Pharisees

Beasley-Murray has simply, and quite rightly, identified the stage-clearing and curtain falls between scenes. Is there more to be said? Always. For starters, is it even obvious that chapter 9 forms a single text by itself?

Chapter 9 seems to initiate a new narrative departure in John. Most of chapter 8 consists of a lengthy, turgid, apparently repetitive debate between Jesus and the Jews (vv. 12-59), which begins when Jesus announces that he is the light of the world. When the Jews intend to stone him, as they intended to stone the adulterous woman (8:1-11), Jesus slips away and, as he passes by, he meets the blind man (9:1). Chapter 8 takes place in the temple, but at the end of the chapter, Jesus leaves the temple. New characters, new setting, new story, new passage. It is obvious.

But maybe not so obvious. Chapter 8 begins with Jesus leaving Jerusalem for the Mount of Olives and then returning to the temple in the morning, where the scribes and Pharisees confront him with a woman taken in the act of adultery (8:1-3).[19] But Jesus has been in Jerusalem since early in chapter 7 (7:1-2, 10, 14), and chapter 8 takes place during this same feast. In fact, the setting does not change until 10:22, when Jesus is in Jerusalem for yet another feast, the Feast of Dedication. Chapter 9 and a good portion of chapter 10 are part of the scene begun in chapter 8.

Plausibly, then, John intended 7:1–10:21 to be one long story of what happened to Jesus during the Feast of Booths. The individual chapters may be episodes in that larger story. And just as it would be a distortion to isolate the episode of the third pig from the story of three pigs, so too it may be a distortion to isolate the story of Jesus in debate with the Jews, or Jesus and the adulterous woman, or Jesus and the blind man, from that larger story line.

The structure of chapter 9 is also not as obvious as Beasley-Murray suggests because the end of chapter 9 is disputable. To be sure, there is a neat tie-up (*inclusio*) at the end of chapter 9. At the beginning, Jesus' disciples ask if the man is blind because of his own sin or his parents' (apparently the only two options in their minds), and at the end of the chapter, Jesus returns to the twin themes of blindness and sin (vv. 39-41). But the end of chapter 9 is not so obviously the end of the story.

For starters, as I have just noted, there is no change of scene at the beginning of chapter 10. Worse, there is no change of speaker. Jesus begins a speech in 9:41, and editors of the New Testament, going back to Stephen Langland, have rudely interrupted him with a chapter break. In John's original Greek, of course, there is no white space between "your sin remains" and "truly, truly I say to you."[20] The Good Shepherd Discourse is not a self-standing passage. It is a continuation of Jesus' sharp rebuke to the Pharisees, which actually begins with Jesus announcing judgment on those who see (v. 39). All the while Jesus is claiming that he is the Good Shepherd, the Pharisees are standing right in front of him—Pharisees who, not too long ago, were searching the ground for suitably sized rocks. They are the "hirelings" who leave the sheep to the wolves (v. 13), and Jesus tells them so to their faces. That gives a different tone to the discourse than it has when we snip it from its context, print it on a condolence card, surround it with flowers and chubby cherubs, and market it as "words of comfort" from Jesus. There is certainly comfort here, but Jesus spends most of the discourse making his original audience very uncomfortable.

There is an *inclusio* surrounding chapter 9, but there is also an *inclusio* around 9:1–10:21. After the Good Shepherd sermon, John returns us to the story of the blind man. The division that occurs among the Jews does not have to do with Jesus' discourse, but concerns different interpretations of the healing of the blind man (10:20-21). In fact, 10:19-21 returns us to some of the themes of chapter 8, including the question of whether Jesus is demon possessed (8:48-49).

Is the structure obvious? In one sense, yes, but in another sense, it is not even obvious where the story begins and ends. At both ends of the story, a number of candidates present themselves.

Let us cut through the complications of beginnings and ends, and simplify. Let us stick with John 9. Even in isolation, John 9 is an Irish knot, a Baroque Cantata of text, which will keep us busy for awhile.

As noted above, a reading can follow the thread of the blind man's increasing insight into what has happened to him and who has done it. Who did this? his neighbors ask; he answers, "the man who is called Jesus" (v. 11), and beyond that, he cannot even locate Jesus (v. 12). As the Pharisees attack, his faith takes another step: the man who is called Jesus "is a prophet" (v. 17), a prophet like Elisha. To the charge that Jesus is a sinner, the blind man points to the obvious fact that he can now see (v. 25), and further reasons that since God does not listen to sinners, a man who opened the eyes of a man blind from birth cannot be a sinner (vv. 30-33). The Pharisees are so eager to hear about Jesus that he wonders whether they might be interested in becoming disciples (v. 28). When Jesus reappears, Jesus identifies himself as the "Son of Man" (v. 35), and the blind man calls him "Lord" (vv. 36, 38) and prostrates himself before him (v. 38). The blind man's sight grows ever clearer, as the "man who is called Jesus" becomes "a prophet" becomes "from God" becomes "Son of Man" becomes "Lord."

The story line of the Pharisees goes in the opposite direction. They are the teachers of Israel, and consider themselves experts on the law and disciples of Moses. They are the inquisition of ancient Israel, ready to investigate any apparent departure from orthodoxy. They jump into the fray because Jesus has healed the man on the Sabbath; Jesus is not "from God" because he ignores the Sabbath (v. 15). They have gone so far as to threaten Jesus' disciples with expulsion from the synagogue (v. 22).[21] They know that Jesus is a sinner (v. 24), even though they confess that they do not know where he comes from (v. 29). When the blind man corners them with the undeniable fact that he has been healed, they accuse him: "you were born entirely in sin" (v. 34), something that Jesus has earlier expressly denied (v. 3). By the end of the story, their blindness is obvious. A blind man has been given sight, and they cannot see the implications. This, Jesus says, is his intention in coming: to give sight to the blind and to blind those who think they see (vv. 39-41). While the blind man's melody moves from real and spiritual darkness to increasing insight, the Pharisees are moving in the opposite direction, from professed insight to evident blindness. Their tragic melody crosses the comic melody of the man born blind.

John also displays his masterful control of information. The story could have been told this way: "On a Sabbath day, Jesus passed out of the temple and met a man born blind and healed him. The Pharisees got mad." But that is not the way that John chose to tell the story. The fact that Jesus acts on a Sabbath day (probably one of the Sabbath days of the Feast of Booths) is withheld until the story is moving nicely along. The information is tucked away in verse 14, and only revealed after the introduction of the Pharisees in verse 13. It is an "Oh, by the way" aside, but it calls attention to itself by virtue of its understated nature. And it is of course no accident that the information about the timing of the miracle is given at the same time that the Pharisees show up. This turns the question of Jesus performing a miracle into a question of Jesus' conformity to law, and raises what would be a purely personal event in the life of a blind man to the level of a national crisis.

John does some equally subtle things with the appearance and disappearance of Jesus. From the beginning of John's gospel, Jesus has proven himself to be the One born of the Spirit (1:32). His voice is audible, but he is as elusive as wind, his origin and destination a mystery (3:8). Jesus wisps his way through the Jews who want to stone him. How ridiculous; who can stone the wind? "Where is He?" the blind man's neighbors ask, and he does not know (v. 12). Of course not. Who has seen the wind?

Jesus' elusiveness is integral to the story. Jesus is named as the speaker in verse 3, and that brief instruction to his disciples continues to verse 6. But when he makes clay and addresses the blind man directly, he is not named (vv. 6-7). And besides, the blind man is not reading the text, so he did not see the words "Jesus answered" in verse 3. Somehow he learns that Jesus is the one addressing him (v. 11), but what he experiences is a voice out of the void, a voice breaking into the darkness. It is the Spirit-born Jesus, blowing where he wills.

And once Jesus has acted, he leaves. John does not even let us see him go. The last thing we know of Jesus is that he sends the blind man to the pool of sending (v. 8), but when the blind man comes back, Jesus is simply gone. There is no "and Jesus departed." He just leaves the text, and he stays away for most of the chapter. The blind man names him (v. 11), and John reminds us in verse 14 that "Jesus" opened the blind man's eyes. Otherwise, Jesus' name simply drops from the story until verse 35, when he hears that the blind man has been put out of the synagogue. This means that the blind man goes through a series of interrogations from the Pharisees, and grows in insight and faith through persecution, in the absence of Jesus. He has never seen Jesus, not once. He has only heard a voice and felt a touch on his eyes, and then Jesus slipped away. Only after he is excommunicated does he find Jesus again, see him face-to-face, and worship him. We will look at some implications of this device in the next chapter. For now, we simply note how John has told the story to depict the slipperiness of the Savior.

Jesus, I have written, is named at the beginning of the chapter and several times during the debates between the blind man and the Pharisees, and is named again when he returns to the story in verse 35. Overall, his name occurs seven times in the story. This is not an accident. Jesus is the One born of what John elsewhere identifies as the "seven Spirits of God" (Rev). He is the One who brings Sabbath—not the oppressive Sabbath of the Pharisees, but the liberating and healing Sabbath of light. He is the complete man, whose number is not 6 or 666 but a combination of 7s. As the complete man, he makes new men, and it is striking that John 9 is the sixth of the signs that Jesus performs, the sign from the sixth day, the sign of a new Adam.

Nor is Jesus' name the only numerological play that John makes in the passage. On Beasley-Murray's "obvious" outline, there are seven scenes in the drama. A heptamerous arrangement is fitting for a story that centers on a debate about Sabbath-keeping, and a story that includes, as we saw in the last chapter, a number of echoes of the creation account of Genesis 1–2 (light, clay, new birth). The word *eyes* occurs ten times in chapter 9 and again in 10:21, and as late as 11:37, this celebrated miracle is still buzzing among the Jews. That makes, for those counting, a total of twelve references to the blind man's eyes in the Gospel of John, a number that no doubt holds some promise of light for the twelve tribes of Israel. *Blind* is used thirteen times in the chapter and once again in 10:21, making a total of fourteen. The blindness is doubly complete, but Jesus, the light of the world, comes to dispel the darkness with a light brighter than the darkness is dark.

Melody on Melody

The inclusio that brackets chapter 9 indicates the possibility that the chapter is chiastically arranged. If we use Beasley-Murray's divisions, that clue turns into a theory:

A. Jesus opens the eyes of the blind man, who did not sin, 9:1-7

B. Neighbors question the blind man, 9:8-12 ("man called Jesus")

C. Pharisees interrogate the blind man, 9:13-17

D. Pharisees interrogate the parents, 9:18-23

C'. Pharisees interrogate the blind man again, 9:24-34[22]

B'. Blind man confesses Jesus as "Lord," 9:35-38

A'. Jesus blinds the Pharisees, who are in sin, 9:39-41[23]

Every textual structure leaves out some features, but this structure is fairly neat. A and A' share terminology of blindness and sin. By their contrast, B and B' display the opposite poles of the blind man's progression in faith, from his puzzled "man called Jesus" to "Lord, I believe." The two interrogations by the Pharisees (C and C') match neatly. That leaves the unique center, D, the only scene in the chapter where the blind man's parents appear.

In a book happily back in print, John Breck argues that chiasms are not "balanced" structures, but instead are dynamic literary devices. He suggests that chiasms should be read "helically," moving not just from A to B to C to B' and so on, but from A to A', B to B', C to C', and so on. Read in this way, the text has a centripetal pull toward the central section. The corresponding sections, Breck argues, are related in the same ways that the strophes of a verse of Hebrew poetry are related. He says there is a "what's more" relationship between the corresponding lines: A and, what is more, A'.

Can we make sense of the story of the blind man if we read it helically? Yes.

A. Jesus heals a man born blind, who did not sin→

A'. What is more, the Pharisees are blinded by their sin.

B. The blind man confesses Jesus as his healer→

B'. What is more, the blind man comes to confess Jesus as Lord.

C. The Pharisees doubt and interrogate the blind man→

C'. What is more, they accuse Jesus as a sinner and cast the man out.

D. The Pharisees threaten the parents with expulsion.

Breck suggests yet another level here. As we read the narrative helically, there is a "what's more" relationship as we move from A/A' to B/B' to C/C':

A/A'	Jesus gives sight and blinds.
B/B'	What is more, the blind man confesses Jesus.
C/C'	What is more, the Pharisees intimidate but cannot silence him.
D	What is more, the Pharisees threaten excommunication against anyone who confesses Jesus.

From these considerations, the story of John 9 appears to be differently focused than we might have guessed. Reading the story linearly, straight through as written, it is about Jesus' power to give light and sight, and about the blind man's growth toward confession of Jesus. Read chiastically and helically, the story confronts us with the brutal tactics of the Jewish leaders, who have become so hardened to Jesus that they seek not only to kill him but to expel anyone who confesses him. We will say more about this in chapter 6.

Verse 22 makes sense as the center of this story, the central point of the chiastic structure. But the introduction of the man's parents in verse 18, and the Pharisees' interrogation of them, is something of a puzzle. It is not wholly anticipated: the disciples mention the man's parents as soon as they see the blind man (v. 2), in raising the question of intergenerational sin and judgment, but there is nothing at the beginning of the chapter that would lead us to expect the parents to appear in the story or for them to be structurally central. What stands out about the parents is their fear of expulsion (v. 22). Their evasive answers to the Pharisees stand in contrast to their son's increasing boldness in the face of intimidation. Perhaps there is a clue to their role in the narrative in the fact that the word *parents* is used six times in the chapter. In a chapter concerned with Sabbath, with its sevens entwined with sevens, the parents fall short. They are people of the sixth day, not people of the Sabbath.

This numerological clue suggests that the generational divide represents a covenantal divide. The parents of the blind man have not sinned, but they still live in the darkness of the old covenant.

[handwritten margin notes: "the evangelion in of creation"]

They are fearful of being expelled, even though, as it turns out, when one is expelled from the synagogue, one ends up meeting Jesus the light just outside the door. The parents are not the bullying Pharisees; they are the bullied, and perhaps more to be pitied than blamed. But they are not the future of God's kingdom.

John 9 has a complex structure, but it is also part of a structure. A number of proposals have been offered that link chapter 9 with the surrounding chapters in various ways. Some students of the gospel have suggested that John's gospel as a whole is organized as a chiasm. According to David Deeks, it works like this:

   A. Prologue, 1:1-18
    B. Lamb of God, 1:19-34
     C. Discipleship, 1:35-51
      D. Marriage feast, 2:1-12
       E. Death and resurrection, 2:13-25
        F. Baptism, 3:1-21
         G. Meditation, 3:21-36
          H. Living water and worship, 4:1-45
           I. Healing, 4:46-54
           I'. Healing, 5:1-30
          H'. Living water and worship, 6–7
         G'. Meditation, 7:1–8:59
        F'. Baptism, 9:1–10:21
       E'. Death and resurrection, 11:1-57
      D'. Marriage feast, 12:1-26
     C'. Discipleship, 13:1–17:26
    B'. Lamb of God, 18:1–19:42
   A'. Epilogue, 20:1-31[24]

My intention is not to defend this structure in detail but only to point out that, if accurate, this outline of John links John 9 with Jesus' nighttime discussion with Nicodemus in John 3. We have already (chapter 4) noted verbal and conceptual links between the passages, but these would be strengthened and extended if the structural connections were there as well. John 9 would appear to be even more evidently a passage about baptism.

The first twelve chapters of John have frequently been labeled the Book of Signs because of John's emphasis on Jesus' miraculous *semeia*. In these chapters, there appear to be seven signs:

1. Water to wine, ch. 2
2. Child raised from deathbed, ch. 4
3. Paralytic healed, ch. 5
4. Feeding of five thousand, ch. 6
5. Crossing the sea, ch. 6
6. Blind man receives sight, ch. 9
7. Lazarus raised from the dead, ch. 11

There is a complex and overlapping background to this scheme. The number seven suggests a link with the seven days of creation,[25] and would very provocatively link the healing of the blind man with the creation of Adam, confirming the patristic link between the clay of John 9 and the dust of John 2 (see chapter 4 above). There are also seven feasts in the calendar of Israel (Lev 23), which themselves overlay the seven days of creation. John 9 is linked with the Feast of Tabernacles (see chapter 4 above), which adds another layer to the structure. Robert Houston Smith likewise links the seven signs to seven of the plagues. In that sequence, the healing of the blind man corresponds with the darkness of the land. In Exodus, the death of the firstborn follows, while in John's reverse exodus, Lazarus is raised.[26]

M.-E. Boismard suggests a variation on this proposal, discovering a seven-day sequence in the entire gospel that links with the seven days of creation:

Day 1: 1:19–2:12: Light
Day 2: 2:13–4:54: Firmament
Day 3: 5:1–6:71: Bread
Day 4: 7:1–9:41: Lights in the heavens
Day 5: 10:1–11:57: Living things
Day 6: 12:1–19:42: Man; creation of Eve
Day 7: 20–21: Sabbath and resurrection[27]

If this is correct, then the blind man's story matches the creation of the heavenly lights that rule the day and night. The blind man not only is given light but ascends to shine in the sky like a star, becoming a son of Abraham, or rises to rule the day in union with the living sun.[28]

Alternatively, the entire book can be understood as a tour through the tabernacle. The opening chapter, which introduces the Lamb of God who comes to take away the sins of the world, brings us to the bronze altar for sacrifice. Chapters 2–4, with their focus on water, are at the laver. Chapters 4–7 center on the feeding of the five thousand, in which Jesus distributes the bread of the presence from the golden table. In chapters 8–13, John lingers at the lampstand, musing on Jesus as the light; and the Upper Room Discourse, especially chapter 17, displays Jesus as the intercessory priest, raising his hands before the golden altar. John is at pains to show us that the empty tomb is the new holy of holies. The slab on which Jesus' body no longer lies is flanked by angels, like the ark, and Peter, like a high priest, is the first to enter.[29] On this scheme, the theme of light in John 9, already associated with creation and the Feast of Tabernacles, is given a fresh dimension, linked with the golden light, the lamp on the lampstand that is the disciple (cf. Matt 5).

CONCLUSION

So which is it? Is John organized chiastically? Does its structure follow a priest's progression through the sanctuary? Is John 9 telling the story of the blind man, the story of Jesus, or the story of the Pharisees? Is the chapter arranged as a chiasm, or in some other way?

There is no need to decide among these alternatives, which are not really alternatives. John is all of these things together, all these overlapping and interacting structures at once. John 9 is, like the rest of John, a polyphonic composition, a cantata to rival Bach's.

Six

Texts Are about Christ

Application

Totus Christus

Scripture is about Christ, but the Christ of Scripture is not only himself but also his body. The Christ who is the subject matter of Scripture is the *totus Christus*.

This theme is arguably the center of Augustine's entire theology, and it is certainly the center of his hermeneutics. In *On Christian Teaching*, Augustine, drawing on the writings of Tyconius the Donatist, makes this the first rule of interpretation:

> knowing as we do that the head and the body—that is, Christ and His Church—are sometimes indicated to us under one person (for it is not in vain that it is said to believers, You then are Abraham's seed [Gal 3:29], when there is but one seed of Abraham, and that is Christ), we need not be in a difficulty when a transition is made from the head to the body or from the body to the head, and yet no change made in the person spoken of. For a single person is represented as saying, He has decked me as a bridegroom with ornaments, and adorned me as a bride with jewels and yet it is, of course, a matter for interpretation which of these two refers to the head and which to the body, that is, which to Christ and which to the Church. (3.31.44)

Tyconius' first rule holds together the christological and the moral, redemptive history and application. There is no need to choose between a christocentric and an ecclesiocentric reading of the Bible, because the ekklesia is only ekklesia as the body of the

Christia The New Testament writers also read the Old Testament as a record of the *totus Christus*.

To be specific: is the story of Cain and Abel a story about Jesus' innocent suffering and death, or a story about the persecution of the church? Obviously, it is both. Jesus' blood speaks a better word than the blood of Abel (Heb 11), and yet John warns his readers not to become Cainites who hate their brothers (1 John 3). Is the story of the exodus a type of Jesus' work or a type for the church? Obviously, both. Jesus passes through the water of John's baptism and enters the wilderness to be tempted, and he also speaks of the "exodus" of his death and resurrection on the Mount of Transfiguration (Luke 9). But Paul also makes it clear that our own baptisms are replays of the exodus, and having been baptized in cloud and sea, we face the same temptations that Israel did (1 Cor 10). Paul understands the Old Testament to speak not only of the church but specifically of the sacraments. The sea is baptism, and the manna and water foreshadow the Eucharist.

The breakdown of this Augustinian hermeneutical principle has been one of the main sources of interpretive confusion among Protestants. If the Bible is about Christ, some preachers and interpreters conclude, then any direct application of Scripture to the life of the believer introduces works and threatens to collapse into moralism. Other preachers insist that the Bible be made practical, so that the stories of David are read not as foreshadowings of Christ but as stories that teach us courage, faith, and tricks (e.g., spittle on the beard) for dealing with oppressive fathers-in-law and kings. The first has the head, the second has the body. Neither has the whole Christ.

TOTUS CHRISTUS IN JOHN 9

We can ask the same questions of John 9: Is it about Jesus? Or is it about us? It is about Jesus, since it records a sign that Jesus performed. It is also a story about Jesus in the sense that the experience of the blind man foreshadows later events in the life of Jesus. Jesus heals the blind man, who is then tried by the Jews, just as Jesus himself has been put on trial by the Jews in previous chapters of John's gospel. These trials of Jesus all anticipate the

Christ is all in all.

great trial before Pilate and the Jews, the capstone of John's gospel. Like the blind man, Jesus will give a good confession under intense interrogation and threats. Jesus will be crucified outside the gate, as the man is cast outside the synagogue.

Insofar as he is a Christ type, the blind man fulfills Old Testament shadows just as much as Jesus does. His suffering is Christic suffering, the suffering of the true Israel that fulfills the story of Israel. Humming John 9 in the "key of exodus,"[2] we hear the blind man move from the darkness of Egypt through the waters of sending and into the wilderness of trial. In the wilderness, Israel is harassed by various threats, above all the Amalekites (Exod 17), against whom Yahweh makes war throughout the remainder of the Old Testament. This plotline of liberation, healing, and illumination followed by trial is repeated throughout the Bible. Israel and the heroes of Israel regularly face vicious opposition at the very moment they are delivered. Moses is delivered from Pharaoh as an infant, but later flees Egypt for fear of Pharaoh. David's home in Ziklag is assaulted by Amalekites when he is in the final stages of his ascent to the throne (1 Sam 30). Jesus later will pass through his own exodus, and though he will personally ascend to his impregnable heavenly throne, his enemies attack his body, leading Jesus to confront the persecutors with, "Saul, Saul, why are you persecuting Me?" The blind man is yet another type of the true Israel, and in John 9, the Pharisees stand in the position of the Amalekites, nipping at the heels of Israel by attacking the weak and the stragglers.

Whatever tropology, whatever practical application, we derive from the story of the blind man is rooted in this allegory—christological typology. We follow the example of the suffering disciple because he is himself a type of the suffering Messiah, who then in turn becomes a type of the suffering church.[3]

John 9 is the fruit of Old Testament texts, showing that Jesus (and the Christlike blind man) is the antitypical fulfillment of Old Testament shadows. John 9 is also a seed, which germinates and grows and produces a new series of interpretations and applications. The plants that grow from John 9 are of two related kinds. On the one hand, John 9 generates a series of typological

example of

literal to
analogy to
tropilgy to
anagogy

analogies: the blind man is a type of Jesus, but he is also a type of several other characters and incidents later in the gospel and beyond. On the other hand, the example of the blind man, which is simply the example of Jesus, becomes a model for imitation. His example is enriched by similar and contrasting episodes else-where, and this lends thickness to our tropological applications. On the one hand, the blind man's experience foreshadows the actions and experiences of other characters; on the other hand, his actions tell us what we ought to do.

To see how this works, we need first to remember the blind man's growing perception of Jesus' identity as he is interrogated and bullied by the Pharisees, and we need to remember that this happens in Jesus' absence. There is a hidden meaning in that.

When we get to John 15–16, the blind man's story line is gen-eralized. Jesus warns the Twelve in the Upper Room Discourse that the world will hate, persecute, and reject the disciples as they have done to Jesus (15:18-24). As the disciples bear witness to the One with whom they have been "from the beginning" (15:27), the world will become more intensely hostile, and will go so far as to "make you outcasts from the synagogue" and to kill disciples of Jesus (16:1-2). All this will take place after Jesus has gone away from them with a promise to return (14:1-4). What Jesus describes is exactly what happens to the blind man: Jesus "goes away" and is nowhere to be found; the Jews mount an assault on the blind man; he witnesses faithfully; they cast him out of the synagogue; and there, Jesus "returns" to him, not leaving him an orphan. In the light of John 15–16, the story of the blind man ceases to mean merely "this is what happened to a blind man" and comes to mean "this is what hap-pens to everyone who comes to the light." The meaning of John 9 changes because of events that come later. The meaning of John 9 changes, expands, because a later word is spoken.

It does the same again when we get to John 18. Here we have another disciple under pressure from the Jews. Peter is standing in the court of the high priest—a significant location—warming himself by the charcoal fire, when a slave girl recognizes him. She says, "You are not also of this man's disciples, are you," and

Peter, fearful, replies, "I am not" (18:15-17). In an earlier chapter, I suggested that the blind man's "I am" statement (9:9) should be understood in the light of Jesus' "I am" statements scattered throughout the gospel. The blind man is becoming a disciple of the great "I am" and finding his identity in being a disciple of Yahweh incarnate. His being is sustained by fellowship with the One who is. Peter denies that he is a disciple, using the negative of the same sentence spoken by the blind man. He is not only denying that he follows Jesus; he is denying the identity of Jesus-Yahweh and, in so doing, denying his own identity. Peter is not—not Peter the rock, not a disciple, not a faithful man. The blind man stood firm with "I am" under a barrage of questions and the threat of excommunication. Peter is toppled by a maidservant.

This later "I am not" from one of the Twelve lends an additional layer of meaning to the blind man's "I am." In the light of the later text, the blind man is not only a witness to the "I am" but also a contrast to Peter. He is not-Peter as well as like-Jesus. Peter should have paid attention. He should have drawn a tropology from the story of the man born blind, the faithful Christlike witness.

Once more: the experience of the blind man is replicated yet again at the very end of the gospel. Jesus disappears from the story after his death and is placed in a tomb. On the first day of the week, Mary Magdalene and the other women find the empty tomb and later encounter the risen Jesus. Jesus returns to them after a little while, just as he came to the blind man after a little while. The reappearance is especially dramatic in the case of Thomas and Peter. Thomas will not believe until he has seen Jesus, but once he does, he confesses him as "Lord" (20:28), just as the blind man did. Peter, the "I am not" disciple, is reunited with Jesus at the sea, at a charcoal fire, around a meal. Reunited with Jesus, he is sent to tend lambs and sheep.

Let us take John 9 further into the New Testament and see where it might lead.[4] As we saw in a previous chapter, the narrative of John 9 is constructed, rather oddly, so as to put the Pharisees' interrogation of the blind man's parents at the chiastic center. This is not obviously the main episode in the story, and

its presence in the center of the text's labyrinth is something of
a disappointment. We had hoped to find treasure or a dragon, and
instead we find parents, and timid ones at that.

But we should assume purpose behind John's arrangement
of things, and so we can ask: if the blind man is a prototype of
later disciples, what might the parents typify? Their most notable
achievement is to deflect and evade the Pharisees because of their
fear of being cast from the synagogue. They know that their son
has been healed, and they have been told that Jesus did it. But
they hesitate. They do not want to leave the synagogue behind,
and so they send the Pharisees back to their son: Do not intimi-
date and bully and threaten and put pressure on us. Instead, do all
that to our son (9:21). He is of age. He can take it.

The man's parents remind us of Adam. Adam sees the ser-
pent, stands right there while it tempts Eve, but instead of intervening, he leaves Eve to handle it herself: "She is of age; talk to
her." These parents also remind us of people subsequent to Jesus,
namely, the Judaizers and their temporizing fellow travelers who,
fearful of persecution and loss and death, stuck around the synagogue and kept as quiet as possible about Jesus. In the light of
John 15–16, we can see the story of John 9 as an allegory of discipleship; in the light of Galatians, we can see it as an allegory, a
typology, of later conflicts in the apostolic church. It is not so surprising that the confessing blind man in John 9 stands in contrast
to the denying Peter in John 18, for Peter will later act with the
same timidity as the blind man's parents, as he withdraws from
table fellowship with Gentiles under pressure from the leaders of
the Jerusalem church (Gal 2:1-10).

We can find a further application of the story of the Christic
blind man in the fact that he receives vision through washing.
From the rest of the New Testament, we know that baptismal
washing is the initiatory rite of entry into the Christian church.
Baptism uses water; the blind man washes in a pool and comes
back seeing. Is there a connection? Is there an implicit theology
of baptism here?

The church fathers thought so. In one passage, Ambrose sums
up a patristic consensus on the passage:

In one instant we see both the power of his divinity and the strength of his holiness. As the divine light, he touched this man and enlightened him. As priest, by an action symbolizing baptism he wrought in him his work of redemption. The only reason for his mixing clay with the saliva and smearing it on the eyes of the blind man was to remind you that he who restored the man to health by anointing his eyes with clay is the very one who fashioned the first man out of clay, and that this clay that is our flesh can receive the light of eternal life through the sacrament of baptism. (*Letter* 67.5)

He exhorts his hearers, "You, too, should have come to Siloam. . . . Let Christ wash you, and you will then see. Come and be baptized, it is time."[5] What can we learn about baptism from John 9? Much in every way.

Baptism is the washing that opens the eyes and, by doing so, lets the light of Jesus flood in, so that the baptized can shine with light. Baptism puts us face-to-face with Jesus, the glory of God, so that we are transformed from glory to glory. John 9 not only shows how Jesus fulfills the creating act of the first day but also points to how the church participates in that re-creation. When the church baptizes at the command of Jesus, it is causing the light of Jesus to shine more brightly from the hill, the lampstand. John 9 shows that the creation event is about the *totus Christus*, the Creator Jesus and the people he makes into sub- and re-creators. Jesus has work to do, but he corrals the disciples into that work: "*we* must work the works of Him who sent me" (v. 4; emphasis added). Baptism is a commission, a sending. The baptismal font is not a fishbowl but a pool of sending. Every baptism takes place in Siloam, and every baptism unites the baptized with the One Sent. Baptism sets us aflame and sends us out as lights into the deep darkness. It opens our eyes and sends us into the world of the blind. It calls us to bold faithfulness in the midst of intense pressure. Baptism grants us a share in the suffering of Jesus, making his enemies our enemies even as it makes him our friend.

We might even go so far as to consider John 9 a text in favor of infant baptism. After all, the blind man washes and is illuminated before he knows anything about Jesus, certainly before confessing Jesus as Lord.[6] He confesses Jesus only after enduring intense Pharisaic interrogation.

Is John 9 preachable? Yes; it reveals Jesus. It reveals the way of discipleship. It provides an inspiring example of faithfulness in the absence of Jesus. It teaches us the meaning of baptism.

But we cannot stop there. If we stop with tropological applications to the church, we are in danger of falling back into a Spinozist separation of reason and faith, religion and the rest of life. The *totus Christus* principle needs to be pushed further.

JESUS AND OEDIPUS

Jesus is the head of the body, but Jesus is also head of all things for the church (Eph 1:21-23) and the One in whom all things hold together (Col 1:17). Jesus sums up not only the history of Israel and the aspirations of the people of God, but the history of man and the aspirations of the human race. This expansion of the *totus Christus* principle has hermeneutical import as well: if the Scriptures speak about Jesus, and if Jesus is the head of all things for the church, then the Scriptures speak about everything. Tropologies founded on the *totus Christus* principle thus open out into a biblical theory of history, a biblical literary and cultural criticism, a biblical political theology.

We cannot draw everything we might from John 9, but we can make a beginning. Let us begin with literary criticism.

I propose nothing new. The church fathers regularly read ancient literature typologically, seeing in it anticipations of the Christ. Many believed the Jewish Scriptures had been widely distributed in the ancient world, so that Plato and others were consciously employing biblical categories.[7] But their reading was also based on their conviction that Jesus is the key to all human history, culture, art, and literature.

Christ was the "true Orpheus," who brought his bride back from Hades, and Odysseus tied to the mast was a type of Jesus on the cross, resisting the siren temptations of the world. Eustathius, twelfth-century bishop of Thessalonica, repeats a commonplace about the plant Hermes gives Odysseus to protect him from Circe's magic:

By Hermes Homer most tellingly indicates the *logos* and by *moly* he indicates *paideia*, our spiritual education that is to say; for this can only be developed with great travail, *ek molou*, and by means of suffering and misfortune. The root of moly is black because the beginnings of *paideia* are always dark as shadows and extraordinarily ill-formed. Therefore our spiritual development is as the carrying of a heavy load and in no wise sweet. Yet moly has a flower and it is white as milk, for the end that *paideia* aims at and seeks to achieve, lies before us in gleaming brightness and all is sweet and satisfying. Hermes it is who gives us this moly, and this is nothing less than those *logos*-inspired directives which do not by any means lie ready for the human understanding to grasp. For moly comes from God and is a gracious gift.[8]

Four centuries later, Queen Elizabeth's tutor, Roger Asham, says the same:

That swete herbe Moly with the blake roote and white floore, [which is] given unto hym by Mercuries, to avoide all inchantmentes of Circes. Whereby the Divine Poete Homer ment covertlie (as wise and Godly men do iudge) that love of honestie and hatred of ill, which David more plainly doth call the feare of God: the onely remedie against the inchantementes of sinne. The true medicine . . . is, in Homere, the herbe Moly, with the blacke roote, and white flooer, sower at the first but sweete in the end . . . the divine Poete . . . sayth plainlie that this medicine against sinne and vanities, is not found out by man, but given and taught by God.[9]

This was a central method of Christian literary criticism until the sixteenth century, and it reflects a profound insight into the supremacy and universality of Christ.

Blindness, Sight, and the Light of the Gods

A consideration of Sophocles' *Oedipus the King* in the light of John 9 is especially suitable for this purpose.[10] Sophocles' play shares a number of literary themes and techniques with the Gospel of John, and especially with John 9. Both texts play on the ironies of blindness and sight. The tense exchanges between Oedipus and the blind seer Tiresias could have been drawn from the gospel. Oedipus mocks the prophet: "You've lost your power, / stone-blind, stone-deaf—senses, eyes blind as stone!" and "Blind, / lost in the night, endless night that nursed you! / You can't hurt me or anyone else who sees the light— / you can never touch me."[11] At the same time, he boasts of his own intellectual prowess:

> Come here, you pious fraud. Tell me,
> when did you ever prove yourself a prophet?
> When the Sphinx, that chanting Fury kept her deathwatch
>   here,
> why silent then, not a word to set our people free?
> There was a riddle, not for some passer-by to solve—
> it cried out for a prophet. Where were you?
> Did you rise to the crisis? Not a word,
> you and your birds, your gods—nothing.
> No, but I came by, Oedipus the ignorant,
> I stopped the Sphinx! With no help from the birds,
> the flight of my own intelligence hit the mark.[12]

Tiresias replies,

> So,
> you mock my blindness? Let me tell you this.
> You with your precious eyes,
> you're blind to the corruption of your life,
> to the house you live in, those you live with—
> who *are* your parents? Do you know? All unknowing
> you are the scourge of your own flesh and blood,
> the dead below the earth and the living here above,
> and the double lash of your mother and your father's curse
> will whip you from this land one day, their footfall
> treating you down in terror, darkness shrouding
> your eyes that now can see the light![13]

John and Sophocles also share stylistic habits, particularly a penchant for ambiguity and double entendres. Vernant has pointed out that the ambiguity of *Oedipus the King* does not arise, as in *Antigone*, from characters who use the same words in different ways (Creon and Antigone have very different conceptions of *nomos*, law); nor does it arise, as in *Agamemnon*, from deliberate duplicity (Clytemnestra welcomes her husband home with a speech that overtly expresses her love and respect but covertly lays out a plot for his death). Rather, the ambiguity of *Oedipus* the play is the ambiguity of Oedipus the character. If the play is full of riddles, it is because the title character is himself a riddle, to himself as much as to others. As a result, he does not know what he is saying and does not understand the meaning of his own actions. When he announces, "By going right back, in my turn, to the beginning [of the events] I am the one who will bring them to light [*ego phano*]," Vernant notes that that *ego phano* is intended to mean "It is I who will bring the criminal to light," but in the event actually means "I shall bring to light that I am the criminal." As things turn out, Oedipus has misjudged himself on every level:

> The Corinthian stranger is a native of Thebes; the solver of riddles is a riddle he himself cannot solve; the dispenser of justice is a criminal; the clairvoyant, a blind man; the savior of the town its doom. Oedipus, he who is renowned to all, the first among men, the best of mortals, the man of power, intelligence, honors, and wealth discovers himself to be the last, the most unfortunate, and the worst of men, a criminal, a defilement, an object of horror to his fellows, abhorred by the gods, reduced to a life of beggary and exile.[14]

In both John's gospel and *Oedipus the King*, the double meanings create a dramatic irony at the expense of the villains of the story.

Oedipus resembles John also in some features of its overall plot. From a middle distance, Oedipus can be read, patristically, as a veiled type of the coming Messiah. As Vernant notes, Oedipus is both *tyrannos* and *pharmakos*, both a king near the gods and the scapegoat expelled from the city. Though the two positions appear to be polar opposites, they are in fact linked, conceptually and in Greek culture. In the *pharmakos* rituals of ancient Greece, the scapegoat was given some of the accoutrements of a king before being ritually slaughtered or expelled from the city. This was fitting because the scapegoat, as much as the king himself, was responsible for preserving the fertility and life of the city.

The king's goodness was the guarantee of the health of the *polis*, and when the *polis* was afflicted, it was the scapegoat's expulsion that restored its health. Jesus is also the scapegoat king, the Lamb of God slain for the sins of the world, the King who rules from a cross. Within John 9, in fact, we have an anticipation of the climax of the story of Jesus, since the blind man is tried as a surrogate for Jesus and eventually expelled from the synagogue, a scapegoat for the scapegoat.

Sophocles links Oedipus' reversal from tyrant to scapegoat both to his self-exaltation, his hubris, and to the symbolism of sight, light, and blindness. At the beginning of the play, the priest of Zeus regards Oedipus as equal to the gods, a status especially evident in his "second sight," his ability to solve the unsolvable riddle of the Sphinx. Oedipus agrees with the priest, and he shows "nothing but scorn for the blind gaze of the diviner whose eyes are closed to the light of the sun and who, in his own words, 'lives by the shadows alone.'" When all becomes clear, however, "it is no longer possible for him either to see or to be seen," as his people avert their eyes from him and he tears out his eyes with Jocasta's brooches. Deprived of sight and of being seen, he becomes powerless. Without eyes, he can no longer scrutinize Thebes as its king and judge. Because he is no longer the object of the admiring gaze of Thebes, he is no longer tyrant.

Vernant recognizes the theological dimension of the reversal:

> Seen from a human point of view, Oedipus is the leader with second sight, the equal of the gods; considered from the point of view of the gods he is blind, equal to nothing. Both the reversal of the action and the ambiguity of the language reflect the duality of the human condition that, just like a riddle, lends itself to two opposite interpretations. Human language is reversed when the gods express themselves through it. The human condition is reversed— however great, just, and fortunate one may be—as soon as it is scrutinized in relation to the gods.[15]

In short, "in the sight of the Immortals he who rises highest is also the lowest."

The theological dimension of the plot is reinforced by language shifts throughout the play. Drawing on Bernard Knox,

Vernant points out that honorifics first used to refer to Oedipus gradually shift to the gods during the course of the play:

> In line 14 the priest of Zeus with his first words addresses Oedipus as sovereign: *kratunon*; in line 903 the chorus prays to Zeus as sovereign: *ho kratunon*. In line 48 the Thebans call Oedipus their savior: *soter*; in line 150 it is Apollo who is invoked as savior, to put an end . . . . to the evil as Oedipus earlier "put an end" to the Sphinx. At 237 Oedipus gives orders in his capacity as master of power and of the throne . . . ; at 200 the chorus prays to Zeus as "master of power and of the thunderbolt." . . . At 441, Oedipus recalls the exploit that made him great (*megan*); at 871, the chorus recalls that amid the heavenly laws there lives a great (*megas*) god who never ages. The dominion (*arxas*) that Oedipus flatters himself he wields is recognized by the chorus to lie, forever immortal, between the hands of Zeus.

In short, "The greatness of Oedipus shrinks to nothing as the greatness of the gods, in contrast with his, becomes increasingly evident."[16] Greatness is a zero-sum game in the world of Sophocles. Humans who grow too great are cut down to size.

Oedipus according to John

As noted above, Oedipus parallels the themes and movement of John 9 in some respects. The Pharisees consider themselves authorities in tradition, solvers of riddles, guides to the blind (cf. Rom 2:17-20). They scorn the blind man as an outcast and a sinner, and consider him unworthy of teaching them anything. In the course of the story, however, they are brought low, their blindness and prejudice exposed. They do not put out their eyes, but that is only because they have not come to recognize their own condition with Oedipal clarity. At the end of the chapter, Jesus condemns their sin, and in the following chapter, he identifies them as hirelings and wolves. The Pharisees' story is a tragic story of unwitting blindness. Importantly, the Pharisees repeatedly declare their understanding; "we know," they say, using the verb *oida*. But their knowledge is as superficial and ineffectual as the knowledge of Oedipus, whose very name contains the verb *oida* and who knows the meaning of the Sphinx' riddle.

At one level, the blind man is also an Oedipus. He comes to sight only to be transformed into a *pharmakos*, expelled from the synagogue. Yet, at a more profound level, the story of the blind man runs in the opposite direction. While the Pharisees protest their wisdom and insight, their blindness is revealed; meanwhile, the blind man moves from blindness to increasing sight. Some are blinded by the radiance of divine light, the light of the world, but not everyone. When the light comes, some gain sight. The ones who are blinded are the ones who think they see already, the ones who love the darkness rather than the light, the ones who try to conceal their evil deeds under the cover of darkness. Others are illuminated by the light, and more than illuminated.

"I am the light of the world," Jesus says, and that is uniquely true of Jesus. He is the uncreated light come into the world in human flesh. But the unique light that is Jesus also illuminates the body, so that it is a body of light. The Christ who is light is the *totus Christus*. The same Jesus who says "I am the light of the world" also says to his disciples, "You are the light of the world" (Matt 5:14). In Matthew, Jesus immediately conflates the image of the disciples as light with the image of them as a city (Matt 5:14-15): you are light; a city cannot be hid; a lamp cannot be hid. The premise of Jesus' final statement is that the city and the lamp are two images for the same reality. The church is the illuminated and illuminating city on a hill. Of course, the church is not light in itself, as if it were its own source of life and brightness. The radiance that emanates from the church is the radiance of Jesus, the light of the world. But the point is, again, that Jesus is light as head of a body of light, as the chief light of a city of light (cf. Rev).

John 9 does more than merely suggest this connection of original light and derived light. It also points to the ways that the church comes to receive and radiate the light that is Jesus. The lamp of the body is the eye, Jesus says (Matt 6:22). This is an odd saying, because we view the eye as receptive and lamps as radiant. Light comes from a lamp through the eye and forms its images, which are transmitted, mysteriously, to the brain. Jesus does not seem to mean, however, that our insides are illuminated by the lamp of the eye. He instead suggests a two-way traffic with the eye. The eye both receives light and gives light; it receives light, in fact, in order to give light. When the eye is clear, light enters and fills the body, so that the body becomes a body of light.[17] Such is Christ's own body.

This is the theology of light behind John 9. The man born blind cannot see light, and therefore he cannot shine with light. He is in darkness and he can radiate only darkness. Jesus comes as the light, re-creates him by clay and water, and he comes back seeing. The remainder of the story is about his increasing illumination, as he gradually recognizes who Jesus is. But it is equally about his growing illumination in the sense that he increasingly radiates the light that is Jesus. Under the intense pressure of the Jews' persecution, he gives more and more light, until his light is so blinding that they can no longer stand it. In order to keep their place pleasantly gloomy, they put him out of the synagogue.

Here is a genuine and profound contrast between the Greek tragedy and the Christian gospel. The Pharisees are Oedipus. They become increasingly tongue-tied before the incarnate word and increasingly blinded before incarnate light. At the same time, the blind man speaks with greater and greater clarity and comes to brighter and brighter light. Without irony or reversal, the blind man is conformed to Jesus. He endures attacks from the Pharisees, just like Jesus. He is ironic at the Pharisees' expense, just like Jesus. He presumes to teach the teachers of Israel; he is filled with light; he is bold under pressure. He even, as we have seen, uses the divine "I am" in answer to his neighbor's questions. In the presence of Jesus, he is not reduced to nothing, but instead becomes an *alter Christus*.[18]

Like Oedipus, the blind man suffers as a result of the opening of his eyes, but somewhat paradoxically, the blind man becomes more and more himself as he engages in debate with the Pharisees.[19] The suffering he endures does not break and destroy him. The opening of his eyes leads to truth, but, in contrast to Oedipus, truth truly does make him free. He would not suffer at all but for Jesus. If he had remained a beggar at the temple gate, he would have avoided the pain of discovery. He is quite literally suffering for Jesus, since he is the Pharisees' handy scapegoat substitute for Jesus. Because he is suffering for Jesus, and his suffering is a quite literal sharing in Jesus' own suffering and trials, his suffering makes him more himself, makes him more fully human.

In short: John, not Sophocles, is the true humanist. John the Jew, not Sophocles the Greek, is the one who exalts man. And the God of Israel, incarnate in Jesus, is the God who lifts men up to share his glory, rather than reducing them to dust.

ENLIGHTENMENT OCULARCENTRISM

At least since Nietzsche, Sophocles has been regarded as one of the great ancient critics of rationalism in both its philosophical and its political guises. Oedipus overcomes the Sphinx in sheer intellectual combat, and reigns peacefully and successfully at Thebes without the assistance of the gods for many years.[20] In Oedipus, Sophocles gives us an illustration of "the noble man who is destined for error and misery in spite of his wisdom" (section 9).[21] The limits of wisdom, the pessimism and tragedy of wisdom, have, Nietzsche recognizes, a theological dimension:

> alongside the aesthetic necessity of beauty run the demands "Know thyself" and "Nothing too much!"; whereas, arrogance and excess are considered the essentially hostile daemons belonging to the non-Apollonian sphere, therefore characteristics of the pre-Apollonian period, the age of the Titans, and of the world beyond the Apollonian, that is, the barbarian world. Because of his Titanic love for mankind, Prometheus had to be ripped apart by the vulture. For the sake of his excessive wisdom, which solved the riddle of the sphinx, Oedipus had to be overthrown in a bewildering whirlpool of evil. That is how the Delphic god interpreted the Greek past. (section 4)

The myth of Oedipus "seems to want to whisper to us that wisdom, and especially Dionysian wisdom, is an unnatural atrocity, that a man who through his knowledge pushes nature into the abyss of destruction also has to experience in himself the disintegration of nature. 'The spear point of knowledge turns itself against the wise man. Wisdom is a crime against nature'" (section 9).

Sophoclean tragic wisdom, with its recognition of the impenetrability of the world, stands in contrast to Socratic wisdom and Socratic aesthetics. According to Nietzsche, the most important law of Socratic aesthetics is as follows: "'Everything must be understandable in order to be beautiful,' a corollary to the Socratic saying, 'Only the knowledgeable person is virtuous'" (section 12). From Socrates we derive our own culture, characterized by "the victory of *optimism*, the developing hegemony of *reasonableness*, of practical and theoretical *utilitarianism*" (section 4).

Socratic logic aims to give brightness and sight, rendering everything transparent to reason. Sophoclean wisdom, though, reveals the truth, as it gestures toward the blindness of reason while giving us brilliant flashes of insight into the reality of the human condition. Underneath the serene, translucent Apollonian mask, tragedy offers glimpses of "the inner terror of nature, bright spots, so to speak, to heal us from the horrifying night of the crippled gaze" (section 9).

The Oedipus myth, thus, enabled Nietzsche to level his critical artillery at what has become known as the *ocularcentrism* of Enlightenment and post-Enlightenment thought and culture.[22] For many in the modern West, the mind has been conceived on the model of the eye. Sight had long been considered the "noblest sense," the source of the most certain knowledge. Testimony from others is suspect; seeing is believing. Descartes' famous thought experiment in the *Meditations* dispenses with tradition and teaching he had acquired through hearing and instruction, and conceives of the most certain knowledge as "clear and distinct ideas." He states his assumption quite explicitly in the treatise on optics appended to the *Discourse on Method*: "All the management of our lives depends on the senses, and since that of sight is the most comprehensive and noblest of these, there is no doubt that the inventions which serve to augment its power are among the most useful that there can be."[23]

Newton understood the function of light and sight differently, "claiming that *only* the perception of external objects and never innate intuitions or deductions are the source of our ideas." Newtonian scientific epistemology was of a piece with the philosophical emphasis on observation in place of speculation, which was associated with Locke, Hume, and the French *philosophes* who drew on their work. Despite the shift in perspective, there is continuity between Cartesian and empiricist philosophies. Martin Jay writes:

> Both Descartes and the *philosophes* influenced by Locke remained beholden to a concept of the mind as a *camera obscura*. Both could say with the Scottish philosopher Thomas Reid, "Of all the faculties called the five senses, sight is without doubt the noblest." Both maintained a faith in the linkage between lucidity and rationality, which gave the Enlightenment its name. And both distrusted the evidence of the competing major sense organ, the ear, which absorbed only unreliable "hearsay." As one of its most illustrious interpreters [Jean Starobinski] has rightly concluded, "Such was the century of the Enlightenment which looked at things in the sharp clear light of the reasoning mind whose processes appear to have been closely akin to those of the seeing eye."[24]

One of the key changes in the evaluation of vision was the legitimation of curiosity. Augustine had set the tone for Western culture with his classification of curiosity as the "lust of the eyes" in 1 John 2, but early modern technological developments, especially the microscope, the telescope, and the mirror, extended the actual range of vision to the very tiny and the very far, and a reevaluation of the probing eye of curiosity eventually accompanied these technical developments.[25]

Frances Yates and Walter Ong have examined the deeper historical roots of this ocularcentric bias. Yates traces the history of the art of memory from ancient rhetorical texts such as the *Ad Herenium* through Renaissance rhetorical strategies and into the early stages of the modern period. For much of Western history, the art of memory involved treating the mind as a space or theater, set about with mnemonic signs that guided the orator. Early on, those who wrote treatises on memory reached "a consensus that the higher and more exclusive art of memory is tied, by natural gift and training, to an ability to visualize the points of a speech."[26] One result of this was the development of a "spatialized" notion of consciousness, a consciousness that eliminated the complexities of time, change, and human interaction.[27] Emphasizing the eye seems naturally to lead to a spatialized view of knowledge, since we can see a lot of things at once but can hear only a word at a time.

Ong, for his part, examines how the pedagogy developed by Petrus Ramus shaped an ocularcentric, spatialized, quantified, stabilized, mathematicized, and impersonal conception of knowledge and consciousness. Ramist pedagogy sought to map ideas and logical connections in an immediately transparent visual fashion, an at-a-glance account of knowledge.[28] According to Ong,

> Ramist rhetoric . . . is not a dialogue rhetoric at all, and Ramist dialectic has lost all sense of Socratic dialogue and even most sense of scholastic dispute. The Ramist arts of discourse are monologue arts. They develop the didactic, schoolroom outlook which descends from scholasticism even more than do non-Ramist versions of the same arts, and tend finally even to lose the sense of monologue in pure diagrammatics. This orientation is very profound and of a piece with the orientation of Ramism toward an object world (associated with voice and auditory perception). In rhetoric, obviously someone had to speak, but in the characteristic outlook fostered by the Ramist rhetoric, the speaking is directed to a world where even persons respond only as objects—that is, say nothing back.[29]

Following Nietzsche, postmodern theory has challenged Enlightenment ocularcentrism. Martin Jay's very large book, *Downcast Eyes*, is a study of the "profound suspicion of vision and its hegemonic role in the modern era" that has appeared in "a wide variety of fields" of French thought in the past few decades. His subjects constitute a who's who of recent philosophy and theory: Sartre, Levinas, Merleau-Ponty, Foucault, Lacan, Barthes, Derrida, Lyotard. Following Nietzsche, postmodern theory has attempted to revive the wisdom of Oedipus, the wisdom of the blinded.

John and Ocularcentrism

John 9 is about blindness and sight, and John as a whole is deeply concerned with light, illumination, enlightenment, and sight. Even the "works of power" found in the Synoptics are reconceived in John in visual terms as "signs." What happens when John 9 enters into dialogue with the cultural dominance of vision in modern Western thought?

On the one hand, John 9's ironic inversions of sight and blindness support some themes of the postmodern critics of the hegemony of vision. At the beginning of chapter 9, the categories of blindness and sight are quite obvious: the blind man is blind, while Jesus and the Jews are able to see. As soon as the blind man's eyes are opened, however, the story gradually unveils the blindness of the Pharisees, leading up to Jesus' declaration that he has come as the light, both to open the eyes of the blind and to seal up the eyes of those who think they see. For John, sight does not unproblematically offer access to reality as it is. John is no empiricist who believes that reality is a strumpet who offers herself to every passerby. She is chaste, and must be wooed.

The Pharisees especially illustrate how distortions of tradition interfere with clear-sightedness. Though the blind man has undeniably been healed, and though the Pharisees cannot deny the reality of the miracle, they are not willing to admit it. Their view of the miracle is shaped by their hostility to Jesus, their preconceptions, their distorted readings of Moses, and their elite social and religious position within Israel. Sight does not give transparent, undistorted access to what is there, but is shaded by preconceptions and passions. John 9 would, in other words, raise a skeptical question mark over the pretensions of modern science.

At the same time, John's gospel is ocularcentric in many respects. In addition to the light symbolism that I summarized above, seeing plays a prominent role in the gospel. Jesus' entire ministry is a ministry of making the Father known, which, in John's parlance, is making the Father "seen": "He who has seen Me has seen the Father," Jesus tells Philip (John 14:9). In John 9 in particular, the giving of sight makes the blind man a new creature. Seeing what the Pharisees cannot puts him in a superior position.

What differentiates John's ocularcentrism from the philosophical ocularcentrism of the early modern period is the specific focus on Jesus. The Logos that brings light is not, as in Descartes or Kant, a human rationality, but the living word who proceeds from the Father and is equal to the Father, the Word that became flesh. Enlightenment, for John, does not come through the process of doubt or through reflection on the transcendental prerequisites for human reason. Enlightenment comes from the light source: the Word that is with the Father from the beginning, the light who lightens every man. Jesus is the light of the world, and the enlightened ones are those who cling to him in faith.

Importantly, too, the light that comes into the world and enlightens every man is also eternally the "Word" of the Father (1:1). In defending himself against the attacks of the Pharisees at various points, Jesus appeals to the testimonies of John, the Father, and Moses. He urges the Jews to believe not merely because of what they have seen (the works) but because of what they have heard and read. In the sequel to the story of the healing of the blind man, Jesus identifies the sheep as those who "hear" the voice of the shepherd, not those who see him (10:4). John's position is not really ocularcentric; it is a much richer and more varied viewpoint that does not dispense with the visual but also recognizes the crucial significance of the oral and aural.

John's critique of modern Enlightenment can be extended further. Enlightenment, after all, is itself a metaphor of light, of illumination, and describes, according to Kant, the light that comes to men who put off the self-imposed tutelage of authority and learn to think for themselves: "Enlightenment is man's emergence from his self-imposed immaturity. Immaturity is the inability to use one's understanding without guidance from another. This immaturity is self-imposed when its cause lies not in lack of understanding, but in lack of resolve and courage to use it without guidance from another."[30]

John is also concerned with illumination. Almost as soon as John introduces the Word, he introduces the "Light" that is "in" the word (1:1-4), a light identified with "life." The light that is in the word is the "light of men" and the light that, "coming into the world, enlightens every man" (1:9). At the Feast of Booths, Jesus identifies himself as "light of the world" (8:12), and he repeats the same declaration to the blind man (9:5) and to the crowds at the Feast of Dedication (12:44-47). Jesus, the incarnate word, is the coming in flesh of the light that illumines all.

As we have seen, John is most obviously drawing on the creation account, but he is also drawing on a theology of light that runs throughout the Old Testament and associates light with knowledge, particularly as communicated by the law; with God himself and his glory; and with life.[31] The word of Yahweh is a "lamp to my feet and a light to my path" (Ps 119). When Yahweh appears to Israel at the sea and at Sinai, he comes radiating light. "You are my light and my life," the psalmist declares (Ps 27). In identifying Jesus as light, John is identifying him as the living, embodied Torah, the guide of life; as Yahweh in flesh, whose glory is manifested especially in the cross; as the life of the world.

"Light of the world" also picks up a more specific thread of Old Testament imagery, where Yahweh speaks of a "light to the nations."[32] As the one who "created the heavens and stretched them out" and "who gives breath to the people in it," Yahweh appoints his servant "as a covenant to the people, as a light to the nations." Among the servant's tasks will be to bring light: "To open blind eyes, to bring out the prisoners from the dungeon, and those who dwell in darkness from the prison" (Isa 42:5-7). It is not enough to make his servant the agent for restoring Israel: "I will also make you a light of the nations so that My salvation may reach to the end of the earth" (Isa 49:6). When Israel has been restored, Israel itself will become light:

> Arise, shine; for your light has come, and the glory of Yahweh has risen upon you. For behold, darkness will cover the earth, and deep darkness the peoples; but Yahweh will rise upon you, and His glory will appear upon you. And nations will come to your light, and kings to the brightness of your rising. (Isa 60:1-3)

The earth was created in darkness (Gen 1:2), but Yahweh dispelled the darkness with a word. Darkness descended again upon the formless void of the fallen creation, but Yahweh's servant is the light that makes a new creation. This background confirms our earlier conclusion that Jesus' actions in John 9 allude to the creation of Adam. Jesus is the servant-light who opens blind eyes and dispels the darkness of creation.

John's announcement that Jesus is the source of "enlightenment" for the creation puts him on a collision course with modern Western culture. Reason, for the post-Enlightenment West, was the "light that lightens every man," the "light of the nations" that would bring deliverance from blindness and the darkness of benighted Christendom. For John, enlightenment does not come from renouncing authorities and teachers. Light comes from the one teacher, the rabbi who is himself the Light. Light comes from submitting to the yoke of another, provided that other is Jesus.

POLITICS OF SIGHT

Sight is always politically fraught. It is always about power. To look at a woman in order to lust is already adultery, Jesus said. And more than adultery; it can be an ocular rape, as a man imaginatively strips the woman with his eyes. When a man checks out a woman, it is often the first step of what we call an erotic conquest.

The erotic gaze is already political, and ancient and medieval politics were about vision in a more specific sense. Politics was about spectacle, about being at the center of attention, the object of admiring and envying gazes. As Shadi Bartsch puts it,

> To be at the center of the gaze: at Rome, there was no position more ideologically fraught, more riven with contradiction, more constitutive *and* destructive of male civic identity. It was the position of the general riding in a triumphal chariot through the streets of the city; it was also the position of the criminal marked for destruction by man or beast in the Colosseum. It was the site for the orator, as he addressed a jury and a corona of spectators in the Forum, and it was also the site for the actor, a man marked by *infamis* (without citizen rights) by the same citizenry that patronized his performance.[33]

Medieval kings continued to employ spectacle for political purposes, overwhelming the populace with the brilliancy of their displays. As Foucault pointed out, modern politics can be seen, in part, as a replacement of spectacle with surveillance. Power is still exercised by spectacle (witness Barack Obama's inauguration), but it is more commonly exercised by the threat that we may be seen.

Though sight has always been politically weighted, it has taken a peculiar form in the modern scientific West. The Western method of social science treats the "other" as an object of study, depersonalizing it in the process, as it depersonalizes all objects of study. Sight places us in a position of mastery and superiority over the object of sight. Platonic conceptions of reality, with their upper and lower worlds, have gone out of fashion for many in the modern world, but there is a kind of horizontal Platonism in modern epistemology. The subject regards the object outside himself, and distant from him, as if from a great height.[34]

In modern ocularcentrism, societies and social institutions, though thoroughly human, are objectified as "social things," things to be studied and not to talk back. Johannes Fabian argues that these habits of mind end up treating the other of anthropological research—the non-Western tribe being studied—as an object to be surveyed, summarized, and charted under the gaze of the Western-trained student:

> To use an extreme formulation, in this tradition the object of anthropology could not have gained scientific status until and unless it underwent a kind of double visual fixation, as perceptual image and as illustration of a kind of knowledge. Both types of objectification depend on distance, spatial and temporal. In the fundamental, phenomenalist sense this means that the Other, as object of knowledge, must be separate, distinct, and preferably distant from the knower. Exotic otherness may not be so much the result as the prerequisite of anthropological inquiry. We do not "find" the savagery of the savage, or the primitivity of the primitive, we posit them.[35]

Anthropology becomes what Fabian calls a political visualism when it is allied with a spatialized vision of knowledge and reality. Anthropological data is collected and organized for consumption in a Western setting, and even the most conscientious anthropologist treats the object as a student: "The hegemony of the visual as a mode of knowing may thus directly be linked to the political hegemony of an age group, a class, or one society over another. The ruler's subject and the scientist's object have, in the case of anthropology (but also of sociology and psychology), an intertwined history."[36]

John's Visual Politics

Seeing and being seen is power. Oedipus is king so long as he can watch as a guardian, so long as people look to him for the fertility and success of Thebes. Blinded, he is without power in both respects. His disfigured face is horrific, and he can no longer examine cases or see dangers. In *Oedipus at Colonus*, he has some mystical power, but that power does not translate into political authority. In both ancient and modern ocularcentric systems, the blind are the emblem of powerlessness. They can be watched, studied, examined, and assessed without ever watching, studying, examining, or assessing in return. They are at the mercy of the sighted. The blind are pure objects of scrutiny, never subjects. The Pharisees have assigned the blind man his role: sinner and beggar, and certainly not teacher or judge.

Though the man gains sight, the Pharisees continue to treat him as an object, as visible but not visioned.[37] John's narrative highlights the Pharisaic modes of power. They enter the story because Jesus heals on the Sabbath and the Pharisees are the Torah watchdogs of first-century Israel. The Pharisees are in a tricky spot. Jesus is clearly a sinner; after all, he has violated the Torah, which, by definition, makes him a sinner. Yet they also have to make sense of the fact that the man was born blind. At first, there is a division among the Pharisees. Some insist that Jesus is not from God, while others ask the obvious question, "How can a sinner do such signs?" (v. 16). When they press the man to confess Jesus as a prophet, they stop the interrogation and try another tack. This time, they are completely united. The Pharisees who left open the possibility that Jesus is from God have been silenced, and the Pharisees now speak with one voice. Jesus' opponents close ranks, not only pushing out anyone who confesses Jesus but also silencing anyone in their own school who does not conform to the majority judgment.

They gradually tighten the bindings around the blind man too. As Jerome Neyrey comments,

> Not everyone enjoyed "voice" in the ancient world: Children did not lecture adults, nor slaves their masters. Women had limited public voice in the governments of Greco-Roman cities. Even males did not enjoy full public "voice": Their speech and opinions were of no significance if they had no social significance.[38]

When Jesus opens the man's eyes, however, he also loosens his tongue, giving him voice in the assembly of Israel. The Pharisees do not like it, and proceed to silence the blind man's unauthorized voice. His account of Jesus' sign gets shorter and shorter.[39] Three times he is asked how it all happened, and each time the explanation is thinner, until it is eventually ruled out of order entirely:

> The man who is called Jesus made clay, and anointed my eyes, and said to me, "Go to Siloam, and wash"; so I went away and washed, and I received sight. (v. 11)

> He applied clay to my eyes, and I washed, and I see. (v. 15)

> I told you already, and you did not listen. (v. 27)

The Pharisees' next tactic is to interrogate the man's parents. Perhaps, they think, the man is a plant, part of a vast Jesus conspiracy. Perhaps he was not blind after all, and the whole thing is a hoax. If true, that would enable them to maintain their opinion that Jesus is a sinner while disposing with the pesky evidence of Jesus' power to do miracles. The parents are no help. They are too afraid of the Pharisees to even hint that Jesus healed their son, but they cannot deny that their son was born blind. Frustrated again, the Pharisees fall back into tactics typical of all frustrated people: they become bullies. They have no arguments left, but they cannot let the man stay. So long as he is in the Jewish community, even if he is only standing silently in a corner praising God for his sight, he is a continuing witness to Jesus and an offense to the Pharisees. So they "revile" the man, accuse him of arrogance for trying to teach them, and try to extract a confession of Jesus so they can be justified in kicking him out of the synagogue.

John's repeated emphasis on the Pharisaic knowledge begs for a Foucauldian reading. The Pharisees are confident that "this man is not from God" (v. 16) and "we know that this man is a sinner" (v. 25). On only one point do they admit ignorance: "we do not know where He is from" (v. 29), but that is not really an admission of ignorance but another declaration of knowledge: this man cannot be the Messiah because we cannot check out his origins.[40] At times, their knowledge sounds paternalist: "Now, now, laddie. You're a nobody. We're the experts. Don't get so excited about Jesus." More often, it is nakedly domineering. Having no doubts that they are in the right, the Pharisees impose their knowledge on the Jews. If anyone knows differently, or even presents contrary evidence, they are cast out of the synagogue. The Pharisees have established a regime of knowledge/power that excludes anyone who confesses Jesus, and they mean to protect their privilege of deciding what counts as knowledge.

The Pharisaic interrogation is remarkably brutal. At first, the neighbors are confused, wondering if the seeing man in front of them is the same as the blind beggar they have seen for years (vv. 8-9). The Pharisees exploit this confusion by attempting to detach the man from himself, his past, his parentage, his senses, his reason, his own experience, and his own mind.[41] Finally, they cut him off from his community. It is no exaggeration to call the man a sacrificial victim; the Pharisees are doing their best to tear him limb from limb in order to dominate him.

The episode is a parable of discipleship; it is equally a parable about the abuses of power among a religious elite. It is not only about the Jews, of course, but a cautionary tale for anyone who assumes the garb of priest. By holding the Pharisees up to scrutiny, and a high degree of mockery, the story functions subversively, undermining the pretensions too often associated with religious expertise.[42] The blind man makes the Pharisees look the fool, and the text has the same effect on us, exposing the folly of the scribes. But beware: those who see this most clearly are themselves the scribes, experts in the text, the very ones in greatest danger of becoming Pharisees.

John 9 is a case study of imbalanced power. The Pharisees hold all the cards. They take upon themselves to interrogate the blind man and his parents, to sort through the truth about Jesus. They have the ability to call in other witnesses, neighbors, and parents, and they have the ultimate disciplinary authority to cast people out of the synagogue when they confess Jesus (vv. 22, 34). They can impose a category on the blind man with impunity, and with the blind man having little or no ability to correct: "You were born entirely in sin" (v. 34). They are the ones who can impose their certainty on the blind man and the rest of the Jews through intimidation and threats of exclusion.[43] The blind man is utterly without power of this sort. At the beginning of the story, he lacks even the power of sight. After his eyes are opened, he is roughed up by the Pharisees.

This power imbalance is greatly exacerbated by a moral imbalance that tilts decisively in the opposite direction. For all their status in Israel, the Pharisees are blind leaders of the blind (v. 39). The blind man moves from literal blindness to literal sight in an instant, and his spiritual insight matures under pressure of interrogation. The situation is not just one of oppression, but of the oppression of the sightful by the blind. The blind man sees what the Pharisees cannot, but he has no power to enforce his insight on anyone. In this, the story of the blind man is again an allegory of discipleship and a preview of the later experience of Jesus. Jesus knows what it is in man; he has clear sight, and is himself the source of sight and light. Yet he is surrounded by darkness, put on trial by the blind, and executed by the sightless. Darkness places eternal light in the dock and interrogates it.

Not only the blind man's political situation, but also his response to it, resembles that of Jesus. His responses are a case study in the politics of powerlessness, of how a disciple remains faithful under pressure from the powerful. Most obviously, the blind man maintains a faithful and increasingly accurate witness to Jesus. As we have noted earlier, he describes Jesus as the man who opened his eyes, as a prophet, as One whom God hears; finally, he worships Jesus as the Son of Man. Along the way, he adopts an ever-bolder position in relation to the Pharisees, formulating a sound theological argument for concluding that Jesus is from God (vv. 31-33). When the Pharisees accuse him of trying to teach them, they have a point (v. 34).

Beyond that, the blind man displays the wit of the weak in his responses to the Pharisees. He professes ignorance—"Whether He is a sinner, I do not know" (v. 25)—while at the same time pointing out the obvious to the Pharisees: "one thing I do know, that, whereas I was blind, now I see" (v. 25). He upbraids the Pharisees for their unwillingness to hear: "I told you already, and you did not listen" (v. 27). He uses sarcasm and irony: "You do not want to become His disciples, do you?" (v. 27) and "here is an amazing thing, that you do not know where He is from, and yet He opened my eyes" (v. 30). Given the imbalance of power, and the moral imbalance, of the situation, the blind man adopts a strategy that brings the Pharisees up short, exposes their prejudice and blindness, and parries their arguments. These are the strategies that lead Jesus to teach in parables, by irony and indirection. These are the strategies of discipleship in public discourse where the field is weighted against Jesus.

Judgment of This World

Giving sight to the blind gives them power, at least the power to look back, and many other powers as well. Jesus gives power to the powerless in the same act in which he gives sight to the blind. Once Jesus opens the blind man's eyes, the balance of power has changed. The Pharisees do not recognize it. That is part of their blindness.

John 9, like much of John, is a trial story. Andrew Lincoln has shown that this Johannine trial motif is rooted in the Old Testament notion that God is carrying on a lawsuit with the world. The premise of this lawsuit is that Yahweh "has sovereign rights over the world" by virtue of creation and that "all humanity and especially Israel, with whom God has entered into a special covenantal relationship, owe God acknowledgement and allegiance." By coming to judge, Yahweh will sort out the truth, set things right, vindicate his people, and condemn the guilty.[44]

The dispute in John is whether this cosmic trial is beginning with Jesus, whether Jesus is "its unique divine agent." As soon as

Jesus announces that the Father has given him authority to judge (5:22), the Jews put him on trial. Of course: God the judge shows up, and human beings want to put *him* on trial. It is an old, old story, repeated again and again in the gospel. As at Massah and Meribah (Exod 17), the Jews bring complaints against Jesus after he feeds five thousand (6:41). Chapter 8 is a lengthy trial scene, and chapter 9 is also a trial scene. The Pharisees play prosecutor, the blind man and his parents serve as witnesses, and Jesus is the sinner accused of breaking Sabbath. Throughout the trial, though, Jesus is absent, so the Pharisees are forced to try his "disciple" instead. Many of the Pharisees have already arrived at a verdict before the trial begins. They know that Jesus is not from God, and they search for any avenue of investigation that will support that decision. Finally, they can do nothing but perform a sheer, brutal power play.

In all these ways, the trial of the blind man foreshadows the later trial of Jesus. There, too, the people bring Jesus to the Jews.[45] There, too, the decision has been made before the trial begins. There, too, the Jews pressure and bully to get their predetermined result. There, too, they cast out an innocent man. In both of these trials, however, the tables are turned and the prosecutors are brought to the bar. By the end of John 9, Jesus reaffirms his own judicial role and declares the Pharisees sinners, just as Jesus is revealed as the judge in the midst of his own trial. Though it looks as if Jesus is being condemned, Pilate and the Jews are the ones on trial: "Now is the judgment of this world," Jesus has said of his crucifixion (12:31). Similarly, the blind man turns the tables on the Pharisees and begins to interrogate them. He pins them down with airtight arguments and drives them to self-condemnation.

This reversal of the lawcourt situation is reinforced by the Edenic imagery of the chapter. As noted in a previous chapter, John 9 alludes to the creation account. Jesus is the light of new creation, and he remakes the blind man with clay and spittle, repeating Yahweh's creation of Adam. The Adamic echoes are more extensive, however. When the blind man tells his story, he says that he "received sight" (vv. 11, 15, 18). Several times, though, he or John speaks of the event as an "opening of the eyes" (vv. 10, 14, 17, 21, 26, 30, 32).[46] This can hardly be accidental. John is indicating that what happens to the blind man is analogous in some way to what happened to Adam and Eve when they ate from the tree of knowledge and their "eyes were opened" (Gen 3:7). Jesus opens the man's eyes on the Sabbath (John 9:14), and the day of the fall is arguably also a Sabbath, the seventh day when Yahweh walks in the garden in the Spirit of the day.

The plot of John 9 does not, however, exactly match the plotline of Genesis 2–3. In Genesis, Adam is created from the dust, is tempted by Satan, and stretches out his hand to eat forbidden fruit, and then the Lord confronts him. The blind man's eyes are open at the beginning of the story, before he ever faces the "Satanic" (cf. 8:44) pressure of the Pharisees. Instead of buckling under the pressure, he stands firm, confessing Jesus to be the Christ and fighting off his adversaries and accusers with questions, wit, sarcasm, and logical argument. He is cast out at the end of the temptation scene, but not because he failed. He is cast out because the Edenic synagogue has been corrupted by serpentine Pharisees. When he meets his judge outside the "garden," the judge commends him and receives his worship.

The connection between Genesis 3 and John 9 becomes clearer when we recognize the role of eyes and knowledge of good and evil in the Old Testament. Eyes are organs of judgment. God "sees" and renders righteous judgment; his "eyes are open" to the humble to answer their prayers, and they are open toward the wicked to condemn them. Justice is not blind but wide-eyed. So, too, knowledge of good and evil is a capacity of kings (1 Kgs 3), kings who see rightly and know in order to judge between good and evil. Adam and Eve jumped the gun by seizing the fruit of the tree, but in seizing the fruit, they received a capacity that is good in itself: the capacity to judge good and evil. So, too, the blind man's eyes are opened so that he can see and judge, so that he can enter into the kingdom not merely as a subject but as a co-judge. We saw above that John rather than Sophocles is the true humanist; he is also the true democrat, who, far more than Sophocles, affirms the legitimacy of the judgments of the weak and the outcast.[47] The gospel tells a story of a man who becomes able to return a gaze, scrutinize for himself, and speak what he sees.

He gains voice, and his voice is the voice of a witness and judge. When Jesus says at the end of John 9, "For judgment I came into this world, that those who do not see may see; and that those who see may become blind" (v. 39), he is commenting on the events that have just transpired. The Pharisees' blind interrogation of the once-blind man who now sees is in fact their own interrogation. When they think they are trying the blind man, and Jesus through him, it is they who are being summoned before the court, with the blind man who now sees standing with Jesus as their judge.

Oliver O'Donovan has defined judgment as "an act of moral discrimination that pronounces upon a preceding act or existing state of affairs to establish a new public context."[48] Jesus is the judge, and his acts of judgment follow this pattern. Jesus discerns so that he may pronounce on the state of affairs in Israel, and in so pronouncing, he creates a new public context, the public in which the church will arise as the people of God. In this case, the new public context is the reverse of the prior context. Jesus turns the world upside down in his judgment, giving sight to the blind and blinding those who see.[49]

Though the Father has put all judgment into his hands, Jesus shares this judgment with all those new Adams and Eves whose eyes he has opened. The blind man turns the tables, asking pointed questions of the Pharisees and giving them conclusive arguments in favor of Jesus. They refuse to answer his questions or acknowledge the force of his arguments, and they are judged supremely when they think that they are most forcefully acting as judges. When they cast the man from the synagogue, they are in fact judging themselves, for those who do not believe are "judged already." What appears to be the powerlessness of the blind man is actually the reverse, a position of power and judicial authority. He is an agent of Jesus' judgment on the Pharisees, because he has his eyes opened.

John is himself among the agents of Jesus' judgment of the world, and through his gospel story, we the readers are, Andrew Lincoln argues, "caught up in the continuing cosmic trial":

> At the very least, being faced with having to make a judge-
> ment on the Gospel's witness ought to make readers aware

that, if this witness is not accepted, some other verdict about justice and life is being preferred and endorsed. For readers in the West the pervasive rival modern verdict, reinforced by the advertising business, involves the claim that individual persons, seen as autonomous units, have the right to whatever well-being and happiness they choose, and that these can be found through gaining and consuming a variety of material goods. Where this is the vision of life, the accompanying notion of justice holds that having a disproportionate amount of whatever it takes to gain happiness and security is justified and that exploiting others by various means, including the use of force and violence, in order to gain or maintain this disproportion, may also be justified.[50]

[handwritten: & that is Getting at the Poetic and the Polemic/Political import of each scripture passage]

Good Shepherd

The political import of the passage continues and, if anything, becomes more overt in the Good Shepherd Discourse that follows. Though there is no break in the text, this discourse is less a continuation of the story of the blind man than it is Jesus' continuing commentary on that incident. The Pharisees are supreme examples of the strangers, thieves and robbers, and hirelings that Jesus speaks about. They have excluded the blind man from the synagogue, thereby exercising control over the "gate" of the sheep that Jesus talks about. The sheep will not follow them because they do not recognize their voices, as they recognize the voice of the good shepherd.

Shepherd terminology is political terminology throughout the Old Testament. Yahweh is Israel's shepherd (Ps 80), and Moses, David, and others serve as under-shepherds who lead Israel like a flock. Yahweh promises that he will come to shepherd his people, and also promises that a new Davidic shepherd will lead the people. Jesus is Yahweh the shepherd-king, the new David. As such, he demonstrates proper royal behavior, a politics of self-sacrifice. True shepherds do not attack the sheep, like wolves; nor do they flee when the wolves arrive, as the hirelings do. The true shepherd-king keeps his sheep and protects them, even at the cost of his own life.

Jesus also describes himself as the "gate" of his people. This is relevant to the preceding story, since the blind man has been shown the door in the synagogue. He is cast "outside the gate." So it appears. But Jesus does not accept that the Pharisees have actual gatekeeping functions. Jesus is the gate, the one who stands between the inside and outside, and anyone who wants to be inside has to come through him. But anyone who does come to him is "inside," whatever the appearances. Jesus is, after all, standing just outside the gate of the synagogue when the blind man is cast out, waiting to admit him into his own sheep pen. The gate image is deepened by the fact that the gates were the places of judgment in the ancient Israelite city. Elders gathered at the gates to determine who was permitted to enter and who was going to be cast out. Jesus is taking over this political role, that of gatekeeper.

Jesus as the Son of Man is judge, and he is also judge as the Good Shepherd. As a disciple of the Son of Man and the Good Shepherd, the blind man whose eyes were opened joins his master in judging the world.

CONCLUSION

John 9, in short, opens up an angle for literary analysis, a critique of Enlightenment rationality, and some features of Christian politics. It is about Jesus; it is about the Jesus who is the head of the body, and so is about the whole Christ. It is about the Jesus who is head over all things for his church, the one in whom everything holds together. John 9 is a text about everything, just like every other biblical text.

This makes "Praying the Book" actually feasible. to pray through Titus for self-control, for training in ministry, for marriage leadership

Remember

Recollection → Literal
Recapitulation → Analogy of faith
Reformation → tropology
Renewal → anagogical
eschatology
covenant
I will be their God and
They will be my people

Epilogue

Of the making of books there is no end. Solomon's wisdom applies equally to individual works: a single book cannot really come to an end either. If my argument in chapter 2 is correct, we do not even know what the event of a text is, what to call it, or what it means until long after it has been written and published. How can a book then come to an end? End it must, however. As a practical matter, if for no other reason, there has to be an epilogue, a last page, an index, a back cover.

If that back cover were not looming into sight, I would spend time musing at length over a few other questions. Since the end is near, I can only sketch these musings.

First, the hermeneutical method offered here is very similar to the fourfold method developed by medieval Bible teachers.[1] For the medievals, the literal sense of the text opened out into a christological allegory, which, because Christ is the head of his body, opened out into tropological instruction and, because Christ is the King of a kingdom here yet also coming, into anagogical hope. Though this method is often seen as a threat to a hermeneutics of the letter, I believe, and hope to have shown, that this is not the case. When the text is seen as an event, as a joke, as music; when words are seen as players; when the letter is not seen as a husk but as a necessary and nourishing part of God's verbal bread—when we understand the letter in this way, a hermeneutics of the letter is as poetically and politically potent as the medieval quadriga.

best quote of the book

Second, the setting I have imagined throughout this book has usually been the scholar, pastor, reader, believer alone with Bible. Though helpful for heuristic purposes, that scene oversimplifies and, to some degree, distorts the realities of reading and interpretation. Even the most isolated scholar reads other scholars, listens to lectures, and relies on others. Pastors and Bible teachers go about their work in communal settings, where they listen to as well as deliver sermons, hear as well as speak, and gain biblical insights from their parishioners as much as they pass them on. Preachers come to as many insights into the text during preaching as they do alone in their studies. If that back cover were not creeping up on me, I would spend more time asking how the introduction of this communal dimension affects interpretation, what new metaphors it might bring to light: perhaps "Texts Are Community Property."

Finally, and related to this, interpretation is ultimately a performance. If texts are musical, if they are scores, then the interpreter is not the composer or even the music critic but the performer.[2] A competent performer gets his notes right; a great performer gets his notes right, but aims to achieve more. A great performer wants to get as much as he can from the correct notes he plays. Interpretation is performance in this sense, and no interpreter or reader should be content with getting the words right. But interpretation is also performance in the sense that it is carried out before an audience and before the critics. A preacher is not done interpreting his text when he finishes writing his sermon; the delivery of the sermon is the interpretation. A commentator is not finished when he has made all of his exegetical decisions, or even when he writes up the results; his interpretation includes the publication of those decisions and results, presenting them to the scrutiny and judgment of others. Again we see that interpretation is a communal activity. Interpretation is performance also in the sense that it aims to be timely. Humor depends on timing, and if hermeneutics is about getting it, it has something to do with saying the right thing at the right time.

There is no such thing as a timeless text, or a timeless interpretation of a text. Until the last trumpet, we have no final, complete ending to any book or event. We do not know what the events of the story are or what they mean, not fully, until the story is all done. So I will have achieved all my aims if my performance in this book is judged timely, a word spoken at the right time.

Menuet

BWV Anh. 114

Johann Sebastian Bach

Minuetto

From "Don Giovanni"

W.A. Mozart

Notes

Preface

1   I could make the same sorts of arguments by examining the way Old Testament writers read earlier texts of the Old Testament, following the lead of Michael Fishbane's *Biblical Interpretation in Ancient Israel*. The reading methods of Jesus and Paul are in profound continuity with these Old Testament readers.

Chapter 1

1   This summary of Milosz' views is from Clive James, *Cultural Amnesia: Necessary Memories from History and the Arts* (New York: Norton, 2007), 487–89.

2   James, *Cultural Amnesia*, 487–89.

3   Barbara Kiefer Lewalski, *Protestant Poetics and the Seventh-Century Religious Lyric* (Princeton: Princeton University Press, 1979), ch. 3.

4   Travis L. Frampton, *Spinoza and the Rise of Historical Criticism of the Bible* (New York: T&T Clark, 2006), 55–56.

5   I cite the KJV not because I favor it in every respect over other translations; I do not. I am using it for comparison's sake only.

6   "KJV was born archaic: it was intended as a step back." David Daniell, *The Bible in English* (New Haven: Yale University Press, 2003), 441.

7   The Hebrew *soul* (*nephesh*) does seem to be linked to breath and throat. See Thomas Staubli and Silvia Schroer, *Body Symbolism in the Bible*, trans. Linda M. Maloney (Collegeville, Minn.: Michael Glazier, 2001), 56–67.

8   The verb in Psalm 23:5 is not *mashach* but *dashen*.

9 The story could begin earlier, with the Reformation, with the problems that surround Calvin's use of accommodation. I could begin with certain features of medieval interpretation, or even with patristic reading. For modern biblical hermeneutics, though, the seventeenth century is crucial.

10 Quoted in Roland Bainton, "The Bible in the Reformation," in *The Cambridge History of the Bible: The West from the Reformation to the Present Day*, ed. S. L. Greenslade, 1–37 (Cambridge: Cambridge University Press, 1963), 2. Similarly, citing Eph 2:20, Calvin wrote, "If the doctrine of the apostles and prophets is the foundation of the Church, the former must have had its certainty before the latter began to exist. Nor is there any room for the cavil, that though the Church derives her first beginning from thence, it still remains doubtful what writings are to be attributed to the apostles and prophets, until her judgement is interposed. For if the Christian Church was founded at first on the writings of the prophets, and the preaching of the apostles, that doctrine, wheresoever it may be found, was certainly ascertained and sanctioned antecedently to the Church, since, but for this, the Church herself never could have existed. Nothing therefore can be more absurd than the fiction, that the power of judging Scripture is in the Church, and that on her nod its certainty depends. When the Church receives it, and gives it the stamp of her authority, she does not make that authentic which was otherwise doubtful or controverted but, acknowledging it as the truth of God, she, as in duty bounds shows her reverence by an unhesitating assent. As to the question, How shall we be persuaded that it came from God without recurring to a decree of the Church? it is just the same as if it were asked, How shall we learn to distinguish light from darkness, white from black, sweet from bitter? Scripture bears upon the face of it as clear evidence of its truth, as white and black do of their colour, sweet and bitter of their taste" (*Institutes* 1.7.2).

11 Quoted in Bainton, "Bible in the Reformation," 22.

12 Quoted in Roy A. Harrisville and Walter Sundberg, *The Bible in Modern Culture: Baruch Spinoza to Brevard Childs*, 2nd ed. (Grand Rapids: Eerdmans, 2002), 23.

13 Quoted in J. Samuel Preus, "A Hidden Opponent in Spinoza's 'Tractatus,'" *Harvard Theological Review* 88, no. 3 (1995): 372–73.

14 Preus, "Hidden Opponent," 363.

15 Jonathan I. Israel, *Radical Enlightenment: Philosophy and the*

Making of Modernity, 1650–1750 (Oxford: Oxford University Press, 2001), 199.

16 Ernst Bizer, "Reformed Orthodoxy and Cartesianism," in *Translating Theology into the Modern Age: Historical, Systematic and Pastoral Reflections on Theology and the Church in the Contemporary Situation*, ed. Robert W. Funk, 20–82 (San Francisco: Harper Torchbooks, 1965), 42.

17 Ernst Bizer says that for Meyer, "every exegesis according to which the Bible says something false must itself necessarily be false." Meyer thus arrives at "a negative criterion for correct exegesis" and draws the opposite consequence as well: "every truth which one derives from the Bible also hits upon the true meaning of the scriptural statement" ("Reformed Orthodoxy," 42–43).

18 Israel, *Radical Enlightenment*, 201.

19 Bizer, "Reformed Orthodoxy," 43.

20 Israel, *Radical Enlightenment*, 201.

21 See Israel, *Radical Enlightenment*, ch. 11.

22 Israel, *Radical Enlightenment*, 200.

23 Benedict Spinoza, *A Theologico-Political Treatise and a Political Treatise*, trans. R. H. M. Elwes (New York: Dover, 1951), ch. 15. Citations to Spinoza's treatise will be included in the body of the text, cited as *TPT*.

24 Frampton, *Spinoza and the Rise*, ch. 6. See also Andrew Fix, *Prophecy and Reason: The Dutch Collegiants in the Early Enlightenment* (Princeton: Princeton University Press, 1990).

25 Quoted in Frampton, *Spinoza and the Rise*, 191.

26 The most complete treatment of the subject is Henri de Lubac, *Medieval Exegesis*, trans. Mark Sebanc and E. M. Macierowski, 2 vols. (Grand Rapids: Eerdmans, 1998–2000).

27 Alister E. McGrath, *The Intellectual Origins of the European Reformation*, 2nd ed. (London: Blackwell, 2004), 159. Luther's understanding of justification was likely worked out by 1516, and thus was being developed while Luther was still committed to the framework of the quadriga, modified in the direction of Lefevre.

28 Richard A. Muller, "Hermeneutic of Promise and Fulfillment in Calvin's Exegesis of the Old Testament Prophecies of the Kingdom," in *The Bible in the Sixteenth Century*, ed. David C. Steinmetz, 68–82 (Durham: Duke University Press, 1990), esp. 71, 77.

29 McGrath, *Intellectual Origins*, 161–62.

30 McGrath, *Intellectual Origins*, 163–64. Luther's location of justification within tropology has interesting ramifications for contemporary debates concerning the "New Perspective on Paul" (NPP). In medieval terms, the NPP relocates justification and especially the "righteousness of God" from tropology to allegory, so that justification has to do with God's accomplishment of redemption through Christ rather than primarily with the application of redemption to the believer.

31 As the dates indicate, these debates were taking place even before Spinoza wrote his treatise.

32 Bizer, "Reformed Orthodoxy," 47–48.

33 Quoted in Bizer, "Reformed Orthodoxy," 55.

34 Bizer, "Reformed Orthodoxy," 55.

35 Bizer, "Reformed Orthodoxy," 61.

36 Bizer, "Reformed Orthodoxy," 58.

37 Henning Graf Reventlow, *The Authority of the Bible and the Rise of the Modern World*, trans. John Bowden (Philadelphia: Fortress, 1985).

38 Garrett Green, *Theology, Hermeneutics, and Imagination: The Crisis of Interpretation at the End of Modernity* (Cambridge: Cambridge University Press, 2000), 28.

39 Isabel Rivers, *Reason, Grace, and Sentiment: A Study of the Language of Religion and Ethics in England, 1660–1780*, 2 vols. (Cambridge: Cambridge University Press, 1991–2000), 1:66.

40 Rivers, *Reason, Grace, and Sentiment*, 1:67.

41 Peter Harrison, *"Religion" and the Religions in the English Enlightenment* (Cambridge: Cambridge University Press, 2000), 67–69. It is amusing to see how thoroughly the freethinkers took over specifically Christian doctrines as if they were universal, natural beliefs.

42 Rivers, *Reason, Grace, and Sentiment*, 2:50–84, with an excellent summary statement on p. 51. See also J. A. I. Champion, *The Pillars of Priestcraft Shaken: The Church of England and Its Enemies, 1660–1730* (Cambridge: Cambridge University Press, 1992).

43 Quoted in Rivers, *Reason, Grace, and Sentiment*, 2:69.

44 Green, *Theology, Hermeneutics, and Imagination*, ch. 2.

45 Immanuel Kant, *Religion within the Boundaries of Mere Reason and Other Writings*, ed. Allen Wood and George di Giovanni, Cambridge Texts in the History of Philosophy (Cambridge: Cam-

bridge University Press, 1998), 112. Page numbers in the text are from this edition, abbreviated as *RBMR*.

46 Kant is not bashing Catholicism, because he immediately goes on to remark that there are many "arch-catholic protestants" (*RBMR*, 117).

47 Green, *Theology, Hermeneutics, and Imagination*, 32–34.

48 Green, *Theology, Hermeneutics, and Imagination*, 42.

49 Ian Hunter comments that Kant's "philosophical biblical hermeneutics" is Kant's key method or "spiritual exercise" for "reconciling moral philosophy and revealed theology within a single discipline." *Rival Enlightenments: Civil and Metaphysical Philosophy in Early Modern Germany* (Cambridge: Cambridge University Press, 2001), 349.

50 This is a remarkable deletion of time and history. Each time we make a moral choice, it is as if we are being created anew all over again.

51 Kant is very close to Rousseau here, whose work he deeply admired.

52 Which is, of course, the only way temporal creatures can reason.

53 James Barr, *The Bible in the Modern World* (New York: Harper and Row, 1973), 177.

54 I summarize an evangelical treatment of David's battle with Goliath in "The Quadriga, or Something Like It: A Biblical and Pastoral Defense," in *Ancient Faith for the Church's Future*, ed. Mark Husbands and Jeff Greeman, 110–25 (Downers Grove: InterVarsity, 2008).

55 Of course, many of the great theologians of Protestant orthodoxy were pastors and preachers as well as theologians, and in their biblical teaching, they did not treat the text as a husk to be stripped off and cast away.

56 Peter Enns, *Inspiration and Incarnation: Evangelicals and the Problem of the Old Testament* (Grand Rapids: Baker, 2005).

57 Enns, *Inspiration and Incarnation*, 17 (emphasis added).

58 Enns, *Inspiration and Incarnation*, 29–30.

59 Enns, *Inspiration and Incarnation*, 53.

60 Enns, *Inspiration and Incarnation*, 53.

61 The incarnational model Enns uses does not work well here. Jesus is God in human flesh, but his human words and actions are just as authoritative as his divine words and actions, because the two are inseparable. Precisely as the God-Man, Jesus says, "I

am the light of the world," and it makes no sense to try to strip the human garb from the divine message.

62 Enns, *Inspiration and Incarnation*, 56 (emphasis added).

63 Enns, *Inspiration and Incarnation*, 66.

64 Richard Longenecker, *Biblical Exegesis in the Apostolic Period*, 2nd ed. (Grand Rapids: Eerdmans, 1999), 219.

Chapter 2

1 E. D. Hirsch, *Validity in Interpretation* (New Haven: Yale University Press, 1967), 6–14.

2 Enns, *Inspiration and Incarnation*, 149–51.

3 Nicholas Wolterstorff has argued that the Bible is a double-authored text, in which the human writers are authorized to speak for God and God takes up the text as his own. See his *Divine Discourse: Philosophical Reflections on the Claim that God Speaks* (Cambridge: Cambridge University Press, 1995). Though Wolterstorff's emphasis on the Bible as God's speech is important and true, I am not satisfied with how he works out his paradigm. The analogy allows him to say that God does not necessarily agree with or endorse everything his authorized agents say, but that pushes us right back to where we started—to a husk/kernel dualism. How are we supposed to distinguish between the authorized speech God endorses and the authorized speech he does not? Do we distinguish using the tools of modern historical research? If so, how does God's speech remain authoritative?

4 This riff on the story of the water in the wilderness was an old favorite of the late Edmund Clowney. This interpretation of the Exodus passage is the background for John's deployment of this imagery: Jesus is struck on the cross, and a river of water and blood flows from him.

5 I have dealt with Gal 3–4 at more length in an essay in a forthcoming Festschrift for Norman Shepherd, edited by Andrew Sandlin.

6 David Daube, *The Exodus Pattern in the Bible* (1963; repr., Westport, Conn.: Greenwood, 1979).

7 Victor M. Wilson, *Divine Symmetries: The Art of Biblical Rhetoric* (Lanham, Md.: University Press of America, 1997), 29.

8 Arthur C. Danto, *Analytical Philosophy of History* (Cambridge: Cambridge University Press, 1968), 151 (emphasis added).

9 This is Danto's own example, in *Analytical Philosophy*, 151–52.

10 Danto, *Analytical Philosophy*, 155.

11 I am closely following the argument of David Weberman's "The Nonfixity of the Historical Past," *Review of Metaphysics* 50 (1997): 749–68. I am working from a copy generously supplied by the author.

12 The phrase is from Weberman, "Nonfixity," 6. He distinguishes between "skeletal" and "thick" events.

13 Weberman, "Nonfixity," 8.

14 Weberman's argument depends on his claim that certain relational changes have ontological, not merely epistemic, weight. Not all relational changes have such weight, but some do: "Social phenomena in general exemplify how relational changes and relational properties are constitutive of the core properties of a thing or event since social phenomena fundamentally depend for their very existence on people's belief about and behavior toward those phenomena" ("Nonfixity," 16). Relational changes can be real changes.

15 A somewhat softer version of the thesis: the event does not change, but we do not know what the event was or what it meant until Jesus rises from the dead. That thesis would be sufficient to ground the argument below, but I prefer the stronger version of the thesis.

16 When this happens, it is impossible to fix. A typesetter's error that lodges a misspelling in a text changes the text in a trivial but real sense.

17 Writers issue different editions of their work; the same book can be very different from one edition to the next. Differences in typesetting and layout are also relevant. Translation brings significant complications as well. To keep on task, I ignore these complications here.

18 Umberto Eco, *The Limits of Interpretation* (Bloomington: Indiana University Press, 1994), 53.

19 Speech act theory distinguishes between the locutionary force of an utterance (what is said) and the illocutionary force (what is done with the words said). For my purposes, it is important to note that in normal English, *mean* covers both. "I meant, 'In a few minutes I will push the red button'" expresses the locutionary force, while "I meant it as a joke" expresses the illocutionary force.

20 Speech act theory includes this under the perlocution.

21 When we reread a book, we will say, "It meant so much more to me. It means something completely different from when I first

read it." Hirsch's stern rejoinder—"no, it has a different significance, not a different meaning"—fails because it violates the
normal meaning of mean.

22 Eugen Rosenstock-Huessy, "Man Must Teach," in *Rosenstock-Huessy Papers, Volume I* (Norwich, Vt.: Argo Books, 1981).

23 One of Gadamer's great achievements was to rehabilitate the
role of prejudice in hermeneutics. See Hans-Georg Gadamer,
Truth and Method, trans. rev. Joel Weinsheimer and Donald G.
Marshall, 2nd ed. (New York: Crossroad, 1991), part 2, ch. 1.

24 Sometimes a parody is just too successful for its own good. *Don
Quixote* so thoroughly demolished chivalric romance that we
read nearly every romance ironically. We are all Cervantean.

25 Quoted in Stephen Prickett, *Words and the Word: Language,
Poetics and Biblical Interpretation* (Cambridge: Cambridge University Press, 1986), 4.

26 See chapter 5 below for more.

27 Victor Zuckerkandl, *Sound and Symbol: Music and the External
World* (Princeton: Princeton University Press, 1969), 128–29.

28 Zuckerkandl, *Sound and Symbol*, 137 (emphasis added).

29 Stanley Fish, *Is There a Text in this Class?: The Authority of
Interpretive Communities* (Cambridge, Mass.: Harvard University Press, 1982), 158–59 (emphasis added).

30 Ian McEwan, *Atonement* (New York: Doubleday, 2002), 350.

31 As McEwan has pointed out, the whole novel is from Briony's point
of view. Her idealization of Robbie is part of her atonement for her
lie, and also a hint of her envy of Robbie's attention to her sister.

32 The Coen brothers' film version captures this stylistic feature by
not including any music for most of the film.

33 Thanks to Josh Gibbs for this sharp way of putting it.

34 Thanks to James Jordan for this suggestion.

35 Eco, *Limits of Interpretation*, 29–30.

36 Kevin Vanhoozer makes this crucial point in *Is There Meaning in
this Text?* (Grand Rapids: Zondervan, 1998).

37 David Steinmetz, "Uncovering a Second Narrative: Detective
Fiction and the Construction of Historical Method," in *The Art
of Reading Scripture*, ed. Ellen F. Davis and Richard B. Hays,
54–65 (Grand Rapids: Eerdmans, 2003), 56.

38 David Steinmetz, "Uncovering a Second Narrative," in Davis
and Hays, *The Art of Reading Scripture*, 61.

39 David Steinmetz, "Uncovering a Second Narrative," in Davis
and Hays, *The Art of Reading Scripture*, 65.

40 David Steinmetz, "Uncovering a Second Narrative," in Davis and Hays, *The Art of Reading Scripture*, 64.

41 This is the reason that Austen is hard to transpose into a contemporary setting. Bridget Jones does not live in Austen's world, and so the romantic machinery works differently.

42 Of course, there is a great deal of history between these texts, and it would take a great deal of research to set them completely within their proper setting. I have relied on Richard Weikart's chilling and extremely careful treatment of the subject, *From Darwin to Hitler: Evolutionary Ethics, Eugenics, and Racism in Germany* (New York: Macmillan/Palgrave, 2004). See also Benjamin Wiker, *Moral Darwinism: How We Became Hedonists* (Downers Grove, Ill.: InterVarsity, 2002), and the first chapter of Marilynne Robinson's *The Death of Adam: Essays on Modern Thought* (New York: Picador, 2005).

43 Quoted in Wiker, *Moral Darwinism*, 261.

44 Quoted in Weikart, *From Darwin to Hitler*, 210.

45 Quoted in Weikart, *From Darwin to Hitler*, 211.

46 Quoted in Weikart, *From Darwin to Hitler*, 215.

47 Of course, misreadings may have happy results. Few would take "Go and sell your goods" the way St. Francis did, but most are glad that he understood it the way he did.

48 Quoted in Robinson, *Death of Adam*, 34.

49 Quoted in Robinson, *Death of Adam*, 34–35.

50 Quoted in Robinson, *Death of Adam*, 43.

51 John Wesley, "John Wesley's Explanatory Notes: John 9," Christ Notes, http://www.christnotes.org/commentary.php?com=wes&b=43&c=9 (accessed August 15, 2008).

52 John Chrysostom, "Homily 56 on the Gospel of John," New Advent, http://www.newadvent.org/fathers/240156.htm (accessed August 15, 2008).

Chapter 3

1 Eugene Nida, "Implications of Contemporary Linguistics for Biblical Scholarship," *Journal of Biblical Literature* 91, no. 1 (1972): 86.

2 Moisés Silva, *Biblical Words and Their Meaning: An Introduction to Lexical Semantics* (Grand Rapids: Zondervan, 1983), 38 (emphasis in original).

3 Peter Cotterell and Max Turner, *Linguistics and Biblical Interpretation* (Downers Grove, Ill.: InterVarsity, 1989), 132 (emphasis added).

4 Cotterell and Turner, *Linguistics*, 178 (emphasis added).

5   Anthony Thiselton, "Semantics and New Testament Interpretation," in *New Testament Interpretation: Essays on Principles and Methods*, ed. I. Howard Marshall (Grand Rapids: Eerdmans, 1977), 79 (emphasis added).

6   Cotterell and Turner, *Linguistics*, 130.

7   Having a son-in-law who has worked on a ranch, I sympathize with this line of argument.

8   Walter C. Kaiser and Moisés Silva, *Introduction to Biblical Hermeneutics: The Search for Meaning*, rev. ed. (Grand Rapids: Zondervan, 2007), 57.

9   James Barr, *The Semantics of Biblical Language* (1961; repr., London: SCM Press, 1983), 218.

10 *Violate* is faintly suggestive of hermeneutical rape. Worse, it appears to be serial rape ("virtually every" insight has been "violated"). What does go on in the dark basements of theology libraries after hours?

11 Cotterell and Turner, *Linguistics*, 138.

12 Quoted in Prickett, *Words and the Word*, 31.

13 See the brief summary in David Hill, *Greek Words and Hebrew Meanings: Studies in the Semantics of Soteriological Terms* (Cambridge: Cambridge University Press, 1967), 14–18.

14 Cotterell and Turner, *Linguistics*, 156 (emphasis added).

15 *Scorn* may be too strong, but only slightly. Cotterell and Turner make it clear that what they describe as "discourse meaning" is "*mere* usage" and that lexical meaning is more important than "what is *simply* contextual" (*Linguistics*, 140; emphasis added).

16 James Wood, *How Fiction Works* (London: Jonathan Cape, 2008), 149. The discussion of Roth is on pp. 150–52. Of course, the reader's heart sinks because of Mrs. Elton's insistence, but is buoyed up by the sheer wit of the phrase.

17 Cotterell and Turner, *Linguistics*, 140.

18 Cotterell and Turner, *Linguistics*, 152.

19 Cotterell and Turner, *Linguistics*, 147.

20 Cotterell and Turner, *Linguistics*, 180.

21 The importance of temporality in our consideration of meaning, examined in chapter 2, emerges here again.

22 Bruce Metzger, "The Language of the New Testament," in *The Interpreter's Bible* 7:56, quoted in Barr, *Semantics*, 247.

23 Barr, *Semantics*, 247.

24 Barr, *Semantics*, 108.

25 Barr, *Semantics*, 263.

26 Silva, *Biblical Words*, 137.

27 Silva, *Biblical Words*, 139 (emphasis in original).

28 Silva, *Biblical Words*, 150.

29 John Ciardi and Miller Williams, *How Does a Poem Mean?* 2nd ed. (Boston: Houghton Mifflin, 1975), 101–2.

30 Ciardi and Williams, *How Does a Poem Mean?* 102.

31 I admit I cheated. I looked at the poem first, and have had the poem in mind all the while I have been writing about the phrase.

32 That is to say, Shakespeare's Lear does not exist outside the play. There is some historical basis for the character.

33 C. S. Lewis, *Studies in Words* (Cambridge: Cambridge University Press, 1967), 13. Lewis labels these contemporary senses "dangerous sense."

34 Richard Chenevix Trench, *The Study of Words*, cond. ed. (New York: Funk & Wagnalls, 1911), 7.

35 Ciardi and Williams, *How Does a Poem Mean?* 104–5.

36 The historical relativity of Silva's claim will be addressed more fully below.

37 A concise summary of the history of the etymologizing imagination from the ancients to Dante is found in Ernst Robert Curtius, *European Literature and the Latin Middle Ages*, trans. Willard R. Trask (New York: Pantheon, 1953). On Philo, see Lester L. Grabbe, *Etymology in Early Jewish Interpretation: The Hebrew Names in Philo* (Atlanta: Scholars Press, 1988).

38 Herbert Marks, "Biblical Naming and Poetic Etymology," *Journal of Biblical Literature* 114, no. 1 (1995): 21.

39 Marks, "Biblical Naming," 25–29.

40 All of these examples are from Bruce Louden, "Categories of Homeric Wordplay," *Transactions of the American Philological Association* 125 (1995): 27–46.

41 Howard Eiland, "Heidegger's Etymological Web," *boundary 2* 10 (1982): 47.

42 I defy any reader to pronounce that word without falling into faux Irish; I defy anyone to repeat the word five times without getting a shiver up the spine. My discussion of these poems owes much to Henry Hart, "Poetymologies in Seamus Heaney's *Wintering Out*," *Twentieth Century Literature* 35 (1989): 204–31.

The poems themselves are found in Heaney, *Opened Ground: Selected Poems, 1966–1996* (New York: Farrar, Straus, and Giroux, 1998), 47, 54.

43 Hart, "Poetymologies," 218.

44 Hart, "Poetymologies," 218.

45 Hart, "Poetymologies," 218.

46 Hart, "Poetymologies," 219. He is quoting Sean O'Riordan's *Antiquities of the Irish Countryside* (1942).

47 Cotterell and Turner, *Linguistics*, 175.

48 John uses the word Philo typically used to introduce an etymology. See Grabbe, *Etymology*, 41–43.

49 G. Soares Prabhu makes the interesting suggestion that the Hebrew Siloam "means literally 'a discharge (of waters).'" Prabhu, "The Man Born Blind: Understanding a Johannine Sign in India Today," in *India's Search for Reality and the Relevance of the Gospel of John*, ed. Christopher Duraisingh and Cecil Hargreaves (Delhi: ISPCK, 1975), 69. If this is accurate, it may round out John's usage further. Prabhu connects the discharge of waters to the "living water" of John 4:10, and from there to other passages that speak of springs, springs in relation to women and birth, etc. The pool would thus be linked with the blind man's new birth. As much as I would like this to be correct, I have not found any indication that "discharge" is a proper translation of *shalach*, the closest being Job 12:15.

50 Raymond Brown, *The Gospel according to John*, 2 vols., Anchor Bible (Garden City, N.Y.: Doubleday, 1966–1970), 2:882.

51 There is not, however, a contradiction of fact. The garden of Gethsemane is on the Mount of Olives, and that is where Jesus was arrested. John simply omits the ascent from the Kidron onto the mount, which associates the garden with the low place of the valley.

52 I owe this observation to Douglas Wilson.

53 Paul Duke, *Irony in the Fourth Gospel* (Louisville: John Knox, 1985), 119. The link between the words is so close that some Greek lexicons deal with both in the same entry.

54 See Earl Richard, "Expressions of Double Meaning and their Function in the Gospel of John," *New Testament Studies* 31 (1985): 96–112.

Chapter 4

1 Another way to fill in the blank in the quotation from Cotterell and Turner, above: "He smashed in his head with a hermeneutical theory."

2 These examples are taken from R. R. Reno and John O'Keefe, *Sanctified Vision: An Introduction to Early Christian Interpretation of the Bible* (Baltimore: Johns Hopkins University Press, 2005), 74–75.

3 Dale Allison, *The New Moses: A Matthean Typology* (Minneapolis: Fortress, 1993), 321.

4 Allison, *The New Moses*, 322.

5 Some of this material has been published, in a more technical form, in my article "I Don't Get It: Humor and Hermeneutics," *Scottish Journal of Theology* 6, no. 4 (2007): 412–25.

6 Perhaps he has even appeared in some previous joke. Bartenders in jokes are usually anonymous, so it is impossible to say.

7 The percentage is higher for bartenders in jokes.

8 The self-reflective humor of the scene is enhanced by the fact that the whole film is animated; there is no camera to rotate. There is only a "camera" to "rotate," which raises all sorts of other interesting problems, best explored in Thomas De Zengotita's *Mediated* (New York: Bloomsbury, 2005).

9 This was confirmed for me recently when I was told about a Chinese viewer who was completely lost throughout the entire movie.

10 Not to mention its ambiguities.

11 There are a couple of good ones in Jacob Milgrom, *Leviticus 1–16*, 2 vols., Anchor Bible 3 (New York: Doubleday, 1991), 1:235.

12 Augustine, *On Christian Teaching*, trans. R. P. H. Green, Oxford World Classics (Oxford: Oxford University Press, 2008), book 1.

13 A. R. Braunmuller, introduction to *The Merchant of Venice*, in *The Complete Pelican Shakespeare* (New York: Penguin Putnam, 2002), 285–92.

14 Marjorie Garber, *Shakespeare After All* (New York: Anchor Books, 2005).

15 Braunmuller, "Introduction," 291.

16 This is the heart of Kevin Vanhoozer's objections to intertextuality. For interaction with Vanhoozer, see my article "I Don't Get It."

17 Sandra M. Schneiders calls the man an "alter Christus." "To See or Not to See: John 9 as a Synthesis of the Theology and Spirituality of Discipleship," in *Word, Theology, and Community in John*, ed. John Painter, R. Alan Culpepper, and Fernando F. Segovia (St. Louis: Chalice, 2002), 196.

18 Francis J. Moloney, in *The Gospel of John* (Collegeville, Minn.: Liturgical Press, 1998), 291–92, particularly stresses the plural.

19 We can, perhaps, be more specific. If John 7:53–8:11 is part of the

original text, it indicates a break between the "last day of the feast" (7:37) and the events recorded in chapters 8–9. 8:2 indicates that the day is the day after the last day of the feast, and 9:14 informs us that this day (assumed to be the same day in chapters 8–9) is a Sabbath. According to Lev 23:33-36, the feast lasts seven days and is followed by a Sabbatical eighth day in which "no laborious work" is to be done (v. 36). Possibly, the day of debate with the Jews and of the healing of the blind man is this eighth day, and if so, the Johannine connections of first and eighth day come into play (cf. 20:26).

20   Gary Burge, *John*, NIV Application Commentary (Grand Rapids: Zondervan, 2000), 255–56.

21   George R. Beasley-Murray, *John*, Word Biblical Commentary (Waco, Tex.: Word, 1987), 155.

22   N. T. Wright, *New Testament and the People of God* (London: SPCK, 1992), 113.

23   Theodore Rabb, *The Last Days of the Renaissance and the March to Modernity* (New York: Basic Books, 2006), 55–62.

24   Recall the argument from chapter 2 regarding Danto's Ideal Chronicler and the mutability of the past. There is no contemporary evidence about the effect of gunpowder because there could not be; the inventors of gunpowder did not know what they had done until much later.

25   Wright, *New Testament*, 37.

26   Robert Alter, *The Art of Biblical Narrative* (New York: Basic Books, 1983), is particularly good on the literary conventions of the biblical writers.

Chapter 5

1   Much of the material in this paragraph was inspired by Duke, *Irony*.

2   Robert Houston Smith, "Exodus Typology in the Fourth Gospel," *Journal of Biblical Literature* 81, no. 4 (1962): 329–42.

3   The author could, of course, dispense with periods and sentences, but then the text would partake in a recognizable style—stream of consciousness or something like it.

4   In some respects, I am following the lead of Jeremy Begbie, *Theology, Music, and Time* (Cambridge: Cambridge University Press, 2000). Begbie offers not a theology *of* music but theology *with* music, theology expounded in musical categories.

5   Zuckerkandl, *Sound and Symbol*, 213. I find a similar contrast of text and music, though more muted, in Begbie.

6 Zuckerkandl, *Sound and Symbol*, 217.

7 I am relying on the summary of Roussel's story in Jerrold Seigel, *The Idea of the Self: Thought and Experience in Western Europe since the Seventeenth Century* (Cambridge: Cambridge University Press, 2005), 614–15.

8 Do you have the same reaction to Sonny and Cher as they wake up Bill Murray each day in Punxsutawney, Pennsylvania? Do you laugh the first time they begin to sing? Do you laugh harder the second time? Why?

9 Henry Beard, *Poetry for Cats: The Definitive Anthology of Distinguished Feline Verse* (New York: Villard Books, 1994), 16.

10 Thanks to my neighbor John Carnahan for this one. Citing him as source also deflects any blame for the joke from me.

11 I got the idea of using *The Three Little Pigs* from David Dorsey's *Literary Structure of the Old Testament* (Grand Rapids: Baker, 1999).

12 The chiasm, and most of my discussion, is a summary of Calvin Stapert, *My Only Comfort: Death, Deliverance, and Discipleship in the Music of Bach* (Grand Rapids: Eerdmans, 2000), 206–17.

13 Stapert, *My Only Comfort*, 211–12.

14 Stapert, *My Only Comfort*, 212.

15 Stapert, *My Only Comfort*, 214–15.

16 Steinmetz, "Uncovering a Second Narrative," 54–65.

17 A. Walton Litz, *James Joyce*, Twayne English Authors Series (Woodbridge, Conn.: Twayne, 1972).

18 Beasley-Murray, *John*, 152.

19 For the sake of this discussion, I am assuming that the incident with the adulterous woman is part of the text.

20 In some texts, literally no white space, since some ancient texts do not even divide words from one another.

21 This is often considered unhistorical, and a clue to the dating and context for John's gospel, particularly in the work of J. Louis Martyn.

22 The fact that the blind man witnesses to the Pharisees a "second time" (v. 24) makes his witness a double witness. His deliverance from darkness is confirmed by "two or three witnesses," as Torah requires. Yet the Pharisees, those lawless sticklers for law, refuse to believe.

23 Duke, *Irony*, 126.

24 David Deeks, "The Structure of the Fourth Gospel" in *The Gospel*

of John as Literature: An Anthology of Twentieth-Century Per-spectives, ed. Mark W. G. Stibbe, 77–101 (Leiden: Brill, 1993), 94.

25 Calum Carmichael argues that John runs through the creation week in chapters 1–5, culminating in the healing of the paralytic on the Sabbath. See *The Story of Creation: Its Origin and Its Interpretation in Philo and the Fourth Gospel* (Ithaca: Cornell University Press, 1996).

26 Smith, "Exodus Typology," 329–42.

27 Summarized in Michael A. Daise, *Feasts in John: Jewish Festivals and Jesus' "Hour" in the Fourth Gospel* (Tübingen: Mohr Siebeck, 2007), 43. Daise is skeptical.

28 As explained in chapter 6, there are many indications that the blind man becomes a judge and ruler in the course of the story.

29 W. Wiley Richards, *Riches from the Lost Ark: The Gospel of John and the Tabernacle* (Graceville, Fla.: Hargrave, 1993).

Chapter 6

1 Richard Hays poses these as alternatives.

2 The phrase is from Kurt Queller of the University of Idaho.

3 John 9 is somewhat unusual in the fact that the tropology comes prior to the allegory: the disciple experiences Christ's sufferings before Christ does.

4 My point here is about the canonical order of the New Testament, not the order of composition. Galatians was written before John, though John comes first in canonical order. The events of John 9, further, occurred before the events of Galatians.

5 John MacArthur makes a similar application, though without a sacramental dimension: "The main lesson is this, have you met the true Siloam? Have you met this Christ?" "Jesus Opens Blind Eyes," sermon delivered in 1997, http://www.biblebb.com/files/MAC/GC1525.HTM (accessed August 28, 2008).

6 This possibility is suggested by Larry Paul Jones, *The Symbol of Water in the Gospel of John*, JSOTSup 145 (Sheffield: Sheffield Academic, 1997), 234.

7 Today, this is regarded as a quaint notion, but the basic thesis that Greek philosophers were aware of Jewish writings seems to me historically quite defensible.

8 Quoted in Hugo Rahner, *Greek Myths and Christian Mysteries* (New York: Harper and Row, 1963), 203–4.

9 Rahner, *Greek Myths*, 222.

10 See Jo-Ann A. Brant, *Dialogue and Drama: Elements of Greek Tragedy in the Fourth Gospel* (Peabody, Mass.: Hendrickson, 2004), especially 42–51. The church fathers occasionally mention Oedipus, seeing the story of inexorable fate as a focal point for discussions of predestination and human responsibility. Medieval Christians made much more extensive use of the Oedipus story, and the Theban legend found its way into nearly every language and country of medieval Europe under the cover of the *Life of Judas the Betrayer*, in which the life of Judas is conformed to the legend of Oedipus. For a summary of the legend, see Paull Franklin Baum, "The Mediæval Legend of Judas Iscariot," *Proceedings of the Modern Language Association* 31, no. 3 (1916): 482–83.

11 I am using the translation by Robert Fagles in Sophocles, *Three Theban Plays: "Antigone," "Oedipus the King," "Oedipus at Colonus"* (London: Penguin, 1984), 181.

12 Sophocles, *Three Theban Plays*, 182.

13 Sophocles, *Three Theban Plays*, 183.

14 Jean-Pierre Vernant, "Ambiguity and Reversal: On the Enigmatic Structure of Oedipus Rex," in *Myth and Tragedy in Ancient Greece*, by Vernant and Pierre Vidal-Naquet, 113–40 (New York: Zone Books, 1990), 118–19.

15 Vernant, "Ambiguity and Reversal," 119–20.

16 Vernant, "Ambiguity and Reversal," 123.

17 Douglas H. Knight has a fascinating discussion of the ancient theology of light in *The Eschatological Economy: Time and the Hospitality of God* (Grand Rapids: Eerdmans, 2006).

18 Schneiders, "To See or Not to See," 196.

19 James L. Resseguie, "John 9: A Literary-Critical Analysis," in *The Gospel of John as Literature: An Anthology of Twentieth-Century Perspectives*, ed. Mark W. G. Stibbe, 115–22 (Leiden: Brill, 1993), 119.

20 For a development of this point, see Peter J. Ahrensdorf, "The Limits of Political Rationalism: Enlightenment and Religion in *Oedipus the Tyrant*," *Journal of Politics* 66, no. 3 (2004): 778–85. Ahrensdorf argues that death is the main obstacle to purely rational politics.

21 Friedrich Nietzsche, *The Birth of Tragedy out of the Spirit of Music*, trans. Ian Johnston, http://records.viu.ca/~Johnstoi/Nietzsche/tragedy_all.htm (accessed August 28, 2008).

22 This is not a wholly modern phenomenon.

23 Martin Jay, *Downcast Eyes: The Denigration of Vision in Twentieth-Century French Thought* (Berkeley: University of California Press, 1993), 71.

24 Jay, *Downcast Eyes*, 85.

25 Jay, *Downcast Eyes*, 65.

26 This is from a summary of Yates in Johannes Fabian, *Time and the Other: How Anthropology Makes Its Object* (New York: Columbia University Press, 1983), 110.

27 This, too, is from Fabian's summary of Yates.

28 Walter Ong, *Ramus: Method and the Decay of Dialogue* (Cambridge, Mass.: Harvard University Press, 1958).

29 Ong, *Ramus*, 287.

30 Immanuel Kant, "An Answer to the Question, 'What Is Enlightenment?'" http://www.english.upenn.edu/~mgamer/Etexts/kant.html (accessed August 28, 2008).

31 See the lucid discussion in Craig Koester, *Symbolism in the Fourth Gospel: Meaning, Mystery, Community*, 2nd ed. (Minneapolis: Fortress, 2003), 141–73.

32 Gunter Reim, *Studien zum Alttestamentlichen Hintergrund des Johannesevangeliums* (Cambridge: Cambridge University Press, 1974), 164–66.

33 Shadi Bartsch, *The Mirror of the Self: Sexuality, Self-Knowledge, and the Gaze in the Early Roman Empire* (Chicago: University of Chicago Press, 2006), 115.

34 See Knight, *Eschatological Economy*.

35 Fabian, *Time and the Other*, 121.

36 Fabian, *Time and the Other*, 122.

37 I am again drawing on the insights of Duke, *Irony*.

38 Jerome H. Neyrey, *The Gospel of John*, New Cambridge Bible Commentary (Cambridge: Cambridge University Press, 2007), 138.

39 Schneiders, "To See or Not to See," 196.

40 The fact that this directly contradicts the earlier argument of 7:27 ("whenever the Christ may come, no one knows where He is from") escapes the Jewish leaders.

41 Dorothy A. Lee, *The Symbolic Narratives of the Fourth Gospel: The Interplay of Form and Meaning*, JSOTSup 65 (Sheffield: Sheffield Academic, 1994), 179.

42 Schneiders, "To See or Not to See," 193. Jerome Neyrey points out that the passage also undermines the popular ancient hier-

archy of origins: "the ancients universally considered a person's 'origins' as significant grounds for ascribing respect and honor: Noble parents and ancestors beget noble offspring, and noble people spring from noble cities or locations." Jesus turns the tables, pointing out that the Jewish leaders do not really know where he comes from and are judging by appearances rather than in righteousness. See Neyrey, *Gospel of John*, 143.

43 Wayne McCready, "Johannine Self-Understanding and the Synagogue Episode of John 9," in *Self-Definition and Self-Discovery in Early Christianity: A Study in Changing Horizons*, ed. David J. Hawkin and Tom Robinson, Studies in Bible and Early Christianity 26 (Lewiston, N.Y.: Edwin Mellen, 1990), 150–51.

44 Andrew Lincoln, "Power, Judgment and Possession: John's Gospel in Political Perspective," in *A Royal Priesthood?: The Use of the Bible Ethically and Politically: A Dialogue with Oliver O'Donovan*, ed. Craig Batholomew, Jonathan Chaplin, Robert Song, and Al Wolters, 147–69 (Grand Rapids: Zondervan, 2002), 151. More fully, Lincoln, *Truth on Trial: The Lawsuit Motif in the Fourth Gospel* (Peabody, Mass.: Hendrickson, 2000).

45 Sjef van Tilborg, *Imaginative Love in John* (Leiden: Brill, 1993), 224, says that when the people "bring" the blind man to the Pharisees, it is the "first juridical word" in the narrative.

46 For those who are counting, that makes seven uses of the phrase in John 9, and there is another in 10:21, referring to the same incident. The numerology underscores the creation themes of the passage.

47 Schneiders points out that the man is never identified by name, and thus becomes an "Everyman." No one is excluded from participation in Jesus' lawsuit with Israel and the world. See Schneiders, "To See or Not to See," 193.

48 Oliver O'Donovan, *The Ways of Judgment* (Grand Rapids: Eerdmans, 2005), 7. I am not persuaded of O'Donovan's claim that the coming of Christ "strips down the role of government to the single task of judgment, and forbids human rule to pretend to sovereignty, the consummation of the community's identity in the power of its rulers" (4). The latter point seems right, that human rulers cannot claim sovereignty, but I am not convinced that "acts of judgment" adequately describes the full scope of legitimate political authority during the *saeculum*.

49 Tilborg, *Imaginative Love*, 229.

50 Lincoln, "Power, Judgment and Possession," 168.

Epilogue

1 I have begun some of these musings in "The Quadriga, or Something Like It: A Biblical and Pastoral Defense."

2 I have reflected a bit more on this in "Authors, Authority, and the Humble Reader," in *The Christian Imagination: The Practice of Faith in Literature and Writing*, ed. Leland Ryken (Colorado Springs: Harold Shaw, 2002), 209–24.

Bibliography

Ahrensdorf, Peter J. "The Limits of Political Rationalism: Enlightenment and Religion in *Oedipus the Tyrant*." *Journal of Politics* 66, no. 3 (2004): 778–85.

Allison, Dale. *The New Moses: A Matthean Typology*. Minneapolis: Fortress, 1993.

Alter, Robert. *The Art of Biblical Narrative*. New York: Basic Books, 1983.

Augustine. *On Christian Teaching*. Translated by R. P. H. Green. Oxford World Classics. Oxford: Oxford University Press, 2008.

Bainton, Roland. "The Bible in the Reformation." In *The Cambridge History of the Bible: The West from the Reformation to the Present Day*, edited by S. L. Greenslade, 1–37. Cambridge: Cambridge University Press, 1963.

Barr, James. *The Bible in the Modern World*. New York: Harper and Row, 1973.

———. *The Semantics of Biblical Language*. 1961. Reprint, London: SCM Press, 1983.

Bartsch, Shadi. *The Mirror of the Self: Sexuality, Self-Knowledge, and the Gaze in the Early Roman Empire*. Chicago: University of Chicago Press, 2006.

Baum, Paull Franklin. "The Mediæval Legend of Judas Iscariot." *Proceedings of the Modern Language Association* 31, no. 3 (1916): 482–83.

Beard, Henry. *Poetry for Cats: The Definitive Anthology of Distinguished Feline Verse*. New York: Villard Books, 1994.

Beasley-Murray, George R. *John*. Word Biblical Commentary. Waco, Tex.: Word, 1987.

Begbie, Jeremy. *Theology, Music, and Time*. Cambridge: Cambridge University Press, 2000.

Bizer, Ernst. "Reformed Orthodoxy and Cartesianism." In *Translating Theology into the Modern Age: Historical, Systematic and Pastoral Reflections on Theology and the Church in the Contemporary Situation*, edited by Robert W. Funk, 20–82. San Francisco: Harper Torchbooks, 1965.

Brant, Jo-Ann A. *Dialogue and Drama: Elements of Greek Tragedy in the Fourth Gospel*. Peabody, Mass.: Hendrickson, 2004.

Braunmuller, A. R. Introduction to *The Merchant of Venice*. In *The Complete Pelican Shakespeare*, 285–92. New York: Penguin Putnam, 2002.

Brown, Raymond. *The Gospel according to John*. 2 vols. Anchor Bible. Garden City, N.Y.: Doubleday, 1966–1970.

Burge, Gary. *John*. NIV Application Commentary. Grand Rapids: Zondervan, 2000.

Calvin, John. *Institutes of the Christian Religion*. Translated by Ford Lewis Battles. Library of Christian Classics. Louisville: Westminster John Knox, 1960.

Carmichael, Calum. *The Story of Creation: Its Origin and Its Interpretation in Philo and the Fourth Gospel*. Ithaca: Cornell University Press, 1996.

Champion, J. A. I. *The Pillars of Priestcraft Shaken: The Church of England and Its Enemies, 1660–1730*. Cambridge: Cambridge University Press, 1992.

Chrysostom, John. "Homily 56 on John's Gospel." http://www. newadvent.org (accessed August 15, 2008).

Ciardi, John, and Miller Williams. *How Does a Poem Mean?* 2nd ed. Boston: Houghton Mifflin, 1975.

Cotterell, Peter, and Max Turner. *Linguistics and Biblical Interpretation*. Downers Grove, Ill.: InterVarsity, 1989.

Curtius, Ernst Robert. *European Literature and the Latin Middle Ages*. Translated by Willard R. Trask. New York: Pantheon, 1953.

Daise, Michael A. *Feasts in John: Jewish Festivals and Jesus' "Hour" in the Fourth Gospel.* Tübingen: Mohr Siebeck, 2007.

Daniell, David. *The Bible in English.* New Haven: Yale University Press, 2003.

Danto, Arthur C. *Analytical Philosophy of History.* Cambridge: Cambridge University Press, 1968.

Daube, David. *The Exodus Pattern in the Bible.* 1963. Reprint, Westport, Conn: Greenwood, 1979.

Deeks, David. "The Structure of the Fourth Gospel." In *The Gospel of John as Literature: An Anthology of Twentieth-Century Perspectives,* edited by Mark W. G. Stibbe, 77–101. Leiden: Brill, 1993.

De Zengotita, Thomas. *Mediated.* New York: Bloomsbury, 2005.

Dorsey, David. *Literary Structure of the Old Testament.* Grand Rapids: Baker, 1999.

Duke, Paul. *Irony in the Fourth Gospel.* Louisville: John Knox, 1985.

Eco, Umberto. *The Limits of Interpretation.* Bloomington: Indiana University Press, 1994.

Eiland, Howard. "Heidegger's Etymological Web." *boundary 2* 10 (1982): 39–58.

Eliot, T. S. *The Complete Poems and Plays, 1909–1950.* New York: Harcourt, Brace, and World, 1971.

Enns, Peter. *Inspiration and Incarnation: Evangelicals and the Problem of the Old Testament.* Grand Rapids: Baker, 2005.

Fabian, Johannes. *Time and the Other: How Anthropology Makes Its Object.* New York: Columbia University Press, 1983.

Fish, Stanley. *Is There a Text in this Class?: The Authority of Interpretive Communities.* Cambridge, Mass.: Harvard University Press, 1982.

Fix, Andrew. *Prophecy and Reason: The Dutch Collegiants in the Early Enlightenment.* Princeton: Princeton University Press, 1990.

Frampton, Travis L. *Spinoza and the Rise of Historical Criticism of the Bible.* New York: T&T Clark, 2006.

Gadamer, Hans-Georg. *Truth and Method.* Translation revised by Joel Weinsheimer and Donald G. Marshall. 2nd ed. New York: Crossroad, 1991.

Garber, Marjorie. *Shakespeare After All*. New York: Anchor Books, 2005.

Grabbe, Lester L. *Etymology in Early Jewish Interpretation: The Hebrew Names in Philo*. Atlanta: Scholars Press, 1988.

Green, Garrett. *Theology, Hermeneutics, and Imagination: The Crisis of Interpretation at the End of Modernity*. Cambridge: Cambridge University Press, 2000.

Harrison, Peter. *"Religion" and the Religions in the English Enlightenment*. Cambridge: Cambridge University Press, 2000.

Harrisville, Roy A., and Walter Sundberg. *The Bible in Modern Culture: Baruch Spinoza to Brevard Childs*. 2nd ed. Grand Rapids: Eerdmans, 2002.

Hart, Henry. "Poetymologies in Seamus Heaney's *Wintering Out*." *Twentieth Century Literature* 35 (1989): 204–31.

Heaney, Seamus. *Opened Ground: Selected Poems, 1966–1996*. New York: Farrar, Straus, and Giroux, 1998.

Hill, David. *Greek Words and Hebrew Meanings: Studies in the Semantics of Soteriological Terms*. Cambridge: Cambridge University Press, 1967.

Hirsch, E. D. *Validity in Interpretation*. New Haven: Yale University Press, 1967.

Hunter, Ian. *Rival Enlightenments: Civil and Metaphysical Philosophy in Early Modern Germany*. Cambridge: Cambridge University Press, 2001.

Israel, Jonathan I. *Radical Enlightenment: Philosophy and the Making of Modernity, 1650–1750*. Oxford: Oxford University Press, 2001.

James, Clive. *Cultural Amnesia: Necessary Memories from History and the Arts*. New York: Norton, 2007.

Jay, Martin. *Downcast Eyes: The Denigration of Vision in Twentieth-Century French Thought*. Berkeley: University of California Press, 1993.

Jones, Larry Paul. *The Symbol of Water in the Gospel of John*. Journal for the Study of the Old Testament: Supplement Series 145. Sheffield: Sheffield Academic, 1997.

Kaiser, Walter C., and Moisés Silva. *Introduction to Biblical Hermeneutics: The Search for Meaning*. Rev. ed. Grand Rapids: Zondervan, 2007.

Kant, Immanuel. "An Answer to the Question, 'What Is Enlightenment?'" http://www.english.upenn.edu/~mgamer/Etexts/kant.html (accessed August 28, 2008).

———. *Religion within the Boundaries of Mere Reason and Other Writings.* Edited by Allen Wood and George di Giovanni. Cambridge Texts in the History of Philosophy. Cambridge: Cambridge University Press, 1998.

Knight, Douglas H. *The Eschatological Economy: Time and the Hospitality of God.* Grand Rapids: Eerdmans, 2006.

Koester, Craig. *Symbolism in the Fourth Gospel: Meaning, Mystery, Community.* 2nd ed. Minneapolis: Fortress, 2003.

Lee, Dorothy A. *The Symbolic Narratives of the Fourth Gospel: The Interplay of Form and Meaning.* Journal for the Study of the Old Testament: Supplement Series 65. Sheffield: Sheffield Academic, 1994.

Leithart, Peter J. "Authors, Authority, and the Humble Reader." In *The Christian Imagination: The Practice of Faith in Literature and Writing,* edited by Leland Ryken, 209–24. Colorado Springs: Harold Shaw, 2002.

———. "I Don't Get It: Humor and Hermeneutics." *Scottish Journal of Theology* 6, no. 4 (2007): 412–25.

———. "The Quadriga or Something Like It: A Biblical and Pastoral Defense." In *Ancient Faith for the Church's Future,* edited by Mark Husbands and Jeff Greenman, 110–25. Downers Grove, Ill.: InterVarsity, 2008.

Lewalski, Barbara Kiefer. *Protestant Poetics and the Seventh-Century Religious Lyric.* Princeton: Princeton University Press, 1979.

Lewis, C. S. *Studies in Words.* Cambridge: Cambridge University Press, 1967.

Lincoln, Andrew. "Power, Judgment and Possession: John's Gospel in Political Perspective." In *A Royal Priesthood?: The Use of the Bible Ethically and Politically: A Dialogue with Oliver O'Donovan,* edited by Craig Bartholomew, Jonathan Chaplin, Robert Song, and Al Wolters, 147–69. Grand Rapids: Zondervan, 2002.

———. *Truth on Trial: The Lawsuit Motif in the Fourth Gospel.* Peabody, Mass.: Hendrickson, 2000.

Litz, A. Walton. *James Joyce*. Twayne English Authors Series. Woodbridge, Conn.: Twayne, 1972.

Longenecker, Richard. *Biblical Exegesis in the Apostolic Period*. 2nd ed. Grand Rapids: Eerdmans, 1999.

Louden, Bruce. "Categories of Homeric Wordplay." *Transactions of the American Philological Association* 125 (1995): 27–46.

Lubac, Henri de. *Medieval Exegesis*. Translated by Mark Sebanc and E. M. Macierowski. 2 vols. Grand Rapids: Eerdmans, 1998–2000.

MacArthur, John. "Jesus Opens Blind Eyes." Sermon delivered in 1997. http://www.biblebb.com/files/MAC/GC1525.HTM (accessed August 28, 2008).

Marks, Herbert. "Biblical Naming and Poetic Etymology." *Journal of Biblical Literature* 114, no. 1 (1995): 21–42.

McCarthy, Cormac. *No Country for Old Men*. New York: Knopf, 2005.

McCready, Wayne. "Johannine Self-Understanding and the Synagogue Episode of John 9." In *Self-Definition and Self-Discovery in Early Christianity: A Study in Changing Horizons*, edited by David J. Hawkin and Tom Robinson. Studies in Bible and Early Christianity 26. Lewiston, N.Y.: Edwin Mellen, 1990.

McEwan, Ian. *Atonement*. New York: Doubleday, 2002.

McGrath, Alister E. *The Intellectual Origins of the European Reformation*. 2nd ed. London: Blackwell, 2004.

Milgrom, Jacob. *Leviticus 1–16*. Anchor Bible 3. New York: Doubleday, 1991.

Moloney, Francis J. *Signs and Shadows: Reading John 5–12*. Minneapolis: Augsburg, 1996.

———. *The Gospel of John*. Sacra Pagina 4. Collegeville, Minn.: Liturgical Press, 1998.

Muller, Richard A. "Hermeneutic of Promise and Fulfillment in Calvin's Exegesis of the Old Testament Prophecies of the Kingdom." In *The Bible in the Sixteenth Century*, edited by David C. Steinmetz, 68–82. Durham: Duke University Press, 1990.

Neyrey, Jerome H. *The Gospel of John*. New Cambridge Bible Commentary. Cambridge: Cambridge University Press, 2007.

Nida, Eugene. "Implications of Contemporary Linguistics for Biblical Scholarship." *Journal of Biblical Literature* 91, no. 1 (1972): 73–89.

Nietzsche, Friedrich. *The Birth of Tragedy out of the Spirit of Music.* Translated by Ian Johnston. http://records.viu.ca/~Johnstoi/ Nietzsche/tragedy_all.htm (accessed August 28, 2008).

O'Donovan, Oliver. *The Ways of Judgment.* Grand Rapids: Eerdmans, 2005.

Ong, Walter. *Ramus: Method and the Decay of Dialogue.* Cambridge, Mass: Harvard University Press, 1958.

Prabhu, G. Soares. "The Man Born Blind: Understanding a Johannine Sign in India Today." In *India's Search for Reality and the Relevance of the Gospel of John,* edited by Christopher Duraisingh and Cecil Hargreaves, 65–76. Delhi: ISPCK, 1975.

Preus, J. Samuel. "A Hidden Opponent in Spinoza's 'Tractatus.'" *Harvard Theological Review* 88, no. 3 (1995): 361–88.

Prickett, Stephen. *Words and the Word: Language, Poetics and Biblical Interpretation.* Cambridge: Cambridge University Press, 1986.

Rabb, Theodore. *The Last Days of the Renaissance and the March to Modernity.* New York: Basic Books, 2006.

Rahner, Hugo. *Greek Myths and Christian Mysteries.* New York: Harper and Row, 1963.

Reim, Gunter. *Studien zum Alttestamentlichen Hintergrund des Johannesevangeliums.* Cambridge: Cambridge University Press, 1974.

Reno, R. R., and John O'Keefe. *Sanctified Vision: An Introduction to Early Christian Interpretation of the Bible.* Baltimore: Johns Hopkins University Press, 2005.

Resseguie, James L. "John 9: A Literary-Critical Analysis." In *The Gospel of John as Literature: An Anthology of Twentieth-Century Perspectives,* edited by Mark W. G. Stibbe, 115–22. Leiden: Brill, 1993.

Reventlow, Henning Graf. *The Authority of the Bible and the Rise of the Modern World.* Translated by John Bowden. Philadelphia: Fortress, 1985.

Richard, Earl. "Expressions of Double Meaning and their Function in the Gospel of John." *New Testament Studies* 31 (1985): 96–112.

Richards, W. Wiley. *Riches from the Lost Ark: The Gospel of John and the Tabernacle.* Graceville, Fla.: Hargrave, 1993.

Rivers, Isabel. *Reason, Grace, and Sentiment: A Study of the Language of Religion and Ethics in England, 1660–1780.* 2 vols. Cambridge: Cambridge University Press, 1991–2000.

Robinson, Marilynne. *The Death of Adam: Essays on Modern Thought.* New York: Picador, 2005.

Rosenstock-Huessy, Eugen. "Man Must Teach." In *Rosenstock-Huessy Papers, Volume I.* Norwich, Vt.: Argo Books, 1981.

Schneiders, Sandra M. "To See or Not to See: John 9 as a Synthesis of the Theology and Spirituality of Discipleship." In *Word, Theology, and Community in John,* edited by John Painter, R. Alan Culpepper, and Fernando F. Segovia, 189–210. St. Louis: Chalice, 2002.

Seigel, Jerrold. *The Idea of the Self: Thought and Experience in Western Europe since the Seventeenth Century.* Cambridge: Cambridge University Press, 2005.

Silva, Moisés. *Biblical Words and Their Meaning: An Introduction to Lexical Semantics.* Grand Rapids: Zondervan, 1983.

Smith, Robert Houston. "Exodus Typology in the Fourth Gospel." *Journal of Biblical Literature* 81, no. 4 (1962): 329–42.

Sophocles. *Three Theban Plays: "Antigone," "Oedipus the King," "Oedipus at Colonus."* Translated by Robert Fagles. London: Penguin, 1984.

Spinoza, Benedict[us de]. *A Theologico-Political Treatise and a Political Treatise.* Translated by R. H. M. Elwes. New York: Dover, 1951.

Stapert, Calvin. *My Only Comfort: Death, Deliverance, and Discipleship in the Music of Bach.* Grand Rapids: Eerdmans, 2000.

Staubli, Thomas, and Silvia Schroer. *Body Symbolism in the Bible.* Translated by Linda M. Maloney. Collegeville, Minn.: Michael Glazier, 2001.

Steinmetz, David. "Uncovering a Second Narrative: Detective Fiction and the Construction of Historical Method." In *The Art of*

Reading Scripture, edited by Ellen F. Davis and Richard B. Hays, 54–65. Grand Rapids: Eerdmans, 2003.

Thiselton, Anthony. "Semantics and New Testament Interpretation." In *New Testament Interpretation: Essays on Principles and Methods*, edited by I. Howard Marshall. Grand Rapids: Eerdmans, 1977.

Tilborg, Sjef van. *Imaginative Love in John*. Leiden: Brill, 1993.

Trench, Richard Chenevix. *The Study of Words*. Cond. ed. New York: Funk & Wagnalls, 1911.

Vanhoozer, Kevin. *Is There Meaning in this Text?* Grand Rapids: Zondervan, 1998.

Vernant, Jean-Pierre. "Ambiguity and Reversal: On the Enigmatic Structure of Oedipus Rex." In *Myth and Tragedy in Ancient Greece*, by Jean-Pierre Vernant and Pierre Vidal-Naquet, 113–40. New York: Zone Books, 1990.

Weberman, David. "The Nonfixity of the Historical Past." *Review of Metaphysics* 50 (1997): 749–68.

Weikart, Richard. *From Darwin to Hitler: Evolutionary Ethics, Eugenics, and Racism in Germany*. New York: Macmillan/Palgrave, 2004.

Wesley, John. "John Wesley's Expository Notes: John 9." http://www.christnotes.org (accessed August 15, 2008).

Wiker, Benjamin. *Moral Darwinism: How We Became Hedonists*. Downers Grove, Ill.: InterVarsity, 2002.

Wilson, Victor M. *Divine Symmetries: The Art of Biblical Rhetoric*. Lanham, Md.: University Press of America, 1997.

Wolterstorff, Nicholas. *Divine Discourse: Philosophical Reflections on the Claim that God Speaks*. Cambridge: Cambridge University Press, 1995.

Wood, James. *How Fiction Works*. London: Jonathan Cape, 2008.

Wright, N. T. *New Testament and the People of God*. London: SPCK, 1992.

Zuckerkandl, Victor. *Sound and Symbol: Music and the External World*. Princeton: Princeton University Press, 1969.

Scripture Index

Author Index

Subject Index

CPSIA information can be obtained
at www.ICGtesting.com
Printed in the USA
LVHW091932221220
674910LV00004B/51